CHRISTIAN IMPERIALISM

A volume in the series

The United States in the World

edited by Mark Philip Bradley, David C. Engerman,
Amy S. Greenberg, and Paul A. Kramer

A list of titles in this series is available at www.cornellpress.cornell.edu.

CHRISTIAN IMPERIALISM

Converting the World in the Early American Republic

Emily Conroy-Krutz

Cornell University Press
Ithaca and London

First published 2015 by Cornell University Press

Printed in the United States of America

Library of Congress Cataloging-in-Publication Data
Conroy-Krutz, Emily, author.
   Christian imperialism : converting the world in the early American
republic / Emily Conroy-Krutz.
      pages cm. — (The United States in the world)
   Includes bibliographical references and index.
   ISBN 978-0-8014-5353-3 (cloth : alk. paper)
   1. Missions, American—History—19th century. 2. American
Board of Commissioners for Foreign Missions—History. 3. Political
messianism—United States—History—19th century. 4. Christianity and
politics—United States—History—19th century. I. Title.
   BV2410.C66 2015
   266'.02373—dc23   2015006493

Cornell University Press strives to use environmentally responsible
suppliers and materials to the fullest extent possible in the publishing
of its books. Such materials include vegetable-based, low-VOC inks
and acid-free papers that are recycled, totally chlorine-free, or partly
composed of nonwood fibers. For further information, visit our
website at www.cornellpress.cornell.edu.

Cloth printing   10 9 8 7 6 5 4 3 2 1

And he said unto them, Go ye into all the world, and preach the gospel to every creature. He that believeth and is baptized shall be saved; but he that believeth not shall be damned.

—Mark 16:15–16, King James Version

The kingdom of the Lord Jesus is a kingdom of order.

—American Board of Commissioners for Foreign Missions, instructions to the Sandwich Islands missionaries, 1819

Contents

Acknowledgments

I consider myself very lucky to have worked with the United States in the World editors on this book. Amy Greenberg first suggested that I talk to Michael McGandy at Cornell University Press about my work, and I am so glad that she did. Michael has been a wonderful editor: supportive and generous, and always patient with a first-time author. Mark Philip Bradley, David Engerman, and Paul Kramer were so helpful as I revised my manuscript, particularly in discussions about how to talk about empire and imperialism. Amy Greenberg has been helpful with this project for many years. I have had to pinch myself to believe my good luck in having her shepherd this book through to its completion. Her insights about empire and the early republic have helped me enormously, as has her friendly encouragement throughout.

I received much-appreciated financial support for my research from the American Association of University Women, the Center for American Political Studies at Harvard University, and the history department of Michigan State University. Librarians at Houghton Library at Harvard, the School of Oriental and African Studies Library at the University of London, Regent Library at Oxford University, the British Library, and the Clements Library at the University of Michigan were incredibly helpful while I was in the archives. The interlibrary loan staff at Michigan State University also helped bring the American Board to me in East Lansing, for which I am very grateful. Thanks also to Bill Keegan for the beautiful maps.

This project began at Harvard University, where I had the incredible good fortune to study with Nancy Cott, Walter Johnson, and Laurel Ulrich. Ian Tyrrel was a great help toward the end. These four historians are all rightfully well known for their excellent scholarship, and I feel very lucky to have had the benefit of their distinct perspectives. Nancy has been a wonderful adviser and I have been so glad to continue to benefit from her mentorship even after Harvard. The history department at Michigan State has been a wonderful home from which to work on this book. I am very grateful to have such supportive colleagues and friends there.

Much of the materials in this book were initially presented at conferences of the Society for Historians of the Early American Republic, the American Studies Association, the Organization of American Historians, the Society of Historians of American Foreign Relations, the Southern Historical Association, the Rothermere American Institute at Oxford University, and the Religion in American Life Conference at King's College London. My thanks to the audiences and commenters at these presentations who helped me to refine my arguments. I have also been very lucky to find wonderful colleagues and friends in the Religion and United States Empire workshop. Conversations at these conferences, whether at the seminar table or over coffee, have helped me to fine tune the arguments here about missions, imperialism, the United States in the world, and the early republic. Big thanks for these conversations go to Eric Burin, Cara Burnidge, Katelyn Crawford, Kara French, Lindsay Keiter, Gale Kenny, Brandon Mills, Ashley Moreshead Pilkington, Barbara Reeves-Ellington, Ann Marie Wilson, and Ben Wright. Rachel Van and John Demos provided some timely help on Singapore and mission schools, respectively. Liam Brockey provided some much-appreciated advice about titles.

A few generous friends and colleagues read an early draft of the entire manuscript and I owe them tremendous thanks. David Bailey, Edward Blum, Mary Kupiec Cayton, and Christine Heyrman were all extremely helpful in pushing me to clarify my argument and make my claims as directly as possible. Rosemarie Zagarri and an anonymous reader for Cornell provided incredibly thoughtful suggestions for revision that greatly strengthened the book. Christine and Mary deserve my particular thanks alongside Amy Greenberg for supporting this book through the entire process. Early discussions with both of them helped me imagine what this book might look like, and conversations throughout the revision process helped to shape its final form. Their encouragement always came at precisely the moment it was most needed, and I am so grateful.

Writing this book would have been a very different process indeed if it were not for the love and support of my wonderful family. My parents and my sister have encouraged me every step of the way. Dad should be pleased to find a (very) little bit of Jefferson in here, and I hope Mom will think that this connects to contemporary discussions of the links between the church and the world as much as she always assured me that it did. More than anyone else, though, I am forever thankful to Jeff for sticking with me through this process. I don't know if he expected that the acronym ABCFM would come to roll off his tongue so easily, but that it does is a testament to the ways that he has supported this project and its author for all these years. Thank you for listening, thank you for arguing with me about whether the American Board was an "it" or a "they" (you're right, it's an "it"), and thank you for distracting me when I needed it. The book and I are both the better for your loving support. Thanks also go to Lizzie, who excels in the area of distracting her mother when it is time to think about things other than the conversion of the world in the early republic.

Prologue

An American Missionary in London

In August 1811, Adoniram Judson was full of hope. His sister-in-law would later remember this young divinity student as an "erect, commanding figure . . . glowing with celestial fire, laboring intensely to excite in his hearers an interest in those high and holy themes that so fill[ed] his own vision."[1] We might picture him in a like manner, burning inside with excitement and expectation, as he sailed from London to New York, reflecting on the travels he had already undertaken, and those that lay ahead of him. For Judson was to become a missionary, and this trip to London had secured British support for his mission to India. Now he could know for sure that he would be able to answer his calling to go out into the world and spread the Gospel, to make his home in what he called the "heathen world," and to attempt to bring it into God's kingdom. He was to be one of the first foreign missionaries from the United States.

As he sailed home to the United States, Judson felt himself ready to begin America's work in the conversion of the whole world. At twenty-three years of age, he and his brethren in the American Board of Commissioners for Foreign Missions (ABCFM) were prepared to leave their homes for the rest of their lives. Taking leave of family and friends, they would "dwell on the other side of the world, among a heathen people," as he explained it to his fiancée, Ann Hasseltine. This was something new for Americans, whose mission work had previously focused on Native Americans living within their own borders. For the generation before Judson, mission projects were met with little enthusiasm or support. By the time that Judson was in college, though, a rising group of evangelical Protestants looked at the world around them and heard it beckon. They described themselves as having a "passion" for missions, and their enthusiasm was infectious. Within the next four decades, American missionaries could be found throughout the world, and American Protestants throughout the country supported them. Judson's trip to London marked the beginning of something new as well as the continuation of something begun long before he ever set foot in India.

Judson's trip to London began, in a sense, much earlier than when his ship first left in January 1811. We could see it as beginning at the founding of the ABCFM in 1810, or the so-called Haystack Meeting at Williams College in 1806, or even in the departure of British Baptist William Carey for India in 1792. For Judson, it was reading *The Star in the East*, a book by a British chaplain to the East India Company, that made him resolve to personally take part in the work of world missions not even a year after he first made a public profession of faith and became a church member.[2] These events all spoke to the transatlantic nature of Judson's and the Board's imagination of their work. They help us to understand why Judson was traveling to London in the first place, and why India was the destination he ultimately hoped to reach. For American Protestants of Judson's era, foreign missions opened up a new opportunity to do God's work in the world.

Importantly, it was an opportunity that they experienced as Americans. By 1834, American missionaries would write of their hopes that America would continue to "act a conspicuous part in the evangelization of the world," for this would be the best way for the country to "manifest her gratitude for her distinguished civil and religious privileges and ensure their perpetuation to numerous generations of descendants." Missionary work, then, was an American duty and would help to extend the blessings of American religious culture around the world and into the future. At the same time, American missionaries of Judson's era identified strongly with Great Britain. Their religion connected American evangelicals to Christians in England and around the world. Much of the early years of the mission movement would be spent trying to work out how religion, the nation, and empire ought to relate to each other. The Board's very formation reveals the competing claims on missionary identity.

The Board had been founded in 1810 at the request of Judson and his classmates at Andover Seminary as a way for American Christians to participate fully in the world mission movement. Inspired by what they understood to be the movements of the Holy Spirit and Providence in the British Empire, they felt called to join in these evangelical efforts. Reading British reports of the spread of Christianity in the East, they came to believe that the time had come for all Christians who were able to take part in global evangelization. Americans, they were sure, were indeed able. "The object of missions to the heathen cannot but be regarded, by the friends of the Redeemer, as vastly interesting and important," the Board's leaders wrote at this time. As they attempted to raise interest and funds for their project, they informed readers that "the Lord is shaking the nations; his friends in different parts of Christendom are roused from their slumbers; and unprecedented exertions are making for the spread of divine knowledge, and the conversion of the nations." Even in "our own country," this "missionary spirit is excited." Yet there was still much work to do, and millions to evangelize. "A new scene, with us, is now opening," the Board wrote.[3]

If this felt very new to Americans, British missionary organizations seemed to be authorities with nearly twenty years' experience. And so, when the Andover students proposed the creation of an American missionary society, it was only natural that their leaders would turn to London for support and guidance. On Christmas day 1810, Samuel Worcester, the corresponding secretary of the new board, instructed Judson to travel to England bearing letters for the directors of the London Missionary Society (LMS). At a time when other Americans set themselves apart from the British and emphasized the importance of independence, these evangelicals looked instead to partner with them. Judson was to announce the creation of the Board and learn what arrangements might be made for a formal connection between the London and American societies. Worcester was particularly concerned about money and whether American Protestants would be able to undertake so expensive a project as foreign missions. Accordingly, he hoped that the London Missionary Society might be willing to support financially the four American missionaries (Judson, Samuel Newell, Samuel Nott, and Gordon Hall) without removing them from the direction of the Board. Judson was also supposed to learn as much as possible about where the missionaries might go, what they had to do to prepare themselves, and "generally . . . whatever may be conductive to the missionary interest."[4]

Judson endured a difficult transatlantic trip during which French privateers boarded his ship. Unable to speak French, he found himself completely at their mercy and was briefly jailed in France. The excitement of these Atlantic travels were not discussed much in the evangelical press, for to emphasize the difficulties that Judson had faced would be to point out the risks that all future American missionaries would take. Those dangers could emerge even before the missionaries disembarked at their future mission stations. As French, British, and American ships navigated the seas during the turbulent years of the Napoleonic War, what hope of success did a few American missionaries have? Few would have blamed them if they had expressed fear or concern, but Judson and his brethren were driven by a conviction that the hand of Providence was guiding them into their work.

If they wanted proof of God's favor, they needed only to look at how Judson survived his imprisonment. At first it had seemed hopeless, and Judson dreamed only of returning to Boston and to the Christians that he knew there. But he would come to feel that this was only God's way of preparing him for the difficulties of missionary life. A way to safety was soon opened for him. Being marched through Bayonne on his way to prison by the French crew, Judson protested his treatment loudly in English in the hopes of being understood by someone he passed. A Philadelphian heard him and promised to help. The next day, he visited Judson in prison and helped him to escape by hiding him under his cloak (this would not be the last time that Judson would try to escape the clutches of European officials in his pursuit of missionary work). The stranger would then find him shelter with other Americans for six weeks in France before he could leave for England. Whatever dangers he had faced, the way had been opened for Judson to go about his mission work. As befitted his future occupation, he would spend part of his time in Bayonne exhorting the participants at a masked ball of the error of their ways and urging them to turn to the religion of Jesus Christ.[5]

Judson made his way to London just in time for the annual meeting of the London Missionary Society. There, he met with the directors of the society and presented the materials of the new American Board of Commissioners for Foreign Missions along with statements from its four missionaries. The London Society agreed to accept the four Americans as missionaries of their own society, though they would not agree to Worcester's plan to combine British financing and American governance. This American attempt to maintain independence and authority while requiring almost complete financial support simply did not make sense to their British brethren. If the Americans wanted to be missionaries, the London Society suggested, they could be London missionaries. This was not what

Worcester or the other directors of the new board wanted to hear, though it might not have disappointed Judson too much. After all, he and the others had sent applications to the London Society at the same time that they had approached the Massachusetts ministers. If the Board had not been founded, they would have happily chosen to serve as British missionaries. In their eyes, the nation that supported them mattered less than the cause they were serving, though they would soon find that their national identity mattered a great deal to others.

Sailing back to America, then, Judson had much to look forward to. He and his fellow missionaries would find their way to India, one way or another. That much was certain. But there was still much to be worked out. This close cooperation with the British that he and the directors of the Board envisioned ran the risk of putting Americans again in a dependent relationship with the British. Neither missionary society could agree on how best to navigate these questions of control and cooperation. The difficulties would only worsen after Judson's next trip across the Atlantic, this time destined for India in 1812.

Though the directors of the Board were able to secure enough funding from within America to send out its first missionaries, this did not mean that they left the questions of their relationship with Britain behind them. A generation after the Revolution, as their country prepared to go to war with England, they remained Anglophilic in an era politically dominated by Anglophobia. They remained focused on making a place for America on the world stage even as it was not clear what that place ought to be in the midst of European empires and American democracy. In spite of these lingering tensions, Judson and his brethren set out in 1812 as only the first of the missionaries of the Board. By 1840, they were joined by missionaries in Asia, Africa, the Pacific Islands, the Mideast, Europe, and the Americas. By 1860, the Board had sent out almost thirteen hundred men and women to serve as missionaries and missionary assistants. That was all ahead of Judson in 1811, however. All he knew was that he was going to India, to serve his God as an American missionary in the British Empire.

CHRISTIAN IMPERIALISM

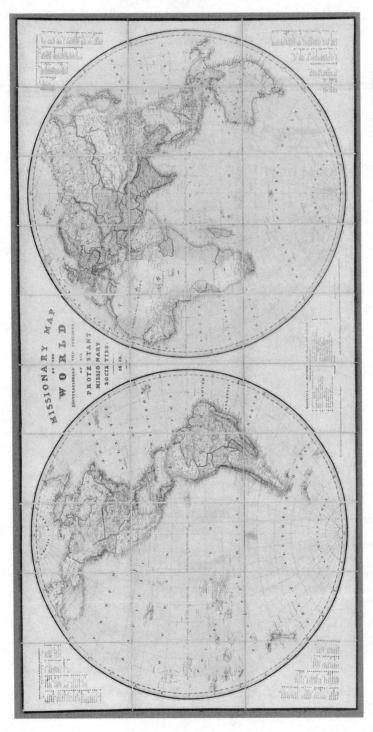

Figure 1. In 1838, the Church Missionary Society published this large map to represent the extent of Protestant missions around the world. The ABCFM was prominently featured among an international group of Protestant missionary societies, all working together in support of the conversion of the world. In the early years of the ABCFM's work, it was important to them to have this kind of recognition of their equality as missionaries alongside other European, particularly British, groups. As the directors of the ABCFM looked over their copy of this map, they could be proud of the wide reach that their nation could claim to evangelize in after only a few short decades. Courtesy of the Wider Church Ministries of the United Church of Christ, ABC 79, Box 1, Folder 1.

Introduction

Christian Imperialism
and American Foreign Missions

In 1803, the directors of the Connecticut Missionary Society described their field of labor in terms of the map of the United States. Look at this map, they said, and you can see the full extent of the field for evangelization by American Christians. With its large swath of frontier to the west of American settlement, this vision of the American mission field conforms to what we think we know about Americans in the early republic. They were focused on the continent and westward expansion. Even as they wrote this description to British missionaries in a spirit of partnership, they did not operate in the same ways that the British did. The British were imperial and global; the Americans were republican and continental.

Thirty-five years later, American missionaries relied on another map, and this one looked quite different. This new image surveyed the whole globe and showed the progress that Protestant missionaries had made in the past several decades. North America was included, of course, and there were many dots representing the activities of American missionaries there. As the map revealed, though, American missionaries were also active elsewhere. In fact, American missionaries were well represented among those who sought to bring about the conversion of the whole world. In contrast to what the Connecticut Society imagined at the dawn of the century, the dots representing American stations were not confined to the North American continent. They could now be found in Africa, Asia, the Pacific Islands, the Mideast, South America, and even Europe. American missionaries now saw their field of labor as encompassing the whole world. Supporters of the mission movement in the 1810s, 1820s, and 1830s embraced this wide scope, seeing the mission movement as an important part of setting their country in its proper place in the world order.

In this book I tell the story of how that map came to be filled in. It is an account of American engagement in the world in the years before the U.S.-Mexican War. By the 1840s, American foreign missionaries had been laboring around the world for nearly three decades. In that time, they had worked hard to bring the whole world, and what they viewed as the needs of all of its people, to the attention of American Christians. The American Board of Commissioners for Foreign Missions was the major institution behind this work. Founded in 1810, the Board and its missionaries worked to convert the world to God's kingdom and to make American Christians aware of the world outside of their own country. If the marks on the map represented the work of individual missionaries focused on particular locations, the map as a whole represented the vision of the American Board and its supporters. For them, all of these spaces were linked. They were all in need of God's grace and capable of joining the ranks of civilized Christians. They were all, in other words, the proper subjects of American missionary exertions.

Globalizing the Early American Republic

The American Board's world map and its history in the first decades of the nineteenth century challenges our understanding of the periodization of American history by introducing us to a group of Americans who had a different way of looking at the world. As an increasing body of literature is showing, Americans in the early republic were not only focused on the continent but were thinking about the globe. India and China, in particular, loomed large in the American imagination. Merchants and missionaries brought goods and stories from the other side of the globe into the United States and helped to shape the ways that Americans thought about the world and their role within it.[1]

Missionaries represented the continuation of a long transatlantic American religious identity, dating from the colonial era and extending through the eras of the First and Second Great Awakenings. In the eighteenth and nineteenth centuries, Christians on both sides of the Atlantic experienced periods of religious revivals collectively known as the Awakenings. Evangelical Protestants felt the world to be filled with the Holy Spirit, which was particularly active in expanding the church by deepening the religious experience of those who were already Christians and by making it possible for new groups around the world to become exposed to Christianity. Prominent preachers traveled across the Atlantic to speak before British and American audiences. Religious groups corresponded across the ocean about the progress of religion in their own locality. They made up what historian Charles Foster has called an "Evangelical united front" that shared common solutions to what were seen as common religious and cultural problems. The American mission movement emerged out of this Anglo-American sense of the importance of religiously motivated benevolent activity that would improve the world.[2]

Foreign missionaries are an essential group for understanding the ways that Americans lived in the world during this era. Missionaries were prominent among the small numbers of Americans abroad in this period, important alongside the merchants and diplomats who helped to determine American foreign relations.[3] The Board was the first and the largest of the nineteenth-century missionary societies operating from the United States. By 1850, the Board was in charge of 40 percent of all American missionary personnel; earlier in the century, its share was higher. Its directors claimed a national representativeness, evidenced in their use of *American* in their title, in contrast to their closest British allies, the London Missionary Society. With much of its leadership based in Massachusetts, it was not the Salem Board or even the Boston Board, although its actual membership never reached the coverage that "American" implied. In many ways, the Board's naming was a statement about what its leaders thought the image of their country ought to be. If they were not actually representative of the United States, they certainly wanted to be. They wanted their country to be the sort of place that would support global missions and find sacred purpose in commercial and imperial expansion.

In the papers of the Board, there are twenty-four fat volumes of letters from men and women anxious to serve as missionaries in the years before the Civil War alone. They would write earnestly about their faith, their sense of calling, and their willingness to sacrifice everything to the spread of the Gospel in the world. Sometimes they would write about the specific places they hoped to go, pointing to India, Africa, Hawaii, Palestine, or the

American Indians. They would include letters of reference from ministers and teachers, all testifying to the particular qualities that these missionary candidates could bring with them into the field: piety and enthusiasm, certainly, but also steadiness of character, talent for language acquisition, and past experience with teaching. These references would even include comments about the health and constitution of the candidates, with implications for how readily they might survive in foreign climates.

These candidate files provide a sense of what sorts of Americans the Board really did represent. They were overwhelmingly from the Northeast, and almost all preached or worshipped in Congregationalist or Presbyterian churches. As time went on, the Board had more missionaries from other regions, although the South and the West never reached the numbers that the North did in its participation in the Board's work. As the century progressed, Christians from other denominations and other parts of the country could support their own missionary societies, many of which corresponded and cooperated with the Board. By the fiftieth anniversary of the Board in 1860, it had sent almost thirteen hundred missionaries out into the world. A little over four hundred of these were ordained male missionaries. The rest were wives, teachers, physicians, printers, and other missionary assistants who had felt the call to do their part to convert the world. Together, they went to forty-one separate missions around the world. They established schools, translated texts, and above all, worked to convert foreign people (whom they called the heathen world) to both Protestant Christianity and an Anglo-American culture that they called civilization. They saw the hand of Providence guiding their steps, even as they met with difficulty and saw few converts to their cause.[4]

Missionaries of the early nineteenth century made their homes away, expecting to die abroad. Yet they still remained connected to America through the written word and prayer. At set times every month, Christians in the United States and the mission field would pause to pray in concert with each other. This spiritual connection worked together with the more material connection of missionary periodicals to link Americans to the missionary world. Missionaries were not only important as representatives of American culture abroad, after all. They were also central sources of information about the rest of the world for Americans at home and, as such, provided Americans with a specific way of thinking about the role of their country in the world.

For example, readers of the Board's monthly periodical, the *Missionary Herald*, could see the globe from their parlors. Opening the magazine, they would read of the work of the Board and its sister organizations around the world. In the August 1826 issue, for example, they would read about the formation of a mission college in Ceylon; a tour in South America; and the activities of missionaries among Native Americans in New York, the South, and the Sandwich Islands. They would read about "Hindoostan," or India, and about the American colony in Liberia. They would also learn about the work of the Bible Society in Russia and in Bengal, the global mission of the American Baptists, and the recent merger of the American Board with its United Foreign Mission Society, which brought far more missions to Native Americans under the control of the Board. The Board understood all of this diverse and global work to be related, and all of it was described for evangelical readers in a short thirty-two pages each month. Explaining the merger with the United Foreign Mission Society, the Board asked its readers if it could "be doubted that the prompt and efficient support of all Protestant missions to the heathen" was the duty of the Christian world, and further, if "the missions which have originated from our own shores" should not "be dear to the hearts of American Christians?"[5] This issue of the *Missionary Herald* is typical of the publications of the Board, then in its second decade of operations, both in the wide scope of its coverage and its identification of duties for American evangelicals as part of the "Christian world" and as "American Christians."

In the first decades of the foreign mission movement, American evangelicals had a dual identity: they were both evangelical Christians who saw themselves as transnational figures taking part in a global struggle for God's kingdom and Americans whose national pride called them to partner with Great Britain in the conversion of the world. If traditional interpretations have described the early republic as continental and republican, the Christian imperialism of the missionaries reveals that this was not a universal worldview. Missionaries and their supporters were, on the contrary, international and imperial in their thinking about their nation in the world. This group of Americans was more concerned with events across the globe than they were with those across the continent, and they were certainly more open to the possibilities of empire than Americans in this era are generally depicted. They hoped that the formal empire of Great Britain would allow for the spread of Christianity and civilization throughout the world. They hoped that they, too, could take part in that movement by working within and alongside the spread of British and American political and commercial influence around the world. The missionaries' imperialism emerged from their sense of their own superiority and their assertion that they had the power to bring foreign peoples into the orbit of their own influence. To truly understand the American early republic, we must include this group of Americans in our narratives.

The American foreign mission movement has been the subject of earlier work, but this early period has not received sufficient attention. It is not a coincidence that the bulk of the previous missionary historiography has focused on periods in American history that are widely understood to be eras of American imperial connection with the rest of the world, either in the colonial era or after 1898. As historians of British missions have demonstrated, missions are very important in the creation and shaping of imperial culture. It is a truism that, geographically, the missionary map followed the imperial map. The relationship between the two has been a consistent source of study for historians of the British Empire, who have seen missionaries as important figures in both the exportation of British culture into the world as well as the importation of the world into Britain. These historians have seen missionaries at times as the first line of empire, as the bearers of social reform, as pragmatic individuals who seized the unique opportunities the empire provided, or as subtle challengers to its logic, depending on the particular context of the mission in question.[6] What, then, ought we make of the American foreign mission movement in a supposedly nonimperial era?

Christian Imperialism and Empire

Empire is a difficult concept for the early American republic. A generation before the beginning of the foreign mission movement, Americans had fought a war against empire and created a new kind of government, one that was rooted in republicanism and local authority. Americans in the first decades of the nineteenth century were busy building their economy, improving internal communication and transportation networks, and expanding their territory into the West. Overseas empire was not a primary concern, certainly not for the U.S. government. And yet the mission movement reveals to us a group of Americans who were thinking about empire and imperialism, and who had a different focus than many of their peers. Religious historian Martin Marty once described the missionaries' early-nineteenth-century emphasis on Asia over North America as "a strange reversal of the general pro-western mentality of the century," and in many ways this is an apt description.[7]

Looking more closely at this group shows, however, that they were not strange, but representative of a larger ambivalence about imperialism in the early United States. These religious Americans were very supportive of empire in theory, encouraging their countrymen to see it as an opportunity for improving the world, while still being quite critical of many imperial practices that they felt did not live up to this possibility. They present us with an alternative early republican view of what America's role in the world ought to have been, an emblem of what I will call "Christian imperialism."

In its most basic political definition, empire refers to a state that exerts political power over an external territory and people. American historians in recent years have reexamined the concept of empire within the history of the United States. Much of this scholarship has focused on the question of whether America is, was, or had an empire. The tradition of American exceptionalism has meant that many historians have traditionally talked about the American past as distinct from European history, particularly with respect to empire and imperialism. Whereas European states may have been imperial, the United States, we have been told, was not for the majority of its history.[8] Certainly the early nineteenth century has not been counted as part of America's imperial era. Yet more recent works have questioned this chronology, pointing to American imperialism earlier in the nineteenth century.[9]

In a world largely defined geopolitically by empires, how did evangelical Americans envision their role in the world? Unsurprisingly, empires and imperialism loom large in their thinking. The American Board was founded in an era of imperialist nation building, European empire building, and imperial conflict across the globe; it is unsurprising that at least some Americans were invested in these politics and thought their country might have a part to play. When these Americans thought about global politics, the expanding British Empire was one of the most significant things that they noticed. It defined the world they lived in. Similarly, this was a time of expansion for the American state. Connections to new places and new peoples meant new fields for evangelization and new communities to welcome into God's kingdom.

This was a way of thinking about empire that had a strong tradition within Great Britain. There, evangelicals understood that empire created a "reciprocal obligation to promote the spread of Christianity," in historian Andrew Porter's phrasing. This was not an uncontested position. Others in Britain had different understandings of the centrality of evangelization to the empire. Evangelicals within Britain criticized the East India Company and other colonial institutions when they did not live up to this standard.[10]

The British missionary understanding of empire was extremely influential for American evangelicals. Many American evangelicals identified strongly with the British throughout these years, at times finding a shared evangelical Christianity far more significant than different national identities. For the participants in the early foreign mission movement, the United States was the partner and inheritor of Great Britain's role as a moral guide for the world; in joining the work of global missions, the United States became Britain's peer. In most of the places where they established their early stations, American missionaries only had access to the place and the people as a result of Anglo-American imperial connections. Instead of rejecting European models, some Americans attempted to apply them to the American context through foreign missions. Their goal was to export an evangelical Protestantism that was Anglo-American in its roots and its culture, and in so doing they made claims about the proper role of the United States in the world.

Conceptions of empire were contested and changing in the half-century after the ratification of the U.S. Constitution. For a nation that had only recently thrown off the shackles of colonialism, this could be a heated topic and was certainly one that required much thought. For those concerned with differentiating the new nation from England, it was important to highlight the ways that the United States was a republic. This never meant, though, that the country would be isolated from the rest of the world. The U.S. economy relied on overseas trade, and much of early American diplomacy sought to open up more of the world to American commerce. The other emphasis of American diplomacy in these years was the expansion of American territory into the western parts of the continent. Thomas Jefferson famously described the new nation as an "empire of liberty" that would spread across the continent, bringing with it the benefits of American citizenship. In practice, this was accomplished not only through purchase (as in Louisiana), but also through violent conflict (as in Florida).[11] Questions of how to govern this new land and the people within it were central to this era. The "liberty" that Jefferson's imperialism promised was explicitly not offered to either enslaved African Americans or to most Native Americans as the country expanded its reach. Indeed, the expansion of slavery was a driving force of early American imperialism, as the demand for land sparked by the cotton boom spread American planters further into the Southwest in the early nineteenth century. This spread of American plantation agriculture

[handwritten marginal note: Though they were liberated, they weren't solitary.]

required the dispossession of Native American land as well as expansion of slavery.[12] By the 1840s, ideas about expansion had developed into the doctrine of Manifest Destiny, which asserted the divine right of the United States to possess an expansive territory that could be acquired through war and the conquest of Native American and Mexican peoples.

None of these ideas were uncontested. Throughout these years, Americans debated among themselves the extent to which America ought to expand and the means by which it ought to do so.[13] From Jefferson's idea of an "empire of liberty" to the ideology of Manifest Destiny, there was plenty of space for Americans to disagree about how their country ought to relate to the rest of the world. Region, class, gender, and politics could all affect the ways that different groups of Americans approached these questions. So, too, could religion. The Christian imperialism of the foreign mission movement was one of many proposals of what America's role in the world ought to be.

Unlike most of the proponents of Manifest Destiny, missionaries were largely Anglophiles, and so their answers to these questions were shaped by British example. The missionaries could join American merchants in encouraging American participation in global networks. These Americans might criticize the British Empire, but they also saw much to emulate. Though Americans were in an inferior position abroad, without the economic or diplomatic power to equal their former colonial rulers, this group aimed to emulate them in many ways.[14] Like contemporaries in England who used the language of justice and humanity to judge the British Empire in the late eighteenth century, these Americans did not see the problems of empire as reason to give up on imperial projects.[15] Rather, they believed that reform was possible, and that empire could serve benevolent ends. Accordingly, some Americans saw a new colony in Liberia as both a potential solution to the problem of slavery in the United States and a way to improve the lives of Africans.[16] For evangelical Christians, imperial connections offered new possibilities for evangelization and improvement. Even though these evangelicals had little reason to expect that they would be successful, most of their early movement was marked by optimism and providentialism. Much of that tone had to do with theology, but much of it also had to do with the ways that American evangelicals applied their understanding of how God worked in the world to their interpretation of global politics.

Christian imperialism was the ideal of these missionaries and their supporters in the United States. As the missionaries discovered when they began their work, empires on the ground did not match their vision of what

empires ought to be. If American missionaries exhibited imperialist thinking in the planning and execution of their work, it does not follow that
they supported empire in all of the forms it took in the early nineteenth
century. Indeed, they could be quite critical of empires that they saw as
being too focused on commerce and power at the expense of benevolence
and religion. The Christian imperialism that the missionaries endorsed was
a dream. It was what they hoped the empires of America and Britain would
look like, and it was what they thought "Christian nations" owed to the
world around them.

Because this Christian imperialism was a vision and not a reality, it is not
necessary here to dwell on the question of whether or not America was an
empire. Instead, in this book I follow the suggestion of Paul Kramer to use
imperialism as a tool of analysis, "something to think with more than think
about." If empire is about states and their power, imperialism is a more flex-
ible term that allows us to think about unequal power dynamics between
groups and their ability to create "relations of hierarchy, discipline, dispossession, extraction, and exploitation."[17] Missionaries certainly did not think
about what they were doing in these terms. Indeed, they were hoping to do
just the opposite: to make everyone equal members of Christ's family and
to counter the exploitation that they believed to be inherent in "heathen"
societies. Yet their way of thinking about the rest of the world was certainly
imperial. It was predicated on their position as Anglo-American Christians
relative to foreign "heathens" of supposedly inferior political, economic,
cultural, and of course, religious status. Central to this way of thinking were
not only ideas about religion and culture but also ideas about race and "civilization." Missionaries began to equate racial and cultural difference with a
hierarchical relationship in which white Euro-Americans were above non-
white peoples across the globe. These missionaries presumed their right to
come into foreign spaces and transform them, relying on their own values
as they judged those around them.

This operational understanding of imperialism allows for a fresh critical perspective not only on the mission movement but also on America's
position in the world in the early republic. Setting aside our assumptions
about the periodization of American empire to think about the meaning
of imperialism, it becomes clear that American missionaries had their own
ideas about what empire ought to look like and how imperial America
ought to be. The Christian imperialism that the missionaries envisioned
had little to do with states. It relied on existing political and economic
networks between supposedly Christian nations and the so-called heathen

world. It expected that these be supportive of efforts to evangelize and improve the world. The missionaries were not primarily focused on the spread of Anglo-American governance; they were concerned with the spread of Anglo-American culture and the Protestant religion, seeing governance as a tool in this larger project.

As Amy Kaplan has reminded us in her study of the culture of American empire, the people of the United States have historically been ambivalent about empire, seeing it as both a dream and a nightmare. For all of the allure of foreign goods that empires promise, there has been the supposed risk of incorporating new and foreign peoples into the body politic.[18] American missionaries of the early nineteenth century were also ambivalent about empire, though in a different way. Insofar as America was going to participate in global commerce and expand its territory, the missionaries insisted, it must also evangelize in these places. In fact, those commercial and political links should, they believed, be in service to their religious goals. They were, then, in favor of empire and imperialism as a general concept, seeing in it great possibilities for the conversion of the world. Yet they could at the same time be quite critical of empire in practice when it failed to live up to this religious and moral ideal.

Over the course of the first several decades of American missionary activity, American evangelists encountered different types of empire: the British East India Company's empire in India, U.S. imperial claims of sovereignty over Cherokee land and people, the settler colonialism of the American Colonization Society in Liberia, and more. Each of these had a distinct model of governance; what united them was their similar approach to the supposed superiority of Anglo-American culture and their assertion of the right to rule over foreign territory and people. This story is about the encounter that American missionaries had with these different types of empire in the early nineteenth century. As they experienced each, they developed a critique of empire that helps us to see new perspectives on how some Americans of this time thought about the role of their country in the world.

These American missionaries saw the expansion of Western imperial power as a potential boon for Christian interests, but they also had high expectations of what that imperialism would look like. Britain and America, they argued, were Christian nations. Accordingly, they ought to practice a Christian form of empire—one that would spread their religion and its connected culture wherever they went. In the first decades of its work, the American foreign mission movement imagined a cooperative approach between missions and empire, whereby imperial expansion provided missionaries with access to the "heathen world" and missionaries helped to spread "civilization" along with Christianity. It was a vision of Christian imperialism; they described it as the spread of the kingdom of God.

So what did real-world empires look like to early American missionaries? Americans began their foreign mission work in India, when it was under the control of the British East India Company (EIC). After the American Revolution, the British Parliament focused on turning this into the jewel of the British imperial crown, and the governing of the British territory in India was controlled both the EIC and Parliament. The EIC's charter was issued by Parliament, and many government officials sat on its Board of Directors; it was through the periodic renewals of that charter that the state asserted some control over EIC-owned territory. In the early nineteenth century, the EIC was not fully secure in its power, and these years would see it attempt to expand its geographic reach while accommodating the interests of native leaders. The commercial government of the EIC and its priorities of profit and stability shaped this period of British imperialism. For the British in the metropole, however, the EIC's territory in India was British territory. It was part of a British Empire that, for evangelicals at least, demanded a religious response from the British people.[19]

Imperialism and empire defined, too, the relationship between the United States and the Cherokee Nation by the early nineteenth century. Though euphemized as "expansion," the westward movement of the white American population involved the purchase and seizure of lands possessed by the Cherokees and the eventual extension of both state and federal sovereignty over the Cherokee land and people. Though previously treated as foreign peoples who needed to be party to treaties, Native Americans during the Jacksonian era increasingly were thought of as a subject people. The Jeffersonian vision of the spread of this republican "empire of liberty" was based on the removal or incorporation of native peoples. The story of the American missionaries in the Cherokee Nation is, in some respects, the story of their (ultimately unsuccessful) resistance to this assertion of an American empire within North America.[20]

Liberia presents a different context, at least in the traditional treatment of the colonization movement. The emigration of African Americans to Liberia has been presented as a movement of colonization that was still non-imperialist. It is understood to be properly part of the history of American reform and American slavery, and is rarely considered within its international and imperial context. This premise, however, is clearly limited.[21] If we look at colonization from the perspective of indigenous Africans, its imperial nature becomes far clearer. Liberia was a settler colony sponsored not by the U.S. government but by the American Colonization Society, although it did receive support through federal and state funding and the navy.[22] The colony's land was acquired through purchase and eventual expansion of the settler population; the relationship between native Africans and Americo-Liberians was never equal (and in fact continues to mark Liberian politics today). This was clear to the missionaries and other contemporaries, who had no problem discussing Liberia as an American colony and referring to the African American settlers as colonists. So clear was the connection between Liberia and other colonial ventures, in fact, that the American missionaries were prompted to reflect on the history of "all colonists" across the world in their discussions of the likely future of Americans in Liberia.[23]

In all of these places and more, American missionaries expected to be welcomed as Americans and as Christians. They believed that their work of evangelization was an important part of imperial projects, or at least that it ought to be. The missions under study here provide the opportunity to discuss the missionary relationship to imperialism, civilization, race, and gender. The American missionaries were not themselves agents of a formal political empire, but this should not stop us from examining the relationship of American missions to imperialism. As these cases reveal, American missionaries were dependent on Anglo-American governance, and they struggled with the tensions that arose at times between their national and religious identities. They worked within territories controlled by imperial power, and by virtue of their role within those places they came into contact with these governing powers repeatedly. Their assumption of their own cultural superiority and their right to alter foreign cultures reveals imperialist mindsets similar to many of these governing powers. When missionaries and the Board debated how involved in politics missionaries ought to be, what they were really asking was what the relationship between the missions and the governing powers should be. These missionaries were always political; their work of evangelization was, even in their own eyes, closely linked to the spread of civilization, and they were deeply invested in politics when they found it to involve morality (as they often did).

Civilization and American Missions

Central to Christian imperialism was the concept of civilization, which missionaries understood to embody important components of a truly Christian culture. Throughout the book, I use the term as they did, to describe a particular type of culture, though for readability I will not place the term in quotations with each use. It is essential to understand how much ideas about civilization structured the ways that the missionaries understood the world in which they lived. This was not a neutral term, but one of judgment about the relative value of different cultures. Anglo-American evangelicals in the early nineteenth century believed that the culture in which they lived was the embodiment of civilization, the pinnacle of human social and cultural organization. Because they were so confident of this, they rarely paused to define what they meant when they talked about civilization, but their discussion contained a few key themes. In defining civilization, they built on Enlightenment concepts of the progression of mankind from savagery to barbarism and finally to civilization, the highest form of social organization. This was in some ways a historical trajectory: all civilizations had begun in savagery. Through the introduction of tools, agriculture, and the like, societies would over time progress to the next rung on the hierarchy. This did not happen at one time for all peoples, however. As some groups progressed, others remained behind. Accordingly, when the "civilized" people of America and Britain looked around the world in the early nineteenth century, they saw people occupying all the different positions on this spectrum.

They often phrased their definition of these categories in negative terms: civilization was the opposite of what savage and barbarous communities were like. Whereas savages hunted to provide themselves with food and sustenance, civilized men farmed and lived in settled communities; whereas savages wandered about in near nakedness, civilized people wore proper clothing. Sexual modesty was similarly an important definition of civilization, in contrast to the (frequently mentioned) supposed obscenity of savage and barbarous women and men.[24] They emphasized the importance of the "useful arts" to civilization, and both British and American missionaries tried to teach these when they could. The most frequently discussed components of civilization within mission literature included a settled agricultural lifestyle; the presence of the arts and skilled trades and the use of technology and tools; monogamous, patriarchal families; a written language and a literate population; and a gendered division of labor that "elevated" women to domestic work. Some variation of these characteristics seemed to define civilization for most Anglo-Americans of the early nineteenth century.

Importantly, for evangelicals all of these components of civilization were deeply enmeshed in what it meant to be a Christian as well. The connection—or lack thereof—between the two has been an important theme throughout the history of missions. Missionaries have debated the issue over the course of the past two and a half centuries at least. At different times and places, for example, missionaries have had a wide range of ideas about how much cultural change needed to occur in order for a person to be considered a Christian. In the first half century of American missionary work, the introduction of Christianity to a "heathen" culture seemed to require the introduction of civilization. As the century progressed, people would debate whether civilization was a prerequisite of Christianity or an effect of it. But at the beginning of the mission movement, supporters were sure that both were necessary for the practice of "true Christianity," as they phrased it. Missionaries were looking for signs of civilization and attempting to implant it as they went about their evangelization. As a result, the missions were sites not only of important religious exchanges but secular ones as well. While American missionaries saw themselves as servants of Christ, they were also partisans of a particular Anglo-American style of civilization.

Because of the perceived connections between conversion and civilization, missionaries and their supporters looked for the spread of Anglo-American power as a providential sign of where they ought to establish missions. Empire, as they understood it, brought civilization along in its wake. This introduction of a community to civilization meant that the way had been cleared for the Gospel. American missionaries thought deeply about what locations they ought to select, and they saw this sort of preparation as very important. The understanding of this relationship meant that missionaries at the beginning of the nineteenth century felt their work to be yoked to the global spread of Anglo-American power. The missionary understanding of imperial expansion as a providential sign that evangelicals could and should begin the work of converting the whole world reveals some of the confusion between the two categories for missionaries and their supporters early in the century. Over the first decades of their work, missionaries' accumulated experiences of actually working within different imperial situations would allow them to begin disentangling the meaning of civilization and Christianity, and the projects of missions and imperialism.

Armed with this understanding of civilization, missionaries and other Euro-American travelers explored the world and its cultures in the early nineteenth century. The missionaries of the Board in this period by and large did not come out of these experiences with a greater appreciation for the diversity of world cultures. While they did incorporate some aspects of foreign cultures—such as local architectural styles—they remained convinced that their Anglo-American culture was the apex of civilization. The concept of civilization that guided much of the early American mission experience was closely entwined with ideas about gender and race. Like economic and social factors, gender and race became important markers of civilization or savagery. For evangelicals, gender norms revealed almost more than anything else how civilized a community was. Race had a more complicated role, as missionaries both believed that God had created all people as one, and yet still identified significant racial difference between themselves and those "heathens" whom they sought to convert, and between different groups of "heathens." What made missionaries want to go out into the world was that they believed that they could change what they saw, and that the "heathen" of the world could eventually become civilized, too.

They had hope for other nations.

Converting the World in the Early Republic

In the chapters that follow I trace American missionaries in a range of imperial contexts as they sought to determine how the American foreign mission movement should relate to empire and political institutions more generally. Beginning in Boston in 1810, in the first chapter I examine the Board's global vision and the ways that it imagined the rest of the world, particularly through the formation of what I call a "hierarchy of heathenism" that helped the Board decide where to send missionaries and when. The next six chapters take place at the actual missions of the Board around the world. Thematically, in each chapter I look at a different type of mission and the relationship between the missions and various types of British and American imperialism. In Bombay, American missionaries attempted to figure out their place within the British Empire and were surprised to find that their sense of a shared Anglo-American identity was not recognized by British officials of the East India Company during the War of 1812. The focus across the chapters is consistently on the ways that Americans viewed the rest of the world, but it is important to remember that these were dynamic encounters in which the so-called heathens were active participants who helped to shape American perceptions of the world. To that end, in chapter 3 I trace the efforts of these missionaries to make converts and the responses of the native Indians to American Christian efforts. If conversion was the goal of the mission movement, it was not one that could be easily accomplished, even as the missionaries assumed that the superiority of their own faith and culture was inherent. Examining the interactions at mission schools and the writings of one early convert reveal the ways that missionaries attempted to work out what it meant to be a missionary in an imperial context.

In the Cherokee Nation and the Sandwich Islands, American missionaries were able to cooperate with governing powers and create settlement-style missions that brought a range of Americans into contact with foreign peoples and spaces. This period of cooperation, covered in chapter 4, was brief in the Cherokee case: Indian removal soon brought the Board into direct confrontation with the governments of the state of Georgia and the United States. In Liberia, missionaries allied themselves with the colonization movement, only to find that the two groups had different ideas about the role of Americans in the world. Chapter 7, on the failed mission to Singapore, is where I look at the attempts of the missionaries to bring American methods into the British Empire and the international crisis that this created. The conclusion of the book returns to a global vision of the Board, this time chronologically focused on the year 1848, as the U.S.-Mexican War ended.

From the beginnings of the foreign mission movement at the turn of the nineteenth century through the 1840s, when the ideology of Manifest Destiny changed the context in which missionaries worked, I consider a developing international vision held by many active and influential Americans. Within two decades of the founding of the American Board, missionaries from the United States operated throughout the world, spreading the Gospel and, often with it, American gender and market behavior. Enlisting a hierarchy of heathenism, the Board mapped out and ordered the cultures of the entire world and placed itself along with Britain at its apex. The beginning of the foreign mission movement marked a turning point when Americans came to see it as entirely appropriate that they should go out into the world and attempt to change it. At first working within and on the margins of the British Empire, and then establishing what might be termed mission settlements, the Board's missionaries acted out their vision of a globally connected America.

By the time that the United States entered what historians have considered its imperial age, American missionaries were already active on a global scale, working out of an evangelical Christian imperialist ideology. That way of thinking brought this group of Americans to view the world with the eyes of imperialists, looking for places where they might exert their influence and power. If American missionaries were seeing the world through an imperial lens even in the early republic, we might ask what we mean when we talk about American imperialism, and where we ought to draw its chronological boundaries. Even as the missionaries found themselves frequently in opposition to the interests of the government, by the late 1840s, much of the same logic that had undergirded the beginnings of the foreign mission movement in 1810 had come to shape the ideology of Manifest Destiny, most especially a hierarchy of humanity with Americans at its peak.

Chapter 1

Hierarchies of Heathenism

When a group of Massachusetts ministers gathered in 1810 to discuss the formation of an American missionary board, their minds were drawn to scripture. As they explained the importance of the work they were about to begin, they returned to Jesus' Great Commission: "Go ye into the all the world, and preach the Gospel to every creature." For evangelical Protestants of the early republic, these words were a command, though a difficult one to enact. Preaching to *all* the world and *every* creature was no small task, and Americans at the beginning of the nineteenth century were not the best-positioned people to take on that responsibility. Without an empire in which to evangelize, and with the Non-Intercourse Act curtailing the possible destinations of American ships, American missionaries did not seem to have many options for overseas missions.

Nonetheless, missionaries and their supporters surveyed the globe in 1810, seeking to learn about the state of the world in order to determine where they might begin their work. As they did so, they translated the "all the world" of scripture into the "most likely" sites of missionary success; it was in these places that the American Board would begin its work.

Missionaries did not want to go just anywhere, after all. The American foreign mission movement as a whole arose only when British missionaries

They were limited so they chose wisely.

reported success in India, and Americans wanted to join in that success. As the lackluster support for Native American missions in earlier decades revealed, missions only gained a major American audience if they could inspire Christians with tales of conversion from heathen paganism to Christian civilization. In the absence of this, missions were the project of a very small minority of evangelical true believers. British success in India, on the other hand, revealed to Americans that success was possible and that there was a mission field "white for the harvest," to use their biblical imagery.[1]

Birth of hierarchy

Inspired by this British example, the American Board attempted to determine which places were ready for missionary work, and which places were not worth the effort, or at least not yet. As it did so, the Board and its supporters created a hierarchy of heathenism that helped them make sense of the seemingly endless possibilities for where to begin the immense task of converting the whole world. This hierarchy ranked the different cultures and peoples of the world with an eye to their level of civilization or depravity, with the ultimate goal of determining who would be most likely to be converted by missionary evangelism. At the top of this hierarchy was the United States itself, along with Britain.

Central to the missionary understanding of the world was the conviction that one's position on the hierarchy could change as one's culture did. These were not fixed positions. Mission work would improve and change these different cultures and communities. The Board and its missionaries sought to find those who seemed to have the potential to move upward toward the supposed Anglo-American apex of both culture and Christianity. Board members noted population size and geography, but far more important were their judgments about culture and their assumptions about what people from that part of the world would be like. Often, these judgments were heavily influenced by their assumptions about the effects of British and American imperial and commercial expansion.

Over the first decades of American missionary activity, this hierarchy guided missionary exertions and helped to determine where missionaries were sent and which missions were prioritized. It was this hierarchy that pointed American evangelicals toward Asia and away from North America in the early 1810s, and it would continue to shape the Board's priorities throughout the early nineteenth century. The ideal mission location would occupy a certain point on that hierarchy somewhere in the middle range. To begin with a culture that ranked too low (as with most Native American tribes) would be an impossible endeavor, Board members felt, while those places nearly or fully "civilized" did not seem to have the same need for missionary efforts.

The main requirement for a place to be considered a good potential mission site was that it could show evidence or potential of civilization. This frequently coincided with proximity to a British or American commercial or imperial presence. A careful study of the Board's decision making reveals not only what missionaries hoped the effects of evangelization would be (the adoption of Anglo-American cultural norms in addition to conversion to Protestant religious beliefs and practices) but also the things that mattered to Americans when they looked at the peoples of the world. In the process of deciding where to focus their evangelizing efforts, the members of the American Board worked to create order out of seeming chaos. The hierarchy that they constructed brought together their ideas about culture, race, and religion with the geopolitical realities of the world in which they lived to rationalize space and help them to go about the work of converting the world.

Civilization and the Draw of Foreign Missions

Both push and pull factors brought American evangelicals into the foreign mission movement. For generations, American Christians had supported mission work to some degree. This work was not overseas but was focused on Native Americans. By 1810, they had come to find this work largely useless. Missionaries saw few converts among the Indians and little enthusiasm for the work from the American churches. This state of affairs did not make them give up on the missionary endeavor, however. News of British missionary success in Asia instead alerted them to a new question. Perhaps their problem was not with missions as such. Perhaps their problem had to do with whom they were trying to convert. The North American continent, they decided, ought to be a lower priority than the rest of the world.

This was a profound shift. As recently as 1805, the Connecticut Missionary Society had insisted that it could not send missionaries even so far as Canada because it was a British colony. It would be inappropriate, the society feared, for American missionaries to be operating in British territory. The immediate postrevolutionary era had divided the Anglo-American evangelical network along regional lines. Though Protestants on both sides of the Atlantic continued to find themselves deeply connected to their brethren across the ocean, the first decades of modern British missionary activity saw a clear delineation between the duties of

No chance of crossing over.

American and British Christians. The global mission field was divided along political lines, with missionaries from each nation working only in the places controlled by their own government. American missionaries accordingly had focused on the areas in North America that the United States claimed. Meanwhile in India, where the British East India Company had been expanding its territory in the years after the American Revolution, British chaplains and missionaries wrote that the way had been cleared for Christianity in Asia.

Anglo-American mission work had entered a new era in the 1790s, when the Baptist and London Missionary Societies were founded in England in 1792 and 1795 respectively, and across the Atlantic missionary societies were founded in Pennsylvania, New York, Connecticut, and Massachusetts. While the British missionaries worked in Tahiti and India, American missionaries focused on converting Native Americans within the boundaries of their respective states. Along with nonevangelicals, Americans interested in missions turned their attention to the "large tracts of country still unsettled." Just as many of their countrymen saw the future of the country in westward expansion into this new territory, evangelicals initially understood this to the proper domain of their evangelical efforts. Sounding a great deal like Jefferson describing his Empire of Liberty, the directors of the Connecticut Missionary Society expected that within the boundaries of the United States in the aftermath of the Louisiana Purchase, "the field for missionary labors will therefore be extending itself for many years, if not ages."[2]

In spite of these differences in scope, the directors of mission societies at the turn of the nineteenth century corresponded across the Atlantic, elected each other honorary directors of their own societies, and generally considered themselves "engaged in the same glorious cause."[3] The Great Commission was a shared project of all Christians, in their understanding, and Americans were responsible for spreading the Gospel through America. American and British missionaries imagined the conversion of the world, at home and abroad, as part of a single project in which each group had its own role working in the regions to which each had access and could rely on the protection of its home government. This larger project aimed to convert the whole world to an Anglo-American model of Protestant Christianity, defined not only by its theology, but also by its culture. Civilization was one of the benefits of the religion they preached, according to American and British missionaries in this period, and they sought to reform the gender relations, agricultural style, property ownership, dress, and recreation of the cultures that they encountered. For both British and American Christians,

Comes from spreading Civilization

the expansion of their respective nation's territory demanded the evangelization of the peoples who lived within their territories.[4]

Within a few years, however, this sense of optimism about the evangelization of North America was waning, and this had everything to do with the ways that missionaries and their supporters thought about Native Americans. For a number of years, missionaries had described the "heathen on our borders," or Native Americans, as living "in a truly deplorable state of ignorance and barbarity." They might even have been "in many respects more unfavorable to the reception of the Gospel, than . . . the inhabitants of the South Sea."[5] This comparison referenced the contemporaneous London Missionary Society mission to Tahiti, which Americans knew about because of their correspondence with British evangelicals throughout this period. It is indicative of changes that were beginning to emerge in American Protestant thinking, particularly as American missionaries began to think about the world beyond the North American continent. Connecticut Christians were well aware of what British missionaries were attempting on a global scale. As evangelicals in New England struggled to generate interest in their message among Native Americans, they read in the religious press and in their correspondence with England about the apparent success that British missionaries enjoyed in their early missions to India and Tahiti. Why was it, they wondered, that the British were finding converts when the Americans were not? These comparisons led them to begin thinking about what might make some groups more likely to convert than others.

The colonial and missionary literature reaching New England in the first decades of the nineteenth century was extremely influential to this way of thinking. American evangelicals were eager consumers of the news of British missionary efforts. As early as 1800, the reports of the London Missionary Society and its missionaries in Tahiti, South Africa, and India were printed in the American religious press. These dispatches were shared frequently enough that even the nonevangelical *Christian Observer*, a publication of the American Episcopal Church, informed its readers that by the time the annual report from the London Missionary Society reached its desk in 1805, "the greatest part of the information which it contains, respecting the progress of their missions, has already been communicated to our readers."[6]

Americans could read about India's readiness to convert to Christianity in the writings of Claudius Buchanan, whose sermon "The Star in the East" received a ready audience on both sides of the Atlantic. William Carey, the British Baptist missionary in Serampore, was similarly widely read. Both of

[margin note, handwritten: Origins of heirarchy / hierarchy]

these authors made specific reference to India and to the Christian community's responsibility to the subcontinent. Buchanan insisted that the time had come "for diffusing our religion in the east."[7] The new access to India provided by the expansion of the British Empire required a Christian response, they said. Given the rich Anglo-American evangelical network and the participation of Northeastern merchants in trade with Asia, it was only a matter of time before this sentiment extended to American Christians as well.

Among those who were reading Buchanan and Carey were a group of divinity students at Andover Theological Seminary, including Adoniram Judson, Samuel Nott, Samuel Newell, and Gordon Hall. In 1810, they approached a group of ministers in Massachusetts to ask if they might create an American foreign missionary society. These students explained that their minds had "been long impressed with the duty and importance of personally attempting a mission to the heathen," and that after a serious and prayerful period of consideration of their likelihood of success and the difficulties they might face, they had decided to devote themselves "to this work for life, whenever God, in his providence, shall open the way."[8] These hopeful missionaries asked if they ought to offer themselves to one of the European missionary societies, or if an American group might be formed to support them. In response, those ministers created the American Board of Commissioners for Foreign Missions.

These students met such quick approbation of their project because they were not alone in their sense that the time had come for an American involvement in foreign missions. For America was in the midst of a series of religious revivals known as the Second Great Awakening, and Protestants throughout the country were talking about how their religious convictions required social, and even political, response. Within the churches, they worshiped in more emotionally expressive styles, proclaiming a faith that the world could be made perfect if only individuals and societies accepted the grace and salvation of Jesus. For these Christians, individuals could gain salvation only through belief in Jesus Christ. For those Protestants who would come to support missions, this was an inclusive vision, for it meant that salvation was possible for all, if only individuals could learn of Jesus and his church. Conversions, they believed, could occur on a large scale. They looked around them, at home and farther afield, and worried about the souls of those who did not yet believe. Those who embraced the mission movement were particularly concerned about those who did not yet have

[handwritten marginal note:] Beginnings of foreign missions in America

access to the word of God. They threw themselves into reform movements with a wide range of social and political aims, including increased access to the Bible and education, the colonization of African Americans to West Africa, the end of slavery, the defense of Native Americans against forced removal from their ancestral lands, and more.

It was out of this rich mix of religious revivalism and social reform that the foreign mission movement was born. Among those who felt this way were a group of students at Williams College in 1806. During a rainstorm, they gathered for shelter under a haystack. They prayed together, and decided to dedicate their lives to the cause of missions. They formed a missionary society at the college in 1808; a similar group, called the Brethren, was founded at Andover Theological Seminary by many of these same students who had moved on to prepare for lives in the ministry. Between its creation and 1870, the Brethren would produce some two hundred missionary candidates. At Andover, mission-inclined students worked with teachers who were similarly passionate about the duty of American Christians to convert the world.

Americans saw Providential signs in the expansion of the British Empire, in the possibility of passage on American ships to Asia, and in the new knowledge of the world obtained by explorers. Even more, they saw these secular and commercial connections as in fact preparing the way for religious conversion. Empire, they found, laid the groundwork for missions. But empire was not enough: just as the British asserted their power in India, Americans were claiming an even greater right to the land in North America. Yet the Indians in India seemed to respond better to civilizing and Christianizing efforts than the Indians in America. Clearly, they were different kinds of "heathen." After coming to this realization, American evangelicals decided that they could make more of a difference if they focused their efforts elsewhere, turning their attention eastward. But where to begin?

As they attempted to evaluate which places in the world were the best locations for their missionary exertion, missionaries created a hierarchy of heathenism to aid them. This hierarchy considered a variety of factors: population size, government style, geographic location, and above all else, the level of civilization in a given place. The civilizing impulse was a central, if complex, one to the early missionary work. It was not until the middle of the nineteenth century that there would be a concerted effort (although not an entirely successful one) to deemphasize the civilizing thrust

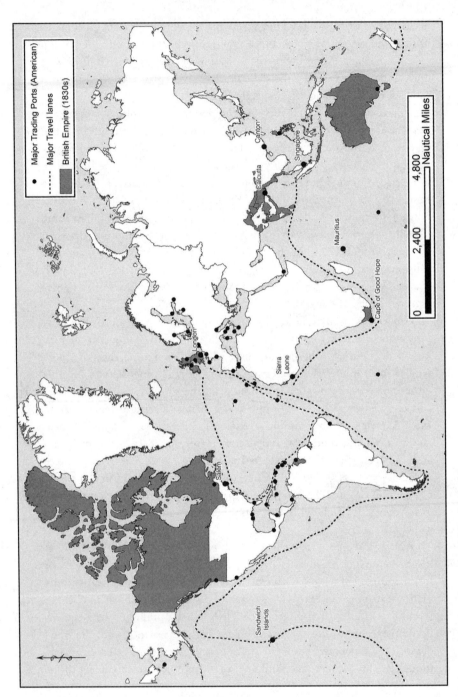

Map 1. Anglo–American commercial and imperial map

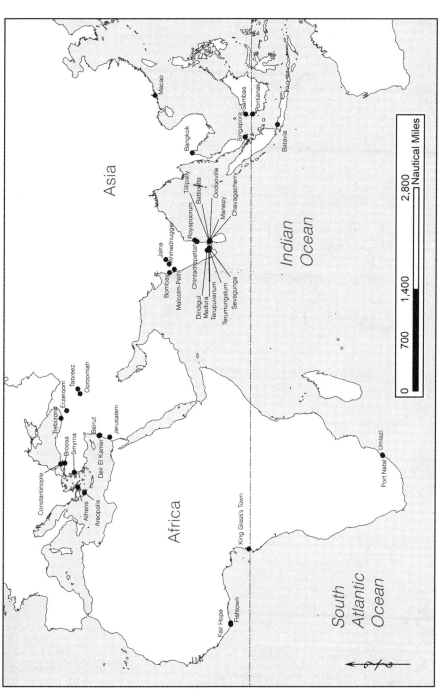

Map 2. ABCFM missions in the world prior to 1844

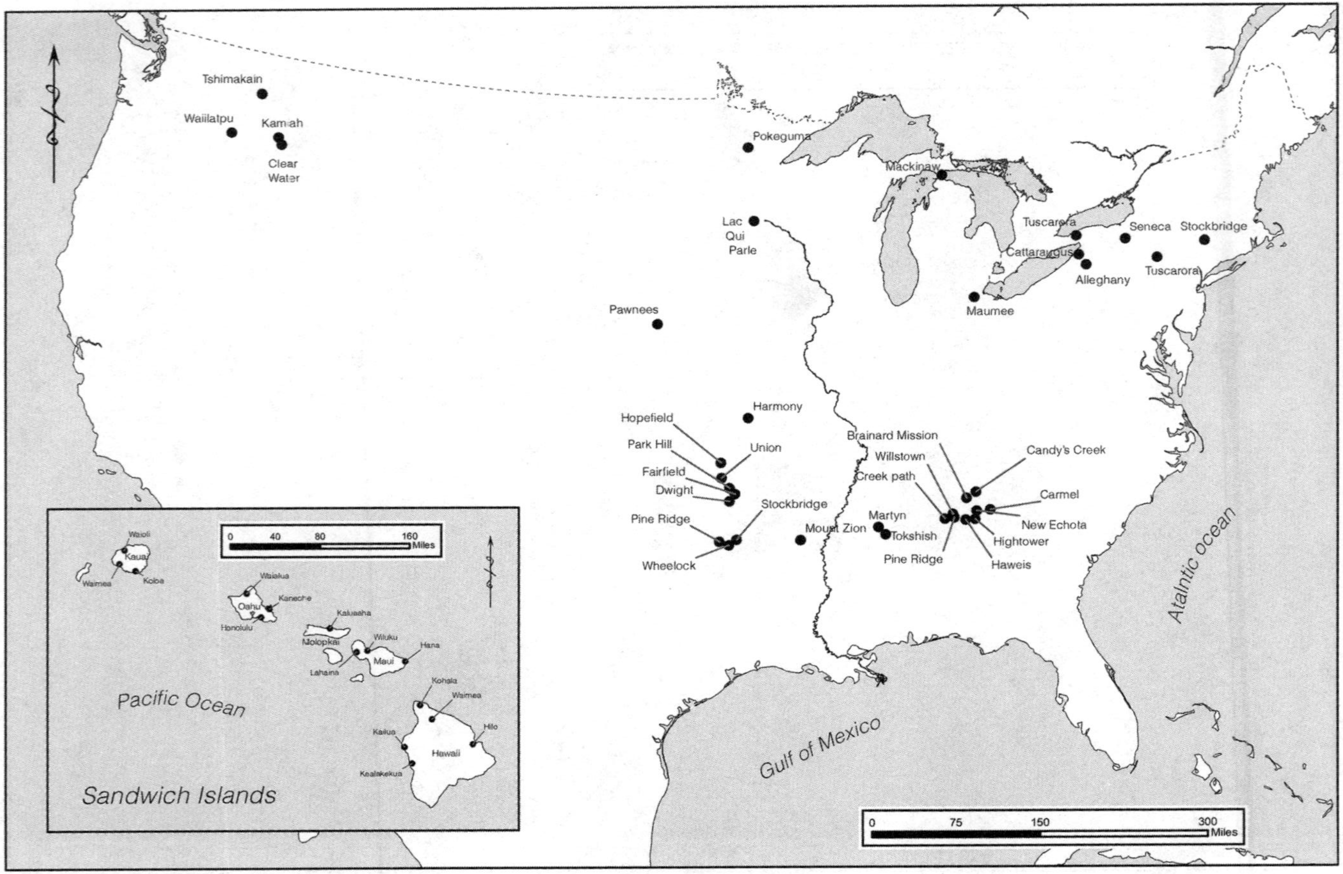

Map 3. ABCFM missions in North America prior to 1844

of conversion efforts and focus on Christ over culture.[9] In the early period, the civilized status of a location, or its potential for eventual civilization, was central to missionary decision making and was perhaps the guiding thrust behind much of the Board's work in its first decades. Accordingly, they considered population size and density, proximity to other "heathen countries," climate, the existing educational infrastructure, and finally, the "condition of the people."[10] That final vague category was perhaps the most important, for it told the missionaries whether they might be heard, and if heard, whether they would be able to spread their word to the maximum number of people possible.

At the top of this hierarchy was civilization, embodied by the United States and Great Britain. They understood civilization to be the ultimate development of human society. As they used this idea to shape their understanding of the world, they built on Enlightenment concepts of the progression of mankind from savagery to barbarism and finally to civilization, the highest form of social organization. Because of the ways that change over time fit into this idea of civilization, missionary supporters could talk about differences across both time and space. Accordingly, when Buchanan urged British and American Christians to work toward the conversion of Asia, he reminded them that once they, too, had been without the Bible. The consequences of sending the Bible to Asia would be "the same as that which followed the giving the Bible to us, while we lay in almost Hindoo darkness, buried in the ignorance and superstition of the church of Rome." Just as these historical Christians had been given the gift of "light and knowledge" in the past, allowing them to become the kind of evangelical Protestants that Buchanan called "true" Christians, so too might the Hindus and Muslims of Buchanan's own day go through a transformation of both faith and culture. This equation of a past "us" with others of the present was central to the ways that missionaries understood difference and progress.[11]

As much as missionaries talked about helping people who were "struggling to rise to civilization," they rarely defined what this would look like specifically. We can see what they meant by examining what they tried to change, what developments they praised, and what aspects of foreign cultures they condemned as savage or barbarous. Industriousness and literacy were among the virtues they most tried to inculcate, as was an improvement of the treatment of women. For evangelicals, these were essential parts of civilization and also essential components of true Christianity.[12] As they discussed their work, they frequently paired the two: they would spread "the blessings of Christianity and civilization" wherever they went.[13] How, exactly, these two goals were linked would be one of the major questions of mission work in this era. In the 1790s, the London Missionary Society, for its part, was convinced that civilization came first. Joseph Hardcastle, one of the directors, explained that an important part of the missionary's job was "to promote the Civilization of the Heathen by instructing them in the useful arts," because this work "bears an important relation to the success of that spiritual work which is our great and ultimate object." At the turn of the century, the London Society explained to the New York Missionary Society "advancement in Civilization seems almost indispensable" to evangelization efforts. In the first decades of the nineteenth century, American missionaries agreed with these sentiments.[14]

Civilization, they believed, could lead to Christianization. Without it, the spiritual work of conversion would be impossible. American missionaries planning new missions around the world expected to do some work to spread civilization with them, but they also understood that their work would be easier to begin if some type of civilization already existed in the places where they were going.[15] Accordingly, missionaries and their supporters looked for the spread of Anglo-American power as a providential sign of where they ought to establish missions. As they understood it, this introduction of a community to civilization meant that the way had been cleared for the Gospel. Frequently, this meant that they looked to do their missionary work in places in or near the expansion of Anglo-American power. And so, as they attempted to judge whether a place had the potential to become civilized, missionaries turned to evangelical and commercial information networks available to them in New England.

Information Networks in Asia

"Some parts of the world have a greater claim to our immediate attention than others," American missionaries Samuel Newell and Gordon Hall wrote in 1818. A large part of the work of foreign missionaries had to do with prioritization—specifically, prioritizing certain places in the world over others as potential recipients for American evangelization efforts. It was difficult, if important, to determine where the missionaries ought to go. Since there were not enough missionaries to actually preach to the entire world, Hall and Newell insisted that "it will be our duty to select the most important places first." As they laid it out for their readers, these selections came down to the extent to which the missionaries could expect that Christianity would be spread once it was planted.[16]

As the American Board began its research into potential mission sites, it was universally understood that the first mission would be somewhere in Asia. Everything that Americans heard about India and its surrounding region made it appear to be exactly the sort of place where the missionaries hoped to work. It was relatively civilized, they believed, with a large population. When the missionaries reached Calcutta, their hopes were initially met: Ann Judson described the city as "the most elegant of any I have ever seen," a compliment that took in both the English and Indian presence.[17] The proximity of the British meant both that the area could be expected to become more civilized and that missionaries could expect protection. As the Board prepared to send its missionaries to Asia, it had considered carefully the choice of the location of its first overseas mission. Based on the information available in New England, the Board decided to send its missionaries to Burma.

As would become clear to the missionaries once they reached Calcutta, however, the information available to them in Massachusetts was far from sufficient and often inaccurate. The reports that the missionaries had read of Burma were misleading, and they determined to find an alternate mission location. Both the initial choice and ultimate rejection of Burma is revealing of what missionaries thought was necessary for mission work, what the ultimate goal of that work was, and the difficulty Americans had in the early republic of actually becoming the equals of Britain in the work of world evangelization.

Without an empire of their own to provide relatively frequent and reliable information, the knowledge American evangelicals could have of Asian culture, society, and politics was severely limited. Their main sources of information were British colonial and missionary reports, alongside American commercial news. After all, through the connections of the first British Empire, Americans had, of course, traded with Asia. Goods such as tea, Kashmir shawls, and porcelain were markers of gentility available to some colonial and early republican Americans. In the years following the 1783 Treaty of Paris, American merchants for the first time were able to trade directly with Indian Ocean markets, and in 1784, the first American ship arrived in India. Within five years, forty American ships traded in the Indian Ocean, and American mariners had become familiar with the ports at the Cape of

Good Hope, the Isle of France (Mauritius), Pointe de Galle, Surat, Madras, Calcutta, Pegu, and Achen. With this commercial contact, many Americans expressed a more general interest in Indian culture and society.[18]

This newfound curiosity about India was not only evident in commercial life. Missionary interest in the region also sparked in this period, suggesting a connection between American commercial and spiritual participation in the world. In Salem, a group of mariners had formed the East India Marine Society in 1799 and opened a museum displaying "natural and artificial curiosities" obtained during travels "beyond the Cape of Good Hope or Cape Horn." The displays of religious objects, musical instruments, weapons, clothing, and other items were meant to represent the East materially to New Englanders for the first time. Because so many Board members and early missionaries were from Salem and the surrounding region, this group doubtless influenced the ways that the early mission movement imagined the East, and the role that missionaries might play there. One can imagine the early missionaries visiting the museum to take a look at the Burmese and other Asian curiosities that were on display prior to their departure.[19]

The links between merchants and missionaries is perhaps best exemplified in the work of Captain Wickes, a mariner based in Philadelphia who was both a correspondent of the British missionaries and a campaigner for their cause. Wickes had carried some of the British missionaries to their station at Serampore in 1801.[20] In the March 1806 issue of the *Panoplist*, an evangelical periodical that would become the organ of the American Board, Wickes appealed for donations to aid the British missionaries in their attempts to translate the Bible into Asian languages. In a matter of weeks, Wickes had collected a significant donation, suggesting not only the power of the press in spreading the word about missionary projects and needs, but also the importance of personal connections between merchant mariners and missionaries for the success of the missionary endeavor.[21]

There were limits, too, to the value of commercial networks in that the merchants did not go where they could find nothing to sell. The Jay Treaty of 1795 curtailed some aspects of American trade in Asia, as it prevented American ships from trading between different Asian ports. Accordingly, American ships only went to places where they could expect to do significant trade. Burma, which the American missionaries saw as an ideal location, was one location that was affected by this policy. American trade with Burma had ceased in 1794, when a shipment of Burmese gum lacquer failed to sell in Salem "at any price." Accordingly, American ships stayed out of Rangoon from the turn of the nineteenth century, and so American missionaries had considerable limits to their knowledge about the place.[22]

Instead of commercial networks, missionaries turned to religious networks and the evangelical press. On Burma in particular, the press also gave reason to hope that the British missionaries had begun to lay the way of the Gospel. Letters from the British Baptist missionaries related the departure of two missionaries for a preliminary trip to Rangoon in 1807, and the eventual establishment of a permanent mission there by Felix Carey and James Chater. In 1808, the *Panoplist* ran its first mention of the mission, relating Carey's optimism about the potential there. Even as one of the two missionaries sent to determine "whether the gospel could be introduced there" declined to join the permanent mission, another filled his place, and two mission families left Serampore for Rangoon.[23]

In addition to the periodical press, a few relevant books were published in the years prior to 1812 that had direct effects on the work of the American missionaries. They read the publications of Claudius Buchanan and Michael Symes, both of which immediately affected their imagined ideal mission sites. Buchanan's reports on the advances in translation efforts were influential, and Americans regarded him as an expert in Asian cultures and civilizations. Symes, however, was the perceived expert on Burma itself, and his book inspired Adoniram Judson to suggest Burma as the location for the first American mission to Asia. His *Embassy to Ava*, which traced his experiences on a 1795 embassy to the Burmese Empire on behalf of the British in Bengal, was published in the United States in 1810.[24] The book gave a glowing report of the empire, and one can see why it would have caught the interest of a potential missionary. Symes's Burma was certainly a heathen nation, but one with decided potential for civilization. His discussion of Buddhism, while not particularly well informed, deemed it "above any other Hindoo commentary for perspicuity and good sense." Further, and importantly for the missionaries, he reported that the Burmese exhibited religious tolerance, which would suggest the possibility that missionaries could operate there without interference from the government. The Burmese showed, he said, "the most liberal toleration in matters of religion. . . . The Birmans never trouble themselves about the religious opinions of any sect, nor disturb their ritual ceremonies, provided they do not break the peace, or meddle with their own divinity Guadma."[25] In their politics, then, the Burmese seemed, if not to have reached the "civilized" status of a Christian nation, at least to have been far from interfering with the activities of

Christian missionaries. This, combined with the New England understanding of the refined goods that could be found in Burma, suggested a level of civilization that would be welcoming to mission work.

A major draw of Burma was that its population was believed to be in the area of 17 million souls ("All of whom are idolaters!" in the phrasing of one writer). That was double the size of the United States at the time. This is a likely overestimate, as modern estimates of the Burmese population at the turn of the nineteenth century place it at 3.3 million. The excitement about this supposedly high population, though, gives a sense of the value of a large population to missionary endeavors. Rather than overwhelming missionaries, a large population, particularly one that was densely settled, suggested incredible potential. If they were able to convert a few people and train native helpers, then those could go out and convert yet more people, and soon a huge portion of the globe would be converted.[26]

From these various sources of information and on the basis of the hierarchy of heathenism, New England evangelicals could hope that they might find success in Asia, and the American Board determined that "the most favorable station for an American mission in the east would probably be in some part of the Birman empire."[27] After missionaries determined that Burma was not, in fact, the somewhat civilized empire they had expected but was rather ruled by a "tyrannical" emperor who was far from friendly to their work, they began to survey the rest of the Indian Ocean region to find a new location. Their search was made all the more dramatic because of the new political context in which they found themselves searching for a new mission, as the United States declared war on Great Britain.

East and West

As the Board honed in on where it might send its eastern missionaries, it did not intend to abandon North American missions entirely. "Though at present the East world appears to hold out the most favorable prospects" for evangelizing, board secretary Samuel Worcester noted, "this Board will not lose sight of the heathen tribes on this continent."[28] British missionaries, though pleased that Americans were becoming interested in Asia, still emphasized the spaces in the Americas where American missionaries might work. William Carey, the British Baptist whose writings about India were so inspiring to American audiences, suggested Americans evangelize Cuba, St. Domingo, and the "back parts of their own country."[29] Americans responded to this sort of advice by taking on a two-pronged approach to global missions: they would move both east and west, with an American counterpart to their Asian mission.

In addition to Burma, they planned to send missionaries to the Caghnawagas tribe in North America. The selection of this tribe mirrored some of the discussion about Asia. It was chosen for the "easy access" American missionaries would have to the tribe, their good disposition toward whites, and their "great influence with their red brethren of other tribes." The tradition of American missionaries evangelizing to North America would continue, though now under the umbrella of foreign missions. The Caghnawagas mission, however, was not to be. The Board could never find a missionary, and it lost interest with all the excitement of the Indian mission during the War of 1812. By the time that peace was declared in that conflict, the Board again began searching for new mission locations.

Just as the end of the war stabilized the mission in South Asia, victory in New Orleans drew the Board's attention toward the Native Americans of the Southeast: the Cherokee, Choctaw, Creek, and Chickasaw. There were, Worcester insisted, "indications of Providence" that the missions to the "heathen" of North America would indeed be possible. The very "finger of God" pointed the Board to these nations, which were, he assured his supporters, destined to become "a distinguished field of Missionary glory." Just as the Board had described Asia earlier in the decade, by 1817 Worcester was calling this region "white already to the harvest."[30]

Worcester was hardly alone in his evaluation of the significance of the historical moment, or of the possibilities for the Indians of the Southeast. The Cherokee in particular had attracted the notice of the Christian public as early as 1807, when Gideon Blackburn began publishing letters about his school for the tribe.[31] Blackburn, a Presbyterian minister in Tennessee, first encountered the Cherokee when he had accompanied some of the young members of his congregation on some of their expeditions during the frontier wars in the 1790s. That experience led him to wonder what could be done to help the Indians, who, as he reflected, "were of the same race with ourselves," and were further intelligent and, he believed, capable of great things if properly trained. This claim that the Cherokee and white Americans were part of the same race highlights the ways that missionaries understood humankind to be essentially unified, even as they believed that there were different ranks and levels. One could, though, improve and move up the levels of the hierarchy of heathenism to eventually become civilized. Over the next few years, he developed a plan for a missionary school system that could in time lead the Cherokee "to become American citizens, and a valuable part of the Union."

By 1815, when the Board was looking for a new mission location, Blackburn's experience was as exciting and inspiring as William Carey's had been the decade before. As Blackburn explained, the value of the mission was in "civilization taking the ground of barbarism," and both his General Assembly and the American Board seemed to agree. Blackburn's reports focused on the assimilation of the Cherokee to American cultural norms: the number of slaves, cattle, horses, mills, and plows they owned; and the amount of commercial activity in which they were engaged. The Cherokee seemed to be becoming civilized, yet Blackburn's school had not made them Christians yet. In many ways, then, the Cherokee appeared to be an ideal location for a Board mission. There was much for them to do, but the way had been prepared. The Cherokee, further, had a sizeable population and a centralized location, both of which were important factors for the Board. Above all, though, it was the proximity to white settlement and the perceived progress in civilization that drew the Board's attention to the Cherokee nation.[32]

A telling absence in the missionary discussion, given its importance later in the century for many Americans' understanding of the role of America in the world, was South and Central America. From time to time, the Board raised the possibility of sending missionaries there, but these were always ultimately rejected. At the time of the Board's founding, Worcester considered South America to be in "so unpromising a state, that the opinion very generally prevalent is that for the pagans on this continent but little can be immediately done." Later in the decade, Rufus Anderson was sent on an exploring tour to Rio de Janeiro, where he reported continual difficulties that missionaries might face there. The "moral character of this people is deplorable," he wrote, going on to describe practices of "bigotry, lust, and barbarous cruelty, not seldom combined in the same individual." There were "discouraging" prospects for schools, and he believed that Board missionaries "would not be tolerated here." The reason for this had to do with Catholicism, which Anderson believed was so deeply entrenched in the government that it would not allow Protestant missionaries to evangelize effectively. They would not be able to "introduce the Bible, or to instruct pupils in the great doctrines of the gospel," he concluded. While they did not consider this to be a heathen land, their anti-Catholicism was strong enough to suggest that it was still not a civilized place and was certainly not worth the effort of their missionary labors. In the years before the Civil War, the Board largely ignored this part of the world as a result.[33]

Commercial Networks and the Sandwich Islands

The mission to the Sandwich Islands (Hawaii) would become one of the most prominent missions of the early nineteenth century. Hawaii was selected as a potential mission site out of a confluence of special circumstances. On the one hand, there was the typical pattern of British example and American emulation: the London Missionary Society had one of its first missions in Tahiti, and their missionaries continued to be active in the Pacific. American attention was accordingly drawn to the region. Americans eagerly read about the travels of Captain Cook in the 1770s, and Protestant readers felt inspired by the relations he made of the vast field of people who did not yet know the name of Jesus. As in India, British example was joined with American commerce. Cook had been accompanied by an American, John Ledyard, who thought that the Sandwich Islands would be an important destination for a trans-Pacific trade in fur. In 1789, the first American ship stopped in Hawaii on its way to China. Within a few years, Hawaii became a regular stop in the Yankee trade to Canton. Sailors and merchants appreciated the food, the women, and the sandalwood. Occasionally, young Hawaiian men would join the ships for their return to the United States. It was some of these men who attracted missionary attention to their home.

Over the first years of the nineteenth century, a number of these youths attracted the sympathy and interest of evangelicals. Some of the young Hawaiians in America had worked on ships. One became a barber and another was a prince, sent by his father to gain an education in the United States. When a group of Yale students found one of these men weeping on the campus of Yale University because he wanted to become educated, supporters of the mission movement took notice. Within a few years, the arrival of these young men was interpreted as a sign that America had been specially selected for the evangelization of Hawaii. The Board established the Foreign Mission School in Cornwall, Connecticut, for these students and others like them. There they were educated alongside youth from Native American nations and China, with an eye to preparing them to return to their home communities trained in both Christian doctrine and academic subjects. It was the Board's hope that they would serve as teachers to their people in secular and spiritual things. As Americans learned from these students about the Sandwich Islands, they came to hope that they might be able to accompany these students back to Hawaii and bear "the offers of mercy to ignorant and perishing multitudes."[34] They were particularly excited by one student in particular, Obookiah, who seemed interested in their cause.

Obookiah had come to America in 1809 at the age of seventeen. His parents had died, and he had persuaded his uncle to let him sail on a Yankee ship with Thomas Hopu, another native Hawaiian who became a student at Cornwall and a convert to Christianity. Obookiah made his way to New Haven, where he was taken into the home of Timothy Dwight, the president of Yale. Dwight educated and converted him, and sent him to the Foreign Mission School when it was started in 1817. Obookiah became a well-known figure among evangelical readers. In 1816, he was one of the five men described in *A Narrative of Five Youth from the Sandwich Islands*.[35] As a student, he would tour New England churches to raise funds for the Mission School. He was celebrated for his conviction of the falseness of the religion of Hawaii and his determination to return home to teach his people and convert them to Christianity.

It was Obookiah who inspired the Board to think about a mission to the Sandwich Islands. When he died of typhus in 1818, enthusiasm for his dream only grew. The missionaries who would travel to Hawaii in 1820 all cited Obookiah's example when they explained why they wanted to become missionaries. He seemed to prove that conversion was possible. Of the four other Hawaiian students at Cornwall, three had also converted to Christianity. For the Board, this was a very promising start. When the missionaries left Boston for Hawaii, they would be accompanied by four native Hawaiians, all of whom had learned about their culture and "civilization," and three of whom shared their religion. They would have native helpers from the beginning of their work, a privilege that Board missionaries experienced very rarely.[36]

The good omens only continued after the missionaries' departure. Quite quickly after the missionaries arrived in Hawaii, there seemed to be still more ways that Providence directed Americans there. Here the promise of commercial and imperial connections aiding the spread of Christianity seemed, at first, to come to fruition. As the missionaries excitedly reported, shortly before the missionaries arrived in Hawaii, the king, many of the chiefs, and indeed, the majority of the Hawaiian people had given up their traditional religion and were looking to hear from missionaries. Missionaries were thrilled to find an open and interested audience. The Board's timing was impeccable. Tamoree, the king of Atooi, had a son being educated at Cornwall. Having heard about the British missions in the Society Islands, he wrote to his son asking him to return and bring with him missionaries who might teach his people to read and write. By the time the letter reached Connecticut, his son was already on his way back to Hawaii in the company of missionaries anxious to do just that. The way seemed to be opened for American missionaries in the Sandwich Islands; it only rested on the missionaries to respond to the clear leadings of Providence. Just as in India, then, British and American trade had prepared the way for missionary efforts. Here they seemed to bear fruit.[37]

For American evangelicals, the Sandwich Islands seemed an ideal mission location because the people of the islands seemed to want them there. From the arrival of the Hawaiian youth in New England at the start of the missionary movement to the arrival of the missionaries in Hawaii just after *kapu* had been abandoned, the way seemed clear for the entry of the missionaries. The example of the Cornwall students made it clear that Hawaiians could be converted and even "civilized." Though Hawaii did not hold the same sort of importance as some of the other locations of early missions in regard to its population size or proximity to other places and people, it had the unique quality of seeming to be destined for American evangelization in the early nineteenth century. For the Boston-based Board, it was significant that they represented the Hawaiians as asking for missionaries to "come over and help us." The phrase would have reminded them of their own history and the founding of Massachusetts. Just as the presence of non-Christian Native Americans had seemed to justify the colonization of Massachusetts long before, the presence of Hawaiians seemingly eager to learn about American ways and Christianity seemed to demand a missionary presence on those islands.

Missions to the Holy Land

When the Board announced the location of its new mission destination in 1819, it introduced new components to the ways that it chose its locations. "If the countries of Southern Asia are highly interesting to Christian benevolence," they began, "the countries of Western Asia, though less populous, are in other respects not less interesting, nor do they present less powerful claims." In contrast to their other missions, the mission to Palestine was explained in terms of its history. This was the place where "those great transactions and events, which involved the destinies of mankind of all ages and all nations, for time and eternity" had taken place. This was where the "labors and agonies of the Son of God" had happened, where "the sciences and the arts," and "civil and political institutions" had all begun. Missionaries who went to the Mideast explained time and again that they were eager to work in these sacred lands. While most of the missions were understood as being designed to move a community forward in time and civilization, this mission looked backward. It was about reclaiming this space to its proper place in sacred history.

The Board began talking about sending a mission to Jerusalem in the late 1810s. Buoyed by increasing support within the United States, the ABCFM was able to think about expanding its reach, and the Mideast stood out as an important place. In many ways, the things that drew the Board toward Jerusalem were very different from what drew them to India or the Cherokee Nation. This was not a matter of Providential imperialism, but rather symbolic significance. As the Board never tired of explaining in the early years of this mission, this was the place where their religion had been born. Yet the region was no longer what it had once been. "The light," as the Prudential Committee explained in its instructions to the missionaries, "has been, for dismal centuries, almost totally extinguished, and the powers of darkness have triumphed and trodden down and led captive at their pleasure." It was now up to the missionaries to rebuild the foundations of the Holy Land.[38]

In spite of the unique symbolic importance that Jerusalem held for American Christians, the reason why missionaries felt it was a possible mission location in 1819 connected to the same ideas about possible mission destinations that shaped their earlier decisions. Missionaries expected to begin working with the Christian community there. While missionaries were quite dismissive of Eastern Christianity, repeatedly stating that it was Christianity in name only, they fully expected to benefit from its presence in the region. Missionaries planned to first appeal to Christians, who they assumed would welcome missionaries and their publications into their homes. The missionaries assumed that, unlike Catholics, these non-Protestant Christians would welcome the scripture they would provide, along with other texts that could, like seeds, be planted and take root. Here it was Christian religious authorities who would provide protection and welcome to American missionaries. From that base, missionaries could attempt to convert the diverse population of Jews, Muslims, and Christians.

As the Board talked about the history of the Mideast, they described "direful changes" since the era of the Bible. Now, the Mideast was made up of Muslim countries that had a population including "many thousands of Jews, and many thousands of Christians, at least in name," who the Board described as being "in a state of deplorable ignorance and degradation." Christian missionaries ought to respond to this situation, the Board urged, and take advantage of the unique possibilities presented by a large population of those "who bear the Christian name."[39] The Board expected that these "nominal Christians" would welcome them to the region and eagerly receive scriptures and tracts from American missionaries. They expected them, further, to help the missionaries spread the word to others. The missionaries had a multipronged approach to this region and believed that Eastern Christians were as in need of conversion as the Jews and Muslims. While Jerusalem was the planned destination of the first missionaries to the region, their travels provided them the opportunity for researching other potential destinations. Smyrna, in particular, seemed a good choice. Again, the same type of logic governed this decision. The presence of Christians there made a ready audience for missionary exertions. The missionaries explained that they "may carry the Scriptures and religious tracts into every town and village throughout those benighted regions" and find Christians who would receive their books "with gladness." The government did not seem to object to the presence of missionaries, nor attempt to interfere with their work, which was an important consideration. Finally, Smyrna was an ideal location for its "frequent communication with all the parts of the Ottoman empire." Like so many of the Board's early mission locations, it was chosen for its proximity to other locations, and its position in commercial and political networks.[40]

Africa, Heathenism, and Race

As the Board went about deciding where they would go—and where they would not—much of their discussion was implicitly about race. The question of civilization and improvability always touched on this theme. Missionaries were optimistic that change could occur, and that once people became civilized and Christianized, all people of whatever color would be brothers and sisters in Christ. This did not mean, however, that they did not share some of the racial concepts of others in their time. Those racial concepts were themselves in flux in the early nineteenth century as racial theories began moving closer to more biological and fixed conceptions of race and human difference. The mission movement confronted these ideas about race and the possibility of change most directly when Africa came up as a potential mission site. In the Board's discussions of Africa, we can see the ways that tensions arose between their idea that change was possible, and their sense of how probable it was within particular groups.

When the Bombay missionaries were traveling in the Indian Ocean, unsure of where their mission might take them, they briefly considered working in East Africa, particularly in Madagascar or the Isle of France (Mauritius). Yet Africa was never high on the list of likely places for missionary success. One of the Bombay missionaries, writing to Boston in 1812, emphasized that "I feel myself and I know the Christian public do a particular propensity to Asia—but God may say *Africa*. If He does we must go."[41] In 1812, they ultimately decided that God was not saying Africa, and there were no references to African mission sites for another decade.

Like South America, Africa was not considered one of the likely sites for American missionary exertions in the 1810s. By the mid-1820s, however, the Board considered western Africa to be "among the most important and accessible fields" globally.[42] Accordingly, mission supporters began trying to plan a mission to Africa. This shift in the evaluation of Africa over the course of the 1810s and early 1820s was the result of a number of factors. For one thing, Americans knew more, or thought they knew more, about Africa. Just as they had earlier cited the population size of South Asia and its position as an entry into East Asia, and China in particular, now they highlighted the large population of West Africa and its potential as a good way to begin working toward the center of the continent. Additionally, missionaries had a new way of understanding how religion worked in Africa. Whereas missionaries in India were attempting to convert "heathens" from one religion to another, American missionaries were convinced that the "heathen" of Africa were without religion entirely: they saw them as a blank slate on whom the missionaries could impart the truth of the Gospel.

Most important, though, was the spread of empire into West Africa. The British colony at Sierra Leone was extremely influential to American missionary thinking, as was the American colony at Liberia. These connections were direct. While the Board had mostly relied on British mission supporters in England to help them plan their work in South Asia, the leaders corresponded directly with colonial officials in Africa as they planned their mission there. The Board's published materials on Sierra Leone stressed the role of William Wilberforce and other antislavery activists, including some heads of the London Missionary Society, in the foundation of the colony, which they saw as being founded with "the most benevolent kind" of motives. The colony would allow "the influence of good men" to travel throughout Africa, they felt. It was this sort of imperial project that the Board wholeheartedly endorsed.[43]

Sierra Leone was a unique colony in the British Empire, founded as it was on antislavery principles. First established in 1787, the settlement in West Africa initially served as a refuge for free blacks and recaptured slaves and was seen as a moral form of empire building.[44] Its initial importance, especially for Americans interested in its progress, though, was in its African solution to the problems of multiracial conflict. During the American Revolution, the British had promised freedom to any slaves who left their masters to fight on the British side. After facing difficulty in London and Canada, several thousand of these migrated to Sierra Leone when it was opened as a British colony.[45]

Watching Sierra Leone gave American missionaries a new perspective on the possibilities of evangelizing Africa. As news from India had done earlier, the correspondence with Britain about its colonies inspired American missionary thought. In Sierra Leone, the colony brought schools, which for many Anglo-American observers provided proof that outside of slavery Africans could in fact be educated and were capable of becoming civilized. One writer noted that Sierra Leone showed how Africans could rise to the high European levels of "industry and laborious exertion" that were considered so important to civilization.[46] This news particularly excited supporters of world mission, as it seemed to prove the ultimate feasibility of their project.

The religious press published several articles a year on the almost one hundred missionaries of the British Church Missionary Society working in Sierra Leone by 1830. These described the geographic extent of the missions, the reception of the native kings to the British presence, the progress of the missionaries in converting individuals, and of course the deaths of the missionaries that occurred.[47] These articles inspired readers with their descriptions of the complete transformation that was possible in African culture and religion through the introduction of missionaries. In the decade before American missionaries began their work in Africa in 1833, only one of these articles had anything negative to say about the missions, and it was similar in tone to articles on the continuity of idol worship among converts in Asia. The bulk of the press, in contrast, focused on the possibility of transformation. Several articles described the changes in Regent's Town, established in 1813 as a refuge for recaptured slaves. Because of its position as a refugee camp of sorts with a very diverse population from twenty-two different ethnic groups, it presented major challenges for the missionaries. In addition to the constant complaints that missionaries throughout Africa (and indeed, much of the "heathen world") had about the gender practices and morality of those they hoped to convert, there was no single language that could be used to communicate with the whole community. It was an unlikely site of improvement.

Yet there was a minister in Regent's Town, Mr. Johnson, who began with a congregation of nine hearers. Within three years, he appeared to have worked a miracle. By then, the town was "laid out with regularity," with buildings of stone including a church, a government house, a hospital, schools, and store houses. Gardens were fenced in and agriculture was conducted on a more regular system, so that the whole population of the town could be called "farmers" with an extensive produce. Even more amazingly to the readers of the *Missionary Herald*, within three years these "most debased and ferocious of savages" were all "decently clothed," swearing and drunkenness had ceased, marriage was becoming common, and church attendance was impressive: between twelve hundred and thirteen hundred could be expected at three Sunday services, and five hundred would attend the daily morning and evening prayers. Large numbers wished for baptism, and "all [had] abandoned polygamy, gregrees, and devil worship." In neighboring towns without the regular influence of a minister, the writer reported, such changes were not evident. For any readers doubting what exactly had sparked this transformation, the *Missionary Herald* explained that it was simply preaching, which had become "the instrument of quickening and giving efficacy to the benevolent measures of government, and of producing this mighty change."[48] For evangelicals looking for proof of the benefits of mission work, and of the possibilities of transformation in Africa, Regent's Town appeared to settle the matter.

If Sierra Leone left Americans with the sense that Christianization and civilization could be possible in Africa, the colonization movement in the United States pushed evangelicals to decide that the time had come for American missionary exertions there. Many of those who worked with the Board felt that missions were necessary to cancel the debt they felt that America owed Africa for the transatlantic slave trade. Only "the gospel of the grace of God" could do this work, and the Board pledged to work with other groups to right the wrong.[49] Those other groups included, most prominently, the American and Maryland Colonization Societies. It was through the colonization movement that the Board saw the evangelization of Africa as a possibility. Just as it included reports on the developments in Sierra Leone, the *Missionary Herald* frequently reprinted reports from visitors to Liberia. These descriptions emphasized the progress of civilization there. The reports were largely positive, with the general message that, considering who these colonists were, the colony was flourishing.[50]

Just as the European imperial presence had been an important selling point for a mission to India, the presence of an American colony in Liberia made it more attractive to missionaries. As it happened, Jehudi Ashmun, the governor of the colony in the mid-1820s had a preexisting relationship with the American Board. A Congregational minister from New York, he had earlier expressed an interest in becoming an ABCFM missionary to South America, before the Board rejected the continent as a possible site.[51] As a colonial official who was committed to the cause of mission, he was an ideal partner for the planning of a mission there, and he promised "the most cordial cooperation" of the Colonization Society to the work of the Board. The colony could offer protection to the mission, as well as medical assistance, groceries, and fabrics. It would also work to obtain a land grant for the mission station.[52] As had been the case in the missionary entry to India, the establishment of an Anglo-American base in the region was essential for American missionaries to feel minimally safe and to find a new space accessible. It was only due to the presence of the colony that the missionaries could be sure of the frequent passage of ships between America and where they were stationed bringing supplies, news, and funds to the mission. Rufus Anderson referred to colonies as "important auxiliaries" that would "greatly facilitate our entrance among the several tribes of the interior" through "the information they collect, the roads they open, and their commercial intercourse."[53] The colony offered less concrete benefits too, especially in "the friendship, sympathies, prayers and support of a large and intelligent body of christian [*sic*] colonists."[54] For the Board, which was accustomed to its missionaries working alongside governments in South Asia and North America that did not explicitly ally themselves with the mission's goals and whose claims of Christian character the Board repeatedly doubted, these assurances from the Liberian colony of both physical and spiritual support were welcome and encouraging.

The combination of these factors—the success of the British in a nearby colony, the presence of an American colony, the apparent ability of the native population to become "civilized," the sense of debt from Americans to Africa—made West Africa an attractive missionary destination in the 1820s. If in 1812, Africa had ranked low on the hierarchy of heathenism, by the middle of the next decade, new developments had made it appear capable of rising in its position. This was not enough to start the mission without a hitch, however. It took a further ten years for the Board to select a missionary who could survive in what they assumed would be the prohibitively harsh climate of sub-Saharan Africa.

Concerns about climate and health made race come to the front of these debates. If conversion assumed that peoples were essentially alike and that one could improve in civilization, the missionaries also exhibited ideas about fixed racial differences in terms of the types of people who could enjoy health in particular climates. Importantly, the African discussions were one of the only times that climate and health entered into these discussions. Missionaries frequently became ill and died in other mission locations, including South Asia, but aside from a general interest in selecting missionaries with strong constitutions, this was never a particular concern for the Board elsewhere. Only in Africa did the Board spend ten years trying to find an African American missionary, who would presumably be better suited to the climate, before ultimately selecting a white South Carolinian, whom they hoped would at least do better there than a Bostonian might.

This tension between the unity of humanity under Christ and the divisions of humanity by racial suitability reveals some of the ways that racial considerations affected the Board's broader decision making. These were years of transition from Enlightenment concepts of race that focused on the environmental construction of race and the diversity of humanity, to an ethnological concept of race that was a precursor to scientific racism. As the American Board thought about Africa and planned its mission, it did so in the midst of an American culture that was also thinking about Africa and Africans and how they related to white Euro-Americans. These years that saw the planning of the American mission to Africa were also the years of the development of the "American School" of ethnology. While not full-blown scientific racism, this was a progression from earlier movements in natural history that increasingly came to think about racial differences and locate them within the body. This movement culminated in Morton's *Crania Americana* (1839) and Gliddon's *Types of Mankind* (1855), but its seeds were in place earlier. Practitioners of phrenology and craniology, for example, put forth ideas about racial difference that would later be more fully developed by Morton. The arguments in Thomas Jefferson's *Notes on the State of Virginia* about racial inferiority as a natural trait are another example of these ideas' presence in American culture prior to 1840. For evangelicals, who were committed to the idea that all people were created by God and thus on some level equal, this transition created new tensions and creative ways of looking at the world and its people.[55]

The leaders of the American Board were sure that environment and race were related, and that different races would respond to a particular climate differently. The Board was very concerned about the health of its missionaries all over the world, and it was a subject extensively discussed in many of its writings. Africa was the only place, however, where this discussion shifted from an individual question of constitution to a general one of racial suitability. It was only in Africa that the Board discussed things like the climate being "so fatal to white men."[56] On the one hand, its concerns were a legitimate response to the high mortality rate for white men and women in tropical climates.[57] Yet this ignored important information about the high mortality rates for African Americans in Africa. The deaths of African American colonists was so well known that one procolonization text of the 1830s even addressed the question of why the movement continued when "it seems as half [of the African Americans] who go die." The leaders of the Board, like many other Americans of the era, remained convinced that black Americans would do better than their white counterparts, in spite of much evidence to the contrary. Indeed, this was a frequent defense of the institution of slavery in the South, where it was believed that whites were not as well suited to labor as were their African-descended slaves.[58]

The Board's eventual decision to send a white missionary, John Leighton Wilson, revealed some of the logical inconsistencies of this approach. In the absence of a black missionary, the Board decided that a white southerner would have the greatest chances of survival in West Africa because the climate of the South, they asserted, approximated that of West Africa. At the same time that the Board searched for its African missionary, insisting that the Southern and African climates were similar, it frequently sent missionaries to the South from the Northeast in order to improve the missionaries' health. While they believed that an African climate would be fatal to a weak white constitution, they were equally convinced that a Southern climate could greatly increase the comfort and health of northern white missionaries. More was at stake, then, than just the matter of health.

Racial concerns also figured into discussions about where in West Africa to send missionaries. Missionaries used the perceived position of foreign peoples on this spectrum as a major component in their decisions about where to go, and this was no different in Africa. Yet this specificity about particular African ethnicities and their likelihood of being converted existed alongside more complex and ambivalent views about the possibility of Africans in general attaining a position of "civilization." In particular, the Board weighted the information that it gathered about particular nations or ethnic groups, whom they called tribes, against assumptions they had about "the Negro" as a general category.

All of the Board's informants about West Africa provided specific information about the different ethnic groups in the region. In Liberia, two of the primary groups were the Dey and the Vey: colonial officials described the latter as "active, warlike, proud, and [like] all their neighbors, deceitful." The Dey tribe, on the other hand, was "indolent, pacific, and inoffensive in their character; but equally treacherous, profligate, and cruel when their passions are stirred, with the Veys." Neither of these seemed to be good candidates for a mission. Instead, the colonial agent at Monrovia suggested that the mission work with the nearby Bassa, whom he described as "domestic, and industrious, many of them even laborious in their habits."[59] Here, then, the Board was guided by detail and information about differences within a broader racial group. Not all Africans were the same. Just as not all Asians could have been equally suitable for mission work, these different ethnic groups could be expected to respond differently.

Even as it had this sort of specific (if still generalized and biased) information about the local population, the Board simplified the diversity of West Africa to two different groups: "the original inhabitants of the country," whom the Board referred to as "the Negro" (this category would include the Dey, Vey, and Bassa); and "the descendants of Arabs, and other emigrants from Asia," whom it called "the Moor." It was to the former that the Board's missions would be oriented. "The Negro," Rufus Anderson wrote in his instructions for the planning tour of Liberia, "is more mild, liberal, and hospitable than the Moor; and is distinguished by the peculiar warmth of his social affections." They were also typified by "strong attachments to home and country," as well as "the development of feeling, thought, shrewdness, a natural eloquence, and a passion for poetry." It was these whom the missionary would seek to convert, and it was also these with whom the missionaries would have had greater experience in the United States.[60]

The Board's use of a hierarchy of heathenism changed the way that missionaries saw the globe. If the world was marked by commercial networks, imperial spaces, and differing levels of "heathenism," those places that were deemed appropriate mission stations began to look a bit more similar, in spite of geographic distance. Throughout the first decades of the Board's work, missionaries were regularly told to peruse the formal instructions issued to earlier missionaries, wherever they were stationed. Missionaries departing at the same time for divergent locations were frequently issued their instructions together, as when missionaries to South Africa and the Sandwich Islands both left in 1834.[61]

This rationalizing of space is still more dramatic in the ways that the Board depicted the future projections of its work by the 1830s. In their remarkable depiction of the "grand spiritual armies" of the United States and Britain, they portrayed an extremely rational geographic imagining of the world. After two and a half decades of work in global mission, they could depict three "great lines of missions" operating in Africa, Asia, and the Pacific (their American work was not included in this plan). The Asian lines began at Constantinople, moved through Asia Minor at Persia and Afghanistan, and through western India by way of Ceylon. A second line began at Greece, and was projected through Asia Minor by way of Syria and Palestine, ending at Mesopotamia; a third Asian line was projected in southeastern Asia, emanating out of the Singapore mission in two directions: northward through China, Siam, and Mongolia, and southward through "the largest and most important groups of islands in the world." The African missions were described as operating on lines working toward the center of the continent; the Board frequently described the day of jubilee that could be expected when Christians met in the center, and all of Africa had been converted as a result. There was nothing inherently logical about these missionary trajectories. Nothing particularly connected these spaces other than a missionary imagination about what the world ought to look like. Through this process, the Board asserted a rationality on the globe as it sought to imagine the place of American Christians throughout the world.[62]

As the missionaries and officials of the American Board selected the locations for their missions, they developed a "hierarchy of heathenism" that allowed them to rank and evaluate the different peoples of the world and their likelihood for conversion. As became apparent when the missionaries actually began working in these places, their assumptions about what sorts of things would lead to conversion rarely reflected reality. India in particular, where missionaries had such high hopes, was far from a successful field of American evangelism in the early nineteenth century. Yet these categories of culture and civilization continued to be important to the ways that missionaries and their supporters viewed the world. Particularly as new theories about racial difference emerged over the course of the early nineteenth century, this ranking of the world was central to the ways that American evangelicals imagined their place within it. It was precisely because this hierarchy existed and because it was possible to move up toward civilization and Christianity that the mission movement existed. Yet the seeming immutability of racial differences challenged this vision, even as it helped to create the context in which Anglo-American Christians emerged as the leaders of this new world order of the missionary imagination.

Chapter 2

Missions on the British Model

In 1810, several seminary students sent letters to the directors of the London Missionary Society expressing their *"passion for missions"* and asking if they might be received as missionaries for the society.[1] This might not have been news had these students been from somewhere in Britain. Instead, they were from Andover, Massachusetts. At the same time as they reached out to London, these students asked American ministers to form a missionary society within their own country that might send out missionaries into the world. From these two requests, in London and in Massachusetts, the early American foreign mission movement took its shape as a movement based in the United States but deeply connected to events and ideas in England. Both groups accepted these young men as missionaries. In England, the inquirers found themselves listed as missionaries under the London Missionary Society. In the United States, their request led to the formation of the American Board of Commissioners for Foreign Missions.

From its beginnings, the American foreign mission movement was rooted in both the United States and Great Britain. It was the success of British missions that first sparked the American interest in global mission, and it was to Britain that American missionaries and mission boards looked for advice and support. For a time, the American Board hoped for a formal relationship between the two, though ultimately the two groups retained a more casual connection. The Americans would rely on the British throughout the first decades of their work. For it was in the British Empire that the American Board of Commissioners for Foreign Missions established its first mission and many additional missions thereafter. As the Americans began their work in global missions, they modeled themselves on the British, hoping to continue an Anglo-American evangelical network that dated from the colonial era.

Though American missionaries at first hoped to work outside of the British Empire, their first mission would be in Bombay, then under the control of the East India Company. Throughout the period of their planning and establishment of this mission, American missionaries encountered British imperialism and British missions directly. In Bombay, the Board's missionaries encountered the foreign culture that they had read so much about in New England. In their preaching and teaching, they sought to transform India into a Christian civilization, with limited success. In practice, foreign missions worked differently than American missionaries had envisioned prior to their departure. It was here that they first developed their understanding of the difference between secular and Christian imperialism.

If the missionaries thought their careful selection of a relatively civilized location with proximity to the British Empire would make their work somewhat easy, they found that they were mistaken. Over the first decades of the Bombay mission, the missionaries and the Board came to reconsider the relationship between missions and empire, even as they held fast to the conception of missionary duty as Christian imperialism. As they envisioned it, their work involved cultural transformation to civilization, in addition to the preaching of the Gospel. From a somewhat naïve sense of the easy connection between empires and the conversion of the world, the Board came to see a distinction between the secular and commercial nature of the East India Company and the moral and civilized nature of a truly Christian empire. In their work, they attempted, alongside British missionaries, to push the British Empire closer to a more Christian form of imperialism.

The East India Company and British Missions

American readers were interested in British mission work for a number of reasons. Missionaries provided them with tales of faraway places and peoples, of foreign customs and strange practices. But missionaries also advanced a theological view of world politics that became very appealing to some American evangelicals. Christians, these mission supporters believed, had a duty to follow the Great Commission whenever, and wherever, they could. For many Christians within Britain, the existence of an empire necessitated missionary work. When they saw Britain's colonial empire expanding, they sensed a new and providential opportunity to perform their duty to spread the Gospel. In this context, failure to act was not only a matter of neglecting their duty to the "heathen," it was disobedience against God. British evangelicals petitioned for the addition of a "pious clause" into the East India Company's charter when it came up for renewal in both 1793 and 1813, and missionary societies continued to send missionaries to the region despite the danger of government opposition.[2]

The East India Company governed over parts of India from its first charter in 1698 until the beginning of the Raj in 1857. Throughout its history, the EIC had a complex relationship to religion and to the idea that part of its goal should be to bring Christianity to India. As historian Penelope Carson has shown, much of this complexity had to do with the type of Christianity that missionaries wanted to bring with them. The EIC maintained an easier connection with Anglicanism than with the various Dissenting Protestant groups. In addition to these denominational concerns, the EIC was consistently worried about the potential for evangelization to disrupt the larger imperial project of commercial gain. Time and again, EIC officials worried that too much missionary work, or the wrong kind of missionary work, could give cause for rebellion against not only the agents of evangelization, but also against the empire more generally. Accordingly, the East India Company resisted the introduction of a pious clause that would have required them to accept missionaries unilaterally.

Mission supporters, though, felt that this pious clause was necessary because not all British subjects shared the EIC's interpretation of the meaning of empire. For British and American evangelical audiences alike, the EIC's reluctance to allow missionaries in British India could be attributed to the presence of a so-called "Anti-Christian Party" within the East India Company. The EIC did not like "the Hindoos to be converted," as one American evangelical explained, and so they kept evangelical Protestantism out of the region. Yet the EIC's reluctance can instead be understood as their attempt to maintain stability. As early as 1806, the army at Vellore faced a sepoy mutiny as a result of the mistaken belief that the British army sought to convert the Indian people. From the perspective of the EIC, it made a great deal of sense, then, to keep the missionaries out.

A fundamental difference of opinion about the purpose of empire kept the two sides from fully understanding the perspective of the other. For EIC officials, the empire was about commerce; for missionaries, it was about the spread of God's word.

Missionaries found ways around government regulations. For example, when British Baptist missionaries William Carey and John Thomas arrived in Calcutta in 1793 and discovered that they could not remain in EIC territory, they instead established their mission at Serampore, then under Danish control. They were able, then, to continue their work. Even when the British took control of Serampore by the early 1800s, EIC chaplain Claudius Buchanan assured Carey that the mission would not encounter difficulties from the government, so long as he would not preach in front of the government house. As the first British missionaries to settle in South Asia, Carey and Thomas's letters were widely read by an Anglo-American Christian audience, even outside of their own denomination.[3] Americans, then, could imagine a type of imperialism that encouraged missionary activity.

Evangelicals on both sides of the Atlantic seemed secure in their understanding that Christian nations were granted empires providentially. Through empires, they saw, they had access to non-Christian people in ways never before possible. God was calling them to begin the work of world conversion, to bring this land that was now part of the British Empire into the Kingdom of God. This conviction, combined with the example of Carey's successful navigation of the East India Company led to cautious optimism on the part of British mission societies that they would be successful in establishing missions in EIC territory during the early nineteenth century. In 1807, the London Missionary Society accordingly planned to send two missionaries, John Gordon and William Lee, to India. First, though, Gordon and Lee would travel to New York. There they would raise funds, taking advantage of the American interest in mission work, and secure passage to India on an American ship that would not require the same sort of passport from the East India Company that a British ship might. The Anglo-American connections of both religion and commerce would allow the British missionaries, perhaps ironically, to enter into the British Empire more easily through America than they might have done directly through England.

Gordon and Lee would not leave the United States for several more years. In the intervening period, imperial and international relations conspired to ground the British missionaries in America. Shortly after their arrival in New York, they learned that the East India Company would not, in fact, allow new missionaries to operate within its territory. Not only was permission required for Europeans or Americans to reside within EIC territory, missionaries as such were explicitly being told that they could not land, and some already in India were being told to stop preaching. Shocked and unsure how to proceed, especially given that they were far away from London, Gordon and Lee sought the advice of the New York Missionary Society, who advised them to remain in New York until more news could be gathered. The London Society soon encouraged them to continue to Asia. The EIC's policies were not expressly antimission, the London Society explained. After all, Carey had been allowed to remain. Clearly, whatever its theoretical concern about the destabilizing potential of missions, the East India Company had permitted select missionaries to remain and had even found their language skills useful to the colonial project as a whole. It was their "duty" to go forward, the LMS insisted, reminding its missionaries that "the Lord will work by his chosen Servants and his own immediate irresistible energy," whatever the EIC might attempt to do. For the London Missionary Society, this was a question of duty, and of what the purpose of empire was. In sending missionaries without authorization, the London Missionary Society challenged the East India Company's authority over India. Instead, British missionaries suggested, the interests of the missionaries, and of Christianity, superseded those of the empire.[4]

More than a year later, the missionaries were still in the United States working as itinerant preachers in New York and Philadelphia (where Lee reported that "many Heathens are to be found in every direction who are 'perishing for lack of knowledge and crying for help'"). It was not the East India Company that kept them from India, but American politics. The missionaries found themselves grounded by embargo.[5] As a result of frustration over the treatment of American commerce and shipping during the war between Britain and France, the American government passed a series of legislation designed to punish the British by withholding American supplies. The Embargo and Non-Intercourse Acts had significantly reduced the traffic not only between the United States and Britain, but also its colonies, including India.

While in the United States, these British missionaries connected with the American side of the Atlantic evangelical network. When missionaries of the LMS, including not only Gordon and Lee, but also the Spratts, the Mays, and Miss Ann Green (whose fiancé died before they could leave for Calcutta; she eventually went overseas as a single woman), were stuck in the United States, they resided in the homes of American missionary supporters, preached in American churches (usually Presbyterian), and occasionally served as missionaries and itinerant preachers in the areas surrounding Philadelphia and New York. "Our friends," wrote John Gordon, "continue numerous and kind." The New York Missionary Society, long in contact with the London Society, served as a substitute governing body. In addition to such organizational connections, British missionaries found themselves the beneficiaries of individual aid, as well. Lee, for example, was given free tickets to Benjamin Rush's lectures at the University of Pennsylvania to prepare him to perform medical services when in India.[6]

British missionaries found a ready community in America for the same reason that the London Missionary Society sent them to New York in the first place: there was a real sense on both sides of the Atlantic that the project of global missions was a shared one between English and American evangelical Protestants. If at the time of the missionaries' arrival in New York, American mission supporters understood that their own part of this project had geographic limits, by the time that the missionaries left, Americans had a very different idea. In 1805, for example, the Connecticut Missionary Society had insisted that it could not send missionaries to Canada because not only was there not enough money, but it was a British territory. It worried that it might seem improper to both U.S. and Canadian authorities to have Connecticut missionaries operating there. A mere five years later, many of these same supporters had founded the American Board. Governance by another nation no longer appeared a conflict for setting up American missions.[7]

Americans saw the move into overseas mission work as representing a shift in Anglo-American relations. Just as the United States, in the political and economic spheres, asserted its national strength and equality with European powers, American Christians claimed a role for themselves equal to that of the British. "If all the circumstances of the case are considered," the American Board reminded its supporters, "we are more able to take an active part in evangelizing the heathen, than any other people on the globe. With the exception of Great Britain, indeed, no nation but our own has the inclination, or the ability, to make great exertions in the prosecution of this design." In making these claims, the Board called on a tradition of Anglo-American evangelical connections from the eighteenth century, but with a new dimension. Then, the two groups were evangelicals from metropole and colony of a shared empire; now, they were separate nations, linked by a common tradition but distinct in political, and perhaps other, affairs.

Throughout the early appeals for support of the Indian mission, the Board emphasized the ways that Americans, too, had a duty to evangelize wherever imperial and commercial networks granted them access to non-Christian peoples. "Though the field is distant, it is not unknown," the Board reminded its supporters. "Distance of place alters not the claims of the heathen, so long as the means of access to them are in our power." Access, they insisted, created a religious duty to go and spread the Gospel. American ships traded in India. The British Empire had established what missionaries believed would be a supportive government there. This, the Board insisted, meant that the Americans had access and had a duty to go forth and convert India. The British Empire clearly required British evangelicals to go about the work of conversion, Americans thought, but because of the close connections between the two countries, it created a duty for them, too.[8]

For decades, American missionary supporters had considered themselves to be "engaged in the same glorious cause" as their British peers. When, in 1802, New Yorkers had elected the president of the London Missionary Society to be an honorary director of the New York Missionary Society, they did so in reciprocation of the "similar act on your part . . . and as an affectionate pledge of our union and cooperation with you." New Yorkers were not the only Americans who corresponded with and felt themselves connected to London. Connecticut mission supporters, too, insisted that while there were some differences between American and British missionaries, they took part in the same "general object . . . the enlargement of the Redeemer's kingdom." By the time that the Board was founded in 1810, the nature of these connections seemed to be even stronger to American observers. As the Board continued its appeal to supporters, it highlighted the importance of American missionary exertions by pointing to the ways that America was fully equal to Britain, and perhaps even more appropriate for the work of world mission. At the time, the British were at war with France and this, according to the Board, distracted them from the full realization of their religious duty. Americans, then free from the vagaries of European imperial struggles, were thus better positioned than the British to take on the mantle of evangelists to the world.[9]

The American independence from the British Empire cut both ways, however. If it freed Americans—for a time—from the imperial conflicts that plagued Britain, it also complicated their missionary interest into India. The entry of Americans into world mission at this time, then, was not simply about a new opportunity granted by the presence of the British Empire, whatever the

[margin handwriting: distracted by war]

Board may have claimed from Boston. As much as the British Empire created opportunities for American evangelicals, it presented problems as well. On the most basic level, this can be seen in the frequent queries from governors in India to the directors of the East India Company in England about the legality of Americans' rights to reside in India at all.[10] Indeed, one of the major factors in the attractiveness of Burma, the initial destination of the Asian mission, was that Burma was "not within the limits of the British empire, and therefore not so much within the proper province of the British Missionary Societies." American missionaries, then, realized that the East India Company might create difficulties for them. While they wanted to take advantage of the benefits of the British presence in Asia, they hoped that mere proximity might be enough to help them without requiring them to submit to an institution that did not completely share their values.[11]

The American position within this previously British project both within and on the margins of the empire was unclear. If British missionaries struggled with the meaning of empire for their work, the implications for Americans were even more fraught. While the Board quite clearly admired much about England, this did not prevent it from criticizing some British customs, or what it saw as the lack of prioritization of religion by the government—both in England and overseas. Nor did it prevent a nascent nationalism from being evident in subtle and overt ways throughout the early years of the Board. The Board was certainly not a nationally representative body; its support came almost entirely from New England, especially in its first years, and its support was largely limited to Congregationalists and Presbyterians. Yet this did not stop the Board from claiming a position of national representativeness.

The Board's members envisioned it as speaking for the country, representing the United States abroad, and doing important work in the religious life of the nation. For them, the Board represented what the United States ought to be doing abroad. The Board's missionaries were always defined simply as Americans, and almost never by their denominational backgrounds. For some of its supporters, the Board's emergence was also explicitly an important statement about the position of the United States. To them, the idea of sending American missionaries under British sponsorship would be an "eternal shame to the United States."[12] Symbolically, the creation of an American missionary society, then, became an important statement of the equality of American and British evangelicals as partners in a shared project.

When the first of the American missionaries to India were ordained, these dual themes of transnational Christian identity and American national

pride were both evident. The ordination of Gordon Hall, Adoniram Judson, Samuel Newell, Samuel Nott, and Luther Rice as Board missionaries
in February 1812 was a public event. Crowds gathered at the Tabernacle
Church in Salem to witness the formal beginning to American missionary
work and to hear Samuel Worcester, the corresponding secretary of the
Board, predict that these five young men were "but the precursors of many,
who shall follow you in this arduous, glorious exercise." In the ordination
sermon, Rev. Leonard Woods, who had taught most of the missionaries at
Andover Theological Seminary, explained the importance of missionary
work through a discussion of the Great Commission and the equal value
of all souls before God. Everyone, even supposed "heathens," needed to
have the opportunity to learn about Jesus, he insisted, and it would be
the work of the missionaries to present them with the opportunity to be
saved. While Woods was clear that nations did not matter to God, as all
were rightly members of God's kingdom, he did pair the United States and
Britain as emblematic of true Christianity and joint partners in the work of
missions. Jonathan Allen, who preached a Farewell Sermon to Ann Judson
and Harriet Newell, the wives of two of these missionaries, continued these
themes but discussed the joint roles of the Christians from the United States
and Britain even more emphatically. These countries, he wrote, could be
expected to "take the most active part in the diffusion of the Gospel among
the heathen nations." While other countries might "profess to be christians,"
it was in England and America that "pure religion" had taken its deepest
roots. "The door for publishing the Gospel among the heathen," he proclaimed, "is, at present, more widely open than at any former period." Now
it was time for Americans to respond to that call.[13]

As much as the early missionary movement exemplified Anglo-American
religious cooperation and affiliation, it also provided occasion for an American evangelical assertion of its ability to operate on the same plane as the
British. As evangelical Christians who were part of an Anglo-American
missionary network, clearly missionaries did not see their work as primarily
a competition between nations, but the Americans were aware of national
differences. The links between the groups were probably clearer in the mission field; for supporters of mission at home, it was easier to feel a pride
in the contributions their country was making toward the conversion of
the world. The published materials in the United States, especially those
oriented toward fundraising, emphasized the Americanness of the American Board a bit more clearly than the personal records of the missionaries
themselves.

Figure 2. On February 6, 1812, the first five missionaries of the American Board were ordained in Salem, Massachusetts. Adoniram Judson, Gordon Hall, Samuel Newell, Samuel Nott, and Luther Rice, aided by their wives Ann Judson, Harriet Newell, and Roxana Nott, prepared to leave in only a few days for India. Within months, the United States would declare war on Great Britain. Courtesy of the Wider Church Ministries of the United Church of Christ, ABC 78.3, Box 1, Folder 1.

Americans in India

If the missionaries would have been happy serving under the London Missionary Society, and if the mission movement itself generally expressed ambivalence about nationalism during these years, this should not suggest that the American identity of these missionaries did not matter. It mattered a great deal. However little they may have expressed it, they went into Asia not as British subjects, but as American citizens. Their experiences abroad over the next few years were shaped by that identity, and their attempts to create an American Christian space in British India was marked in important ways by their national identity. The ability of national background to shape a transnational religious experience can most clearly be seen in moments of conflict, and these Americans arrived in India at precisely such a time. In between their departure from the United States and their arrival in India, the United States had declared war on Great Britain. The missionaries began their work at the dawn of the War of 1812.

In February 1812, British and American missionaries left Philadelphia and Salem for India. Unaware of the developments in the United States that allowed the Americans to be supported by the ABCFM, one director of the London Missionary Society included the Americans in his reports on missionary staff that year.[14] Where, exactly, these five American men and three women were headed was unclear. The Board hoped that they would find their home in Burma, though they left it up to the missionaries once they reached India. Even once the Americans reached South Asia, however, it would take several years for them to establish their mission. Their entry into the region was more difficult than they expected. While they had anticipated some difficulty with the East India Company, this was compounded by the outbreak of the War of 1812.

Four months after the missionaries left the Northeast, the war between the United States and Great Britain began. Within the United States, opposition to the war was strong, especially among Federalists and New Englanders, including many supporters of the ABCFM. The disruption of the Anglo-American evangelical network during these years deeply troubled American evangelicals. Throughout the conflict, American Christians "long[ed] to hear particularly what Christians in Britain are doing."[15] For American Board members it was especially trying, as they had to negotiate the financial and spiritual support of their missionaries with extremely limited access to communication. The missionaries sorely needed that support. Upon their arrival in India, they learned that the East India Company was indeed resistant to a missionary presence, and false reports of still more American missionaries bound for India led EIC officials to be even more concerned. Soon they heard calls for their arrest.[16]

In August 1812, Gordon Hall and Samuel Nott finally arrived in Calcutta after their long journey from Philadelphia. Reunited with Adoniram and Ann Judson, who had traveled on a different ship, they were worried to hear that the Judsons had been ordered to leave and that all of the missionaries were facing the "opposition of government." Police requested that they reboard their ship and return to the United States immediately. Lord Minto, the governor-general who ruled over Bengal for the East India Company, had long expressed concerns about missionary activity, and the Americans quickly began thinking of alternative locations for their work. Return to the United States was simply not an option for them. Such a move would have ended the foreign mission movement before it even began. Surely, they believed, there was another place where they might venture to continue their work.

Largely because of this government opposition to their presence in India, the American missionaries dispersed shortly after their arrival in India. After receiving permission to sail to the Isle of France (Mauritius), Samuel and Harriet Newell left with the company's approval. It was there that Harriet and their newborn baby would die. Ann and Adoniram Judson had become Baptists on their journey to Calcutta and were joined by Luther Rice after his arrival. While Rice returned to the United States to organize American Baptists to support mission work, the Judsons fled British authority, attempting to outrun those who would arrest them on their way to Burma. Of those remaining under the Board's direction, Samuel and Roxanna Nott and Gordon Hall remained in India.

British missionaries, too, were ordered out of the region, though the attempts to remove them never seemed so threatening as the situation of the Americans, due to the wartime context. As Joshua Marshman, the British Baptist missionary who helped both the American and British missionaries petition for their right to remain in India, discovered, the East India Company was particularly frustrated by the British missionaries' attempts to get around EIC procedure by approaching India through America.[17] By March 1813, the British missionaries had departed for England, even as the Americans remained.[18]

If the EIC opposed both American and British missionaries within its territories, we might ask again what difference nationality made. The records of the East India Company about these events reveal in even starker terms the risks that the missionaries faced in India. Just as American mariners were in danger of capture as perceived British subjects, the missionaries were accused of merely pretending to be American citizens. In their litany of critiques of the American missionaries' character, the government officers commented that they "do suspect they are British subjects," and thus would rightly come under the control of the East India Company. These suspicions were not universal, however. Company chairman Charles Grant vigorously objected to their treatment; it was "neither necessary nor warranted." Much of his response focused on the right that the British government had to treat these missionaries as it did. As they were "neither Prisoners of War, nor British Subjects, nor charged with carrying on any correspondence dangerous to the British Possessions," Grant pointed out, the government had no right under "English Law, nor by the Law of Nations" to demand their removal to England. Grant was sympathetic to missions generally and was active in pushing the East India Company to allow evangelism within its territory. His defense of the Americans was probably motivated by these concerns. Grant's commentary reveals that whatever their difficulties, the American foreign mission movement had friends in England outside of mission circles. Yet even these friends had their limits: much of Grant's argument on behalf of the Americans was based in his belief that they intended to leave the EIC's domain when they began their preaching. Could Americans appropriately act as missionaries within the British Empire? This was the question. Its answer was complicated because of the relationship between the missionaries' religious and national identities. While American missionaries proclaimed themselves participants in an Anglo-American evangelical project, they were at the same time American citizens in the British Empire.[19]

Aided by British missionaries in the area and their directors in London, the two men spent the next several months petitioning the East India Company government and debating their ultimate destination. After considering Madagascar and Java as possible destinations, these missionaries decided by late August that they might be able to settle somewhere in the EIC's territory, so long as they found a more favorable governor. Sir Evan Nepean, governor of Bombay, seemed more likely to allow them to evangelize in their territory. He was the president of the British and Foreign Bible Society, and as such could be expected to sympathize with the missionary cause. In November, Hall and the Notts applied to the police for a passport to allow them to travel to Bombay. This was refused, and instead they were ordered to leave for England on the next ship, leaving in a few days. American and British missionaries alike assumed that the EIC wanted to take the Americans as prisoners of war. The government order informed the missionaries that they had "forfeited all claim to the further indulgence" of the EIC by not leaving immediately after their arrival for the Isle of France or the United States. Without a passport, Hall and Nott boarded a ship for Bombay, resolved to face arrest if they were going to be sent to England.[20]

Throughout their difficulties, the missionaries wrote of how they were "fully persuaded that we did right in becoming missionaries, and in coming to the East. We therefore think we are in the path of duty." They even went so far as to request at least two additional missionaries to be sent to India at the earliest opportunity of the American Board.[21] It was with great frustration, accordingly, that the missionaries learned that they would not be allowed to stay in Bombay either, due to the "unfavorable impressions of our characters" that had been given to "the minds of this government" after they had left Calcutta without passports and against the explicit orders of the police.[22]

Within a year of October 1812, the American missionaries sent no fewer than six petitions to government officials in India, to say nothing of their official and unofficial correspondence on the subject of their right to remain in India. These emphasized the ways that the missionaries were unconnected to politics. Their goal was simply, they explained, to do good "by translating the scriptures, by aiding in the education of children, and ultimately by making known the Gospel to some who are now ignorant of it."[23] Such goals, they assumed, would not be at odds with the EIC's purposes. While it was clear that the East India Company did not generally share their understanding of Christian imperialism, the missionaries assumed that the goal of civilizing India was common between the two groups. Accordingly, they focused on these aspects of their work in their correspondence with colonial officials.

To be successful in their efforts to stay in India, missionaries had to placate officials at multiple levels. Locally, they could at times convince a governor that their presence would not hurt the empire, but on a higher level, it was much less certain that they would be granted permission to stay. Their lack of a concrete plan of where they would go further conflicted with the established order of the East India Company. The British missionaries established at Serampore, for example, seemed perplexed by the lack of planning that American missionaries seemed to have completed prior to their arrival in India. While the Americans were happy to allow Providence to direct them to where they would be most useful, this was clearly not the most effective type of behavior within the empire. And so, when the Americans sailed from Calcutta to Bombay, and from Bombay to Cochin, both times without passes, they were eventually refused the right to reenter Bombay because their earlier illicit flight had angered the governor and raised questions about their character. In striking contrast to the British missionaries' respectful behavior toward the EIC's regulations, American missionaries expected to be able to go where they pleased as a result of the holiness of their project. Three times in a period of as many years, the Americans were ordered to England as prisoners and told that their passage was imminent. Throughout these months, the missionaries lived in government buildings, and their mobility was severely limited.[24]

The reaction to the arrival of the *Alligator*, an American schooner that came to Calcutta from Salem in 1813, also demonstrates the precarious position of the American missionaries. The ship carried a packet of letters, books, and money from the Board for its missionaries—it was the first to leave New England for India since the missionaries' departure. As he packed the parcels for the missionaries, Samuel Worcester hoped that it would reach the missionaries soon, and that the "obstruction" caused by the war would "not be long."[25] Yet British officials were convinced that there was a nefarious purpose to the ship's presence in their territory. The ship's crew was arrested and sent to England as prisoners of war, and the American missionaries found themselves under suspicion. In their writings, they described the sense of a shift in their relationship with the government; the *Alligator* was, they felt, the "only ostensible reason" that the British were trying to remove them from the region. The context of British opposition to the American missionary presence seemed to have been completely altered by the war.[26]

Slowly, the East India Company eased its restrictions against the missionaries in the winter of 1813–14. In early December, the police finally allowed Gordon Hall and Samuel Nott to return to shore in Bombay, provided that they surrendered themselves to the police and agreed to go to England when ordered.[27] By March, nothing more had been heard from the police in Bombay, and the mission brethren were reunited there after nearly two years.[28] In May, they began to have great hopes that they would be able to remain, as they had not yet heard otherwise, and by October, the mission had begun its operations, opening schools and working on translation of the scriptures, in the absence of any news from the government about their need to depart. It was in this somewhat unsettled but seemingly stable state that the three requested the Board to send more missionaries to help them in Bombay and to establish a second mission station in Ceylon.[29]

The war seemed by this time to be only an excuse for sending the missionaries away.[30] Rather, the missionaries believed that opposition to the cause was the root of the EIC's attempts to rid India of missionaries, not only American, but also British. As the American missionaries came to spend more time in India, they only became more convinced of the importance of their work and the needs of the native people. In their eyes, the missionaries were on the side of the natives, working to repair what one called the "wretched situation of this land," while the government only tried to hinder those good works.[31] This was in some ways the beginning of the American missionary conception of itself as working in opposition to governments and its critique of secular imperialism. For the missionaries, England, along with America, was the seat of true Christianity in the world, and it accordingly needed to practice Christian imperialism. If the American Board, along with evangelicals throughout the Anglo-American world, thought that the existence of empire created the opportunity for, and indeed a requirement of, a moral and religious response, then the British

Empire, at least the part under the domain of the East India Company, was failing to live up to this promise. How much more important, then, did the missionary presence there seem to be.

Anglo–American Cooperation in India

The links to the London Society sustained the Americans in this time of uncertainty. Throughout this period, the Americans were out of touch with the United States. Those few letters that reached America did so through London, a process that took considerably longer than it might have otherwise. In the face of this, the American missionaries forged much closer ties with British mission supporters. In March 1813, when they were in Bombay and unsure of how long they could remain, Gordon Hall and Samuel Nott sent their first letter to George Burder, secretary of the London Missionary Society, since their initial applications to serve as LMS missionaries. The "very lamentable war," they wrote, made their situation bleaker, and they hoped that Burder could help them get their news to America. Burder, in turn, wrote regularly to the American missionaries, offering support and encouragement to them. Over the course of the war, the letters between the American missionaries and their supporters in London came to resemble those that they sent to their own board. They wrote about their adventures, their progress in evangelization, and their impressions of the people around them. As time passed, their letters focused so much on their sense of the work they had yet to do that the news that the missionaries expected to be sent to England within two months was relegated to a postscript.

The connections between British and American missions during the war were not only spiritual, but practical, as the Americans relied on the London Society and its missionaries for advice, morale, and financial support in the absence of access to the Board. Because of the paucity of ships traveling from New England to India during the war, remittances from the Board were few and far between during these years. The Board eventually appointed agents in Bengal, including William Carey, to assist in its financial transactions in India.[32] When the Board appointed a committee in Calcutta to serve as financial agents for their missionaries, almost all of those they chose were British members of this transnational evangelical network.[33]

When the war ended in March 1815, the Board and its supporters throughout the world rejoiced at the greater ease with which they could now pursue their work. The declaration of peace allowed many aspects of the Anglo-American missionary network to return to normal, with one important difference: now, the American missionaries were more secure in their position in South Asia, and the reopening of trade meant that the Board could dispatch more missionaries to support the Bombay station and establish a new mission at Ceylon. Learning its lesson from the legal troubles of the first group of missionaries, the Board contacted the directors of the East India Company in England on behalf of missionaries James Richards, Edward Warren, Benjamin Meigs, Daniel Poor, and Horatio Bardwell.[34]

The American missionaries continued to operate under the domain of the East India Company, which had control of the region through 1857. While their situation was less tenuous with the conclusion of the war and increased pressure within England to encourage missionary work in India, the missionaries still had to balance their roles as Anglo-American Protestants allied with British Christians and as American citizens operating at the pleasure of the government.[35] The connections between British and American missionaries, unsurprisingly, continued to provide both groups with much-needed camaraderie and support.

The relationship between the East India Company and missionaries in general warmed over the course of the 1820s and 1830s, though the government tended to be more closely connected with the British, rather than the American, missionaries. As Ian Copland has argued, this was a result of several factors. As the mission movement within Britain became more respectable and more evangelicals gradually came to India as EIC leaders, by the 1830s missionaries could expect to receive better treatment from the East India Company. Additionally, the language skills of the missionaries were highly useful to the government. William Carey in particular served as an important teacher of indigenous languages to officials in Calcutta. Other missionaries could provide expert knowledge of native religion and law that was essential to the workings of the government. The EIC even began to support mission-run public schools, entrusting the important work of educating native youth to the labor of the British missions. It was this interpretation of the relationship between missions and empire that the American missionaries had emphasized in their wartime petitions. In the years after peace, they saw the East India Company begin to agree with parts of their claims about the duties of empire.[36]

In spite of this, the American missionaries continued to face instability in Bombay. For even as the East India Company began to take advantage of the benefits that missions could offer to the empire, it also continued to insist that missions could be dangerous. The earlier concerns of the EIC that the mission could lead to social unrest proved to be well founded. There, by the late 1830s, conversions of native Indians of multiple backgrounds could result in mass protests and even Indian parents bringing charges against missionaries for interference with their children.[37] As these reactions made clear, the initial wariness of the East India Company toward missions was a reasonable reaction to local circumstances. Even as individual EIC officials may have been sympathetic to the work of the missionaries, there continued to be a distinction between the two groups; at times their interests were very much at odds. National differences, too, continued to matter. The American missionaries certainly never experienced the sort of alliance with the colonial officials that the British missionaries sometimes did. The relationship between the Americans and the government continued to be defined by insecurity and careful balancing of interests. The Americans remained critical of what they saw as the government's slowness to support evangelical and moral projects.

In navigating the operations of the EIC government, American missionaries relied on their British allies; they were not isolated in India. In all of their work, the American Bombay missionaries continued to be connected to other missionaries in the region and, through their connections to the Board, throughout the world. The joint letters from Bombay sent frequent news about the progress of world mission back to the United States, not only discussing their own progress and that of the American Ceylon mission, but also the possibilities for evangelization in the Mideast and Africa, and the comings and goings of British missionaries in Asia. These links were formalized by the creation of the Bombay Missionary Union in late 1825. The Missionary Union brought together the missionaries of the American Board, the Church Missionary Society, the London Missionary Society, and the Scottish Missionary Society working in Bombay, Surat, Belgaum, and the southern Concan. The group's goal was to "promote Christian fellowship, and to consult on the best means of advancing the kingdom of Christ in this country," and membership and participation in annual meetings was open to any Protestant missionary in the region.[38]

Both the instability of the missionaries' position in Bombay and their continued connection to the British mission movement can be seen in the creation of the Board's second Asian mission. Following Newell's advice, and as a result of the apparent lack of support from the East India Company for any other missionaries to settle in Bombay, the Board planned to establish its next mission at Ceylon. As it was still unclear to the Board in 1815 whether the missionaries would be allowed to remain in Bombay, Board members wondered whether it might be Ceylon after all that would be the site of their first permanent mission. Ceylon was not governed by the EIC, but by British officials. Governor Brownrigg, the governor there, was far more welcoming to missionaries, as his understanding of empire was far more in line with that of the American missionaries.[39] The new missionaries reflected the continual American interest in India, describing it as "the most promising and attractive part of the heathen world."[40] To make it more likely that the new missionaries would not have the same difficulties that the Bombay missionaries had faced, Hall and Newell advised the Board to appeal for help in London before sending the new missionaries abroad. Yet it was not to the EIC that they suggested the Board write, but rather to the London Missionary Society. In the absence of direct permission from the East India Company, they hoped, the new missionaries might be able to go out under LMS instructions and thus be safer from molestation by the EIC in India. Though they had reason to expect that the governor would allow American missionaries to remain in the region, as Hall and Newell had just received this permission themselves, the EIC system was changeable enough to cause concern.[41]

Similarly, the British missionaries provided essential aid and information when new missionaries arrived.[42] The missions helped each other in other ways, as when the American missionaries sent tracts to Surat for distribution before Fyvie and Skinner had their own press.[43] The visit of an Anglican bishop to the region further demonstrated the friendly relations between British and American preachers in Bombay. The bishop's sermon focused on his frustration that anyone but ministers of the Church of England were allowed to preach. This tirade, the missionaries explained, was for the benefit of two chaplains who had worked in alliance with the (Presbyterian) missionaries of the Board. Whatever the wishes of church officials, missionaries and chaplains on the ground found ways to cooperate and support each other's work more often than not.[44]

Individual governors were incredibly important, then, for the interpretation of what the role of religion in the British Empire ought to be. While the East India Company had official policies, governors were able to act somewhat independently in practice, simply because they were so far from London and oversight was diffused among multiple governors. Accordingly, when Bombay received a new governor from the East India Company in 1819, the American mission found itself again negotiating with the British government for their right to remain in Bombay and perform their work as they saw fit. Governor Stuart Elphinstone shared the concerns of the EIC about allowing missionaries to operate within India. In the words of the missionaries, he was "apprehensive of a too rapid advance against the prejudices of the natives, thus endangering the public peace." For the missionaries, this apprehension manifested itself in a reluctance to grant them passports to itinerate on the continent and a general concern about the operations of the mission schools. While the previous governor had regularly allowed the missionaries passage to the continent, Elphinstone was more concerned about keeping the native population calm and removing any fears of the Brahmins that their religion might be "interfered with," as the missionaries explained.[45] This was a reasonable concern; the missionaries had encountered plenty of individuals who held this precise fear, and interference with native religion was of course the goal of missionary work.

When American missionaries talked about the ways that they understood the connections between imperialism and religious change, they tended to support the power of the British. Horatio Bardwell, for example, described one conversation he had with a group of Brahmins who were furious at the rise of the EIC's power, and the attendant decline of their own. In Bardwell's telling, the discussion went from political to religious authority, with Bardwell asserting the value of the British ascendancy because of its link to Christianity. For Bardwell, as with the other American missionaries, the British Empire had value precisely because of its potential for bringing about religious change. Those with whom he was talking, however, did not see the benefits that Bardwell saw in these developments. They "seemed reluctant to admit," he wrote, "that the religion of Christ inculcated peace and kindness to all mankind." The missionary's teachings, then, did little to prevent the mixture of political and religious control in the eyes of those whom they sought to convert. Even as the British distanced themselves officially from the American mission's work, and the American missionaries were critical of some aspects of the EIC's governance, there were profound links between Christianity and British imperial control in the missionaries' eyes. For the missionaries, the needs of the British Empire for stability were meaningless next to the needs of the world for the Gospel. However practical Elphinstone's concerns, the missionaries did not consider them important; the spread of the Gospel was simply a higher priority and was the only reason that they felt empire was justified.[46]

To placate the governor, the missionaries sent a memorial on their schools that stressed the more secular benefits of missionary education with regard to "civilization." In 1815, Governor Evan Nepean had been able to allow the Americans to remain because he had convinced the Court of Directors that the missionaries were only interested in religious instruction, and now they needed to convince Elphinstone of the same. At the time of his appointment, Elphinstone requested that the missionaries submit a paper to him explaining the goals and methods of their schools. It was essential, he wrote, that the missionaries not give "the slightest pretext to the Brahmins to represent their religion as interfered with."[47] Elphinstone appeared somewhat mollified by the missionaries' response and supported the general project of increasing literacy among Indians. The happier relations with the government were demonstrated in 1824, when the missionaries requested some land for burying their dead in the grounds of St. Thomas Church. To their surprise, they were granted not only the land, but a masonry wall to surround it, at "a very considerable expense to the Government." This they took as a "favorable indication" of the government's stance toward the mission in general.[48] They needed such indications since, even though missionaries were now allowed to reside and work in EIC territory, foreigners officially were not. The missionaries, as a result, remained only at the pleasure of the governor, and in 1824 the missionaries were awaiting the arrival of Edmund Frost, a new missionary from the United States. Indeed, it was their knowledge of the government's opposition that had slowed the Board's responses to the Bombay missionaries' repeated requests for additional laborers after the war.[49] Frost was granted permission to remain in Bombay, but the governor encouraged them to be quiet about it: "The less that was said about it the better."[50]

These indications of an improving relationship were not without counterexamples to keep the missionaries somewhat unsure of their position and untrusting of the goals of British imperialism. In 1823, for example, two Indian Jews working for the mission were arrested when circulating six thousand tracts in the bazaars in the Deccan, which had recently come under EIC control. The tracts were confiscated, though eventually returned to the mission, and the missionaries were instructed to refrain from sending any more tracts into the area. The governor urged them to consider that "nothing can be more hostile to the true interests of Christianity, or more dangerous to the public interests" than the distribution of such tracts. The texts were "directed against the Hindoo superstition," which, in the political context of the time, the governor found dangerous; the missionaries were discouraged from distributing any texts in the area that made "any reference to religion."[51]

This interference in their work frustrated the missionaries, unsurprisingly, and they not only published the letters from the East India Company to themselves, but they also printed their response in a circular format for distribution. They asserted there that this was the first time the EIC had interfered in missionary operations (since they had been granted permission to remain in Bombay), and they directed their comments first toward the content of their tracts and then toward the expected response of the natives to that content. They disagreed emphatically with the governor's interpretation of the political context and claimed that their tracts had little in it that could offend Hindus. The books contained "no pointed attacks," they insisted and were being loudly and gladly received by some two thousand natives who surrounded the missionaries' assistants. Their work had never created "the least disturbance" in India, they wrote. Instead, they framed this incident as a conflict between the government and the missionary endeavor generally. The distribution of tracts, they wrote, was simply what missionaries did, wherever they were; this was "the universal expectation of all the friends of missions, and of the Christian public," and they would continue to do so. Hinting at their hopes that this could be a shared project of the church and the government, they highlighted the fact that some politicians were coming to agree that the spread of Christianity "would constitute the only secure basis of that vast empire which the great Ruler and Judge of nations has confided to the guardian care of the British Power."[52]

The American missionaries, then, continued to operate at a difficult intersection of political and religious interests. While they enjoyed some support from the government by the 1820s, this was tenuous, and the missionaries were very defensive of their right to remain in the area and pursue their work as they saw fit. These rights that the Americans asserted were based solely on their religious credentials. Since they shared a religion with the British government, they expected that government to recognize their authority as God's messengers. When the East India Company did not do so, the missionaries critiqued the nature of the British presence in India.

The government's lack of enthusiastic support of their work led the Board to question the value of establishing missions within the British Empire, in spite of the benefits it provided in terms of access. Even when the government allowed them to work, it could interfere with their operations and attempt to keep them from upsetting native populations. As the missionaries thought about what India needed, they believed that their work of evangelization was more important than stabilizing British colonies, though they hoped that their work of civilization could be seen as a shared project. In this judgment they were developing an understanding of what Christian imperialism ought to look like. From their experience in Bombay, they could determine that British imperialism was not necessarily going to be "Christian" in their way of thinking. The prioritization of stability for commercial gain overwhelmed the goals of civilization and Christianization.

The American missionaries did not give up, however. Working with individual governors and other officials who would support their understanding that imperial and commercial access to India required a Christian and missionary response, the Board's missionaries established a Bombay mission that would last for decades. With the support of the British missionary movement, both in India and in England, American missionaries were able to navigate their position within India even during a time of war between their country and Great Britain. Throughout their early years in Bombay, the American missionaries had to develop an argument to justify their presence there. It was relatively easy to insist in Boston that American Christians had a duty to evangelize the "heathen" of India, but explaining to officials of the East India Company why this was so was more difficult. As they did so, missionaries presented different ideas about their identity: as Americans, as Christian missionaries, and finally as American missionaries.

In spite of its rocky beginnings, by 1860, when the Board celebrated its jubilee anniversary, the Bombay mission was quite stable. It had employed twenty-eight missionaries, four assistant missionaries, and their wives over the course of five decades.[53] As new missionaries arrived, they sought the approval of the East India Company's Board of Directors before beginning their work. Even with these numbers and the shift toward better relations with the EIC, Bombay missionaries would continually complain about being understaffed. This was understandable: by the mid-1820s, the mission operated nearly forty schools with some two thousand students. The mission could never have what they considered sufficient numbers of missionaries, both because of funding problems and because the government would not allow so many. So the mission was dependent on the labor of native teachers who did not share their goals of Christianization or civilization. When the Bombay mission opened its schools and began preaching to the public, these difficulties forced them to think deeply about what conversion would look like. As they did so, they realized that converting the world would involve a great deal more engagement with the culture and people of India. If the American Board had hoped in 1810 that the British Empire could provide new access and opportunities for mission work, they learned in Bombay that while this was the case, it did so within a context that limited their potential for success.

Chapter 3

Mission Schools and the Meaning of Conversion

In 1818, the Bombay missionaries published *The Conversion of the World, or the Claims of Six Hundred Millions.* This short text was a call to arms for American Christians, an American response to the writings of Carey and Buchanan that had been so influential to the American missionaries before they left the United States. In the book, Gordon Hall and Samuel Newell laid out their plan for what all Americans might do to advance the cause for world conversion. It would not be difficult, they insisted. In a crude mathematical analysis, they laid out the reasons to expect the mission movement to succeed. Estimating the population of the world to be 800 million, they asserted that some 600 million were "heathens" in need of evangelization. Ever the optimists in their beliefs about what missionaries could accomplish, Hall and Newell estimated that one missionary was needed for every twenty thousand "heathens." Although this meant that thirty thousand missionaries were needed, in contrast to the less than four hundred currently employed by Protestant missionary societies around the world, this seemed a modest number to these ambitious missionaries. One missionary could certainly make a difference among twenty thousand people for a simple reason. "Wherever the gospel is preached and its power experienced," they explained, "native preachers will be raised up on the spot to aid the Missionaries and ultimately to take the work off their hands."[1]

This optimism was not at all justified by what Hall, Newell, and their brethren faced in Bombay. Conversion was difficult and slow. This divergence between their hopes and reality can largely be explained by what Hall and Newell left out of their book: the interests, needs, and agency of those millions of people whom they hoped to convert. If missionaries initially expected that simply telling the story of the Gospel would result in conversion, they soon found that it was much more complicated than that. People did not always want to hear them. Others listened with their own interests. Even some who found power in their Gospel story did not see why accepting it should require the kinds of changes that missionaries demanded.

These difficulties were particularly evident in the educational institutions that missionaries created and attempted to create in Bombay over the first several years of their work there. The schools were supposed to be the place where missionaries could have the clearest access to "heathen" children and could accordingly make the most difference. Here, missionaries reasoned, parents would voluntarily bring their children, anxious to take advantage of the benefits of a Western education and the potential for future employment and advancement that it suggested. Students would be a captive audience, removed from the supposedly pernicious influence of their parents and open to the transforming message of both Christianity and civilization. Graduates would become converts and would go on to serve the mission and its schools in their adulthood. It rarely worked out this way, to the frustration of the missionaries.

In Bombay, as elsewhere at the Board's missions, the missionaries could report large numbers of attendants at church on a regular basis. There was even a steady, if small, stream of people who expressed some interest in conversion. Yet very few of these would be baptized. The first baptism was in 1819, and by the end of the next decade, only eight additional converts were baptized at the Bombay mission. Behind these numbers and in between the lines of the missionary apologies about them is the important story of how missionaries understood conversion and how they sought to judge the sincerity and interests of those they met in Bombay. Here we can see the ways that native Indians shaped the missionary project to their own interests, and the ways that American missionaries desperately sought to remain fixed in their work.

The missionary schools and other missionary discussions of conversion are central sources for thinking about how American missionaries understood their work overseas. Missionaries claimed to be apolitical, but their message did not come without cultural judgments and demands. Many individuals were well aware that the missionary links to the East India Company could mean that their way of life was being challenged in cultural, religious, and perhaps even political ways. Missionary critiques of Hinduism, Islam, and Catholicism, the main religions they encountered in India, did not help them make a case that their concerns were solely religious. Cultural critiques easily blended with religious ones. For in the years of the early republic, missionaries would not alter their assumptions of what it meant to be a "true" Christian, even if it meant limiting the numbers of converts that they could report at their missions. Civilization and cultural transformation remained a key component of conversion, even when it meant that fewer people wanted to join them at the Lord's Table. This was the task of Christian imperialism: to convert the world in its faith and culture in order to bring all the world into God's kingdom.

The Difficulty of Conversion

Conversion was, of course, at the heart of what the missionaries hoped to accomplish as they went about their work. But conversion was a tricky thing to measure. As early as 1814, the Board requested potential missionaries to write compositions on the subject of "the evidence, which should satisfy a missionary that a person, formerly a heathen, is a proper subject for admission to church ordinances." In other words, the Board asked its applicants how they would be able to tell when a conversion was real. Horatio Bardwell, who would go on to serve as a missionary in Bombay, provided an extensive answer to this question. On a basic level, the evidence the missionaries expected of a former "heathen" sounded a lot like what they might expect of an American Christian if they wished to be admitted to membership in a church. They had to display a change within their heart. A convert first needed "repentance towards God and faith, in the Lord Jesus Christ." Adults would also need to display "evidence, that they are the subjects of renewing grace," as well as "a general knowledge of the doctrines of the Bible."[2]

As Bardwell explained how he would determine whether or not to baptize a "heathen" and welcome them into the communion of the church, though, he spoke about particular concerns with how they might display evidence of their inner conversion. He was particularly concerned that missionaries not act too quickly. They must wait for the right time, to be sure that any "hopeful appearances" were not fleeting. A convert's "constancy may be proved by trials and temptations," he explained. "Heathen" candidates for conversion would have to show clear knowledge of the Bible and not simply speculation about the nature of God and Christianity. In India, the missionaries could take comfort in the fact that a convert, simply by being willing to unite himself with the mission family, would be renouncing caste. This in itself could be a powerful sign. Taking such an action was a difficult and weighty decision. Bardwell noted that in so doing, a Brahmin would "expose himself to the malice and scorn of his countrymen," which a missionary could see as a sign of some of the internal changes that conversion was expected to initiate. Simply put, these were high bars for potential converts to pass. Between these high expectations and the fact that native peoples were often satisfied with their own faith traditions, it should not surprise us that so few joined the early mission churches.[3]

However, American missionaries could not require too complete of a change, for they valued their converts precisely for their ability to go forth and evangelize to their own people. A large part of why Hall and Newell thought only one missionary would be needed for twenty thousand was precisely that early converts could serve as assistants to the mission. Native assistants were essential because missionaries well understood that much was lost in translation. Evangelization could be much more effective in one's own language, using examples from daily life. Further, missionaries were not welcome everywhere. People who did not wish to hear a foreign missionary might listen to someone of their own background. As they discussed conversion and education, missionaries stressed the importance of allowing converts to remain somewhat within their own cultures so that they could be welcomed by their communities and allowed to teach and preach in their own right. Converts had to walk the line between demonstrating an acceptance of American Christian norms and remaining legible to their own people.

Historians of missions in recent years have paid particular attention to the ways that conversion did not mean that converts abandoned their own culture and fully assimilated into that of their new religion. Whatever expectations missionaries may have brought to these dynamics, in the field conversion did not mean a complete renunciation of the past. Instead, conversion was a process of change that affected both the convert and the missionary. Converts to Christianity could find ways to incorporate their new faith into their old traditions. Missionaries, too, often changed through the process of living with foreign peoples and having to accommodate their message to the needs and desires of foreign peoples.[4] Such flexibility was precisely what American missionaries of the early nineteenth century tried to avoid in establishing their strict interpretations of what was required for baptism and conversion.

The Bombay missionaries, instead, wanted to be known for the high demands that their religion made of them and any potential converts. "Strip Christianity of its uncompromising demands," one of them wrote, "and neither the heathen, the Musselman, or the baptized infidel, will feel any dislike for it."[5] These demands, in other words, were what made Protestant Christianity the superior religion they were sure it was. Having these high standards was an important way that the American Protestant missionaries differentiated themselves from the Jesuit and other missionaries who had earlier converted some Indians to Catholicism. The Catholic missionaries, to these Americans' eyes, had not required sufficient changes, or not the right kinds. Missionaries complained when one Hindu woman asked for baptism that Catholicism had made this woman believe that all she needed to be converted was a change in dress. "The notion is very prevalent among the natives that for a man to put on a hat, jacket, and breeches, is enough to constitute him a Christian," they wrote.[6] This would not do. While clothing was something that American missionaries did try to change at some of their missions around the world, they knew that a change of dress was not sufficient. Any external changes needed to be the signs of changes that had already happened within the heart, and determining how and when that had happened proved to be difficult.[7]

If Bardwell had thought before his departure that renouncing caste would be a helpful sign of the sincerity of conversion, he soon learned that it was much more complicated than that. Caste was often the major impediment to conversion, the missionaries insisted. American missionaries frequently discussed caste in their descriptions of Indian culture, and they were uniformly critical. As the missionaries were aware, to become a Christian, a person of the high Brahmin caste would lose their status. For many, this was too great a sacrifice. It involved not only social ostracism and potential persecution, but also economic and practical difficulties. Apostates were further prevented from inheriting ancestral property. In addition to the social difficulties that a loss of caste could create, there were economic and practical ones as well. Missionary Cyrus Stone considered caste to be a frequent cause of people giving up their inquiries. One story, for example, described three Brahmins who wanted to be baptized, but had family debts. They believed (and the missionaries seemed to agree) that once these men violated caste and became Christian, they would be immediately thrown into prison. Accordingly, they did not pursue baptism.[8] This was not a solitary story. The public journals of the Bombay mission pointed to caste as a possible explanation for the low numbers of converts at Bombay in comparison to other mission stations repeatedly throughout the 1820s and early 1830s. "If there were no greater obstacles in the way of the heathen here changing their religion, than there are in those pagan countries where no caste exists," Cyrus Stone wrote, "multitudes would ask for baptism, and perhaps by attending more constantly on the means of grace, might be really converted." The missionaries would time and again refer to individuals whom they had met in their travels who had become convinced of the truth of Christianity, but who would not become Christian for fear of what others would say or do.[9]

Stone may have been right that caste was an important obstacle for conversion, but this was in large part because the American missionaries made it so. Caste was just one of the cultural systems in India that the missionaries found backward and prohibitive to their work and that they repeatedly and openly criticized. Caste differences, they believed, made Brahmins lazy and the lower castes deluded. It prevented people from being educated, industrious, and in a word, civilized. Further, it created false divisions among people that were at odds with Christian teachings. Their response to those concerned about violating caste was that a Christian should rather obey God than submit to the rules of man. Perhaps not surprisingly, very few others saw things fully in that way, and the mission had a small number of Hindu converts. Even those who were willing to join with the Christians in the face of external opposition could have difficulty with issues surrounding caste because within the church, the American missionaries insisted that caste differences not be recognized.

Other missionaries dealt with caste differently. The missionaries complained of earlier missionaries, both Jesuit and British, who had "humored" converts who wanted to continue upholding caste divisions, going so far as to divide the communion table according to caste. For these missionaries, caste was akin to social class, and entirely possible to incorporate into Christian practice. To change it would be a social, not a religious, matter. American missionaries, though, saw it as a completely arbitrary and unchristian division among people. This was one of the few points on which American missionaries criticized their British brethren, finding them far too complacent about the policies of the British Empire. Among their own converts, they would eventually count members of multiple castes, and they expected all to be able to come together within the church. One of the major motivations for building a chapel within Bombay concerned exactly this issue. The missionaries were frustrated by Brahmins who had tried to keep lower-caste men from entering worship services before the missionaries owned their own building. Having their own building, they explained, would allow them to welcome everyone more easily.[10] The shared living arrangements of missionaries and their students and some converts were particularly troublesome to Brahmins, as was the communal eating both within the mission family and at communion. Taking part in the religious life of the mission thus went hand in hand with abandoning caste. For the missionaries, this was an important statement of the sincerity of one's conversion and willingness to devote one's life to Christ; for potential converts, it was a high demand, resulting in very low numbers of converts.[11]

Missionaries found idolatry, too, to be a major impediment to conversion in India. The missionaries talked about idolatry in contexts as varied a Hindu holidays, Muslim burial practices, and Catholic celebrations of Holy Week. Idolatry, then, was not a problem with any particular religion so much as it was a problem with the entirety of the indigenous culture that Bombay missionaries encountered. Idol worship, to the missionaries, meant both the actual worship of man-made manifestations of the divine and also the incorporation of images and certain physical rituals into worship services. They saw it everywhere they looked, and they preached against it whenever they had the opportunity. Missionaries were well aware, further, that this stance cost them some potential converts. Many, they reported, would "lose at once all anxiety to hear" the Gospel on learning that the missionaries would require them to give up their idols.[12] To Hindu Indians, idols clearly had a different importance than the missionaries could recognize, with cultural, traditional, and family meanings. Yet the missionaries saw the decimation of idol worship to be a major part of their work.[13] In the pantheon of cultural and religious practices that the missionaries attempted to quash, the idea that gods resided in man-made representations infuriated them particularly. Missionary Allen Graves, for example, described meeting with an old weaver one day to whom Graves preached about the "shameful character of Hindoo idols." Like many of the people the missionaries described, the weaver decided to divide his worship "between the idols and Christ." This was insufficient, Graves replied. If the weaver did this, he would "perish together" with his gods; a complete transformation and total rejection of the old ways was required for true conversion. The weaver did not request baptism.[14]

As they made these critiques of Hindu practice, the missionaries also critiqued the nature of Hindu belief. Correcting what they saw as Hindu misperceptions of the divine concerned more than just religion: it became a matter of benevolent reform as well. The most famous example of this type of missionary activism concerned *sati*, or the practice of widows self-immolating on the funeral pyre of their deceased husbands. American missionaries, like the British, saw this as a barbaric practice that needed to end, and even before the first missionaries left for India, it was one of the things that Americans thought missionaries ought to be concerned with. The wives of the missionaries were instructed in their farewell sermon to teach Indian women "that they have immortal souls; and are no longer to burn themselves, in the same fire, with the bodies of their departed husbands." Changing this practice became a matter of political action as well as religious conversion. Images of mission work included engravings of sati, intended to raise American awareness of, and horror about, the practice.[15] American missionaries spoke of other practices in similar terms, paying particular attention to hook vows, illustrating this practice, too, in their letters. Figure 3 depicts a woman who had recently had a child and had come to pay homage for this blessing through an act of physical exertion. Two iron hooks were placed through her skin, and her body was swung from the hooks. Missionaries described this as "a barbarous and frantic scene," likening this devotional behavior to "tortures in order to compensate the imagined deity for the blessings which they supposed they had successfully implored of him." The missionaries were deeply troubled by what they interpreted as the Hindu understanding that one needed to debase oneself to secure divine favor.[16]

It was not merely the physical pain that the missionaries found upsetting; rather, they focused on the idea that it was through such pain that people could find God's favor. This seemed more than anything else to reveal the "deplorable" state of the "heathen," and in comparison, the elevated state of American Christians, freed from such delusions. Lest their American readers miss the points that the missionaries hoped to make through the telling of these stories, they exhorted: "Christian! Behold this thy deluded, perishing, fellow creature! . . . Be entreated to inquire faithfully with yourself how much you ought to do, and how much you might do to send abroad among the heathen that gospel which is able to make them wise unto salvation through faith in Christ." In this sort of direct appeal, the missionaries reminded their audience of the benefits of American Christian civilization even as they entreated the public to provide more support for their work.[17]

Figure 3. The missionary illustration of "hook vows" was never published but was sent to the directors of the American Board as part of the missionaries' collective journal as a way to highlight the missionaries' horror at the practice. Courtesy of the Wider Church Ministries of the United Church of Christ, ABC 16.1.1, v. 1.

These direct appeals, also, could help account for why the mission was not as successful as it had hoped to be regarding baptisms. Conversion was a sensitive subject for the Bombay missionaries. Especially once the Cherokee mission began reporting converts, the missionaries in Bombay repeatedly apologized for their slow progress. "Though we are left to mourn over the unfruitfulness of our own labors," they wrote, "we cannot but rejoice that others have the happiness of seeing the blessing of the Lord upon the work of their hands."[18] In 1833, twenty years after the missionaries first arrived in India, they could report only ten former Hindus who had converted to Christianity, and less than five former Muslims. One of these, further, had been censured by the congregation and was no longer a member in good standing. While they had educated thousands of children through their mission schools, none of those students had asked to join the church. Considering the importance of conversion to their work, both in terms of souls that were saved and labor that could help them continue, these were dreary numbers for the missionaries to reflect on.

When they explained their low rates of conversion to the Board, the missionaries tended to use the metaphor of a seed that had been planted. It might take a long time for a sprout to become visible above the soil, but this did not mean that no changes were occurring. It might be "buried and apparently fruitless for a time," they wrote, but could still "spring up at some future period and bring forth an abundant harvest." In due time, they would be able to "reap," and in the meantime they continued in the knowledge that they ought to "continue to labor and pray and hope," confident in the knowledge that "already thousands have heard the glad tidings of salvation from our lips, who probably would have died without hearing them, had we not be sent to them."[19] Nonetheless, in 1819, the missionaries expressed concern that "a single soul has not yet been by our means and to our knowledge brought to a saving acquaintance with the Redeemer."[20]

In spite of this sense that they were not doing enough, the missionaries did not baptize every person who requested it. These sorts of dynamics are suggestive of the ways that some Indians hoped to make use of the mission, and the ways that missionaries attempted to control these encounters. In 1816, an English officer approached the mission to seek baptism for his children and his Hindu mistress. She desired baptism, he said, which made her the first person to request baptism at the mission. Their response to him is indicative of the ways that they would respond to others going forward in the coming years. They refused the request and exhorted the officer "to reflect upon the great sin in which he was living, to repent, and turn to the right ways of the Lord," at which point they would consider baptizing his children. They did not even address the potential baptism of the woman. When he returned a week later, they again admonished him. He was never heard from again. Because he did not come back, we cannot know if the missionaries were employing a practice here that they used often when people presented themselves for baptism: the use of delay as a test. Missionaries were very concerned about the sincerity of potential converts and regularly talked about making people wait before they would baptize them in order to see how genuine their conversion was. If they were willing to wait and remain steadfast in their desire to be baptized, the missionaries could conclude that the conversion was genuine.[21]

When another person presented himself to the mission asking for baptism in 1819, the missionaries still were not sure what to do. They could not tell what his motives were, and they worried about it. His name was Kader

Yar Khan, and he was a Muslim. The first time the missionaries mentioned him in their letters, they seemed entirely unsure what to make of him. Was he genuine? They could not tell. But did they have the right to withhold baptism from him if he was sincere? This, too, was unclear. By the end of that year, Khan became their first convert. Ultimately, he did not give "so clear evidence of a radical change as is given by others in many instances," but they believed him when he professed his faith in Jesus Christ and his dependence on him for salvation. "We therefore indulge the hope that he is truly born of God," they wrote. "If so, may the glory be given to whom alone it is due."[22]

After his baptism, Khan offered to change his dress, his name, and to cut his beard, but the missionaries told him not to. They wanted him to still look much the same. They employed him as a teacher and wanted him to be able to fit in with those he was to teach. It would be "inexpedient," they explained, for him to be "distinguished, in these respects, from a Mussulman." In his former apparel, he might be more easily received by Indian Muslims and better able to speak to them about the nature of a religion of the heart, as opposed to simply an external change of dress and practice. This was a key issue for the missionaries. He would be a missionary assistant, and he would work where they hoped to make the most difference: in the large network of mission schools they established throughout Bombay and the surrounding region.[23]

Indian Culture and Missionary Education

As the missionaries worked out what it would mean for a Hindu or Muslim Indian to become a Christian (or a Christian that the missionaries would recognize as such), many of these discussions took place in the context of the mission schools. The first thing missionaries did when they established their stations around the world was to open a school, not only for the financial support schools could provide them, but also for the importance of training youth in the ways of both Christianity and civilization. Time and again, the missionaries defined education as a central right that was denied to the mass of the people by Hinduism and other non-Christian religions. Under the Brahmins, one missionary explained, learning was discouraged. The priests monopolized education and discouraged the lower castes from "the 'dangerous pre-eminence' of learning." This resulted in the "mental bondage of the Hindoos," which could most clearly be seen in the ignorance "and the consequent degradation" of women in Indian culture. In contrast, missionaries represented Christianity as a religion that required education. People needed to be able to read the Bible and tracts to learn the true nature of God and how to live their lives.[24]

Mission schools, further, were a far more palatable part of their operations to native Indians than itinerant preaching and garnered enthusiasm and some apparent success. If missionaries struggled to find converts, they did not struggle to find students. The Bombay missionaries taught a large and diverse group of students in the area, including Hindus, Muslims, Jews, and those whom the missionaries termed "professed Christians," including Catholics and Orthodox Christians, at a variety of types of schools. When they talked about the schools, they felt that great good could come of simply promoting literacy and circulating the Bible. As the educational branch of the mission grew, both in numbers of schools and geographic reach, some of these hoped-for positive effects were realized. In July 1829, for example, Cyrus Stone could report after his first tour of the mission schools on the continent that profound cultural changes accompanied the introduction of mission schools. Their influence went beyond the students and their families to the villages at large. "The contrast between the moral aspect of the villages where we have schools and where we have not," Stone reported to the Board, "is cheering. As you enter the one all is darkness and death; but as you approach the other you see the rising dawn of heavenly truth glimmering amidst the surrounding darkness."[25] It was this rising dawn that the missionaries hoped to spread across India through the medium of mission schools.

The difficulty that missionaries faced in this work came down to the question of staff and missionary oversight. The schools became sites of major tension between what the missionaries hoped to accomplish and what non-Christian teachers, students, and parents wanted to receive. In these schools, the mission would employ native teachers (usually Brahmins, although they also employed Jews) to teach children in their own languages, using mission-printed texts as their schoolbooks. Native free schools had the advantages of being quite easy to set up and rather popular among parents; barred only by finances, the missionaries were able to establish schools in most of the places they traveled.[26] By 1818, the missionaries in Bombay could report that at four schools some eight hundred boys had been admitted over three years. By 1825, the Bombay mission had charge of twenty-six schools, showing not only the generosity of the American missionary public, who supported the schools through contributions, but also the extent to which these schools could be started and maintained with little direct oversight from the missionaries themselves.[27]

This lack of oversight, however, was the major disadvantage of this plan and was due to language and religious differences as well as distance. While the teachers taught the students to read using scripture and religious tracts, the extent to which that curriculum coincided with a Christian education was limited by the identity of the teachers. Indeed, none of the teachers were Christians themselves and thus had no incentive to convert their students to the church. This, perhaps not surprisingly, led to some problems inside the classrooms. For example, in 1818, the missionaries were excited to report a decrease in the "daily practice of celebrating the praises of heathen gods" within the schools. They hoped soon to be able to "eradicate this evil wholly from the schools under our care," as teachers had gone from openly engaging in non-Christian worship to at least being more discreet.[28] The extent to which such eradication could occur without direct oversight was limited, of course, and reveals the lack of authority that missionaries held over their South Asian schools in this early period. For this reason, the missionaries instituted not only lessons in the chapel for students on Sundays but also religious classes for their teachers on Tuesdays, beginning in 1826. Students and teachers alike from that point forward would be catechized on a regular basis. This was structured something like a Bible class in the United States and was important due to the role of the instructors, who had influence not only over the students, but also their parents.[29]

Even this sort of direct intervention with their teachers was limited in its effects, as evidenced by the struggle over whether the teachers would stand during prayer along with the missionaries. Teachers did not comply with missionary demands as easily as the missionaries expected. Soon after they were required to attend chapel, the teachers refused to stand during prayer. The missionaries took this a sign of their "prejudices," which chapel lessons had been expected to remove. When it became clear that chapel lessons would not remove these "prejudices," the missionaries decided not to employ any teacher who would not comply with their demand. Angry teachers persisted in their refusal, and several of the schools were closed as a result. When the missionaries hired new teachers, some of those who had left returned to their work, but the whole incident revealed both the uneasy power dynamics within the schools and the questionable effectiveness of education to bring about a religious reformation in Bombay.[30] The question that the native free schools raise, then, is why missionaries expected them to be effective means of delivering the Gospel to Asia in the first place. If missionaries had little control over what actually happened in the classroom

Figure 4. This illustration of one of the school bungalows used by Bombay missionaries is indicative of some of the ways that missionaries had to adapt to local circumstances as they attempted to evangelize the population. Courtesy of the Wider Church Ministries of the United Church of Christ, ABC 79, Box 1, Folder 2.

and biblical education would as a result not become a significant part of the curriculum, why were missionaries so dedicated to the use of schools for their work?

The answer to this has two parts, and it is suggestive of the ways that missionaries understood conversion to work as well as what they thought was necessary to be a true Christian. The missionaries believed that simply the practice of reading the scripture, even if under the tutelage of "heathens," could be transformative in the long term. There were frequent stories recorded in the mission journal of individuals who had come to believe in God through introduction to the written tracts and texts of the mission. The ability to read was of central importance, the missionaries believed, both to being "civilized" and being able to encounter God through the Gospel. Further, the enthusiasm of the missionaries for educational projects was matched by that of their supporters at home, many of whom donated specifically to the School Fund of the Board. This faith in the power of education could relate to the rise of the Sunday school movement in the United States at the same time. Like mission schools, Sunday schools were initially designed to provide literacy training to the poor with little direct emphasis on religious education. That such institutions could eventually lead to a religious awakening was a widely accepted logic of the time among evangelical Christians, and they pursued this work both in the United States and abroad.

The Board also hoped that another sort of educational institution could overcome the disadvantages of the free schools. "Domestic education" was a project in which missionaries would adopt children (in their language, they generally described this as "obtaining" or "procuring" them), raise them in the mission family, baptize them, and give them Christian names. This does not seem to have been a way to increase domestic help for the mission family. While children were brought into the mission household as servants, those children would not receive the names given by American patrons, nor would they be baptized.[31] Bringing children into the mission family as members, baptizing them, and raising them as part of the family struck the Board as a "very captivating plan." Evangelicals in the United States, too, were very excited about this idea, and many sent in thirty dollars for a year's support of one child within the missionary household. In 1817 alone, the Board received contributions to support thirty children to be named for New England ministers, missionaries, and prominent members of society. The donors were mostly women's associations, with a few male donors. These mission supporters sent in their donations with instructions to name children for such illustrious figures in American Christianity, both historical and contemporary, as Joshua David Brainerd, John Elliot, Jeremiah Evarts, Jedidah Morse, Samuel Newell, Samuel Hopkins, and Cotton Mather. Only two female children were specified in that year (both sponsored by women's associations), with Sarah Pierce being an interesting name choice, given the educational reforms of the woman by that name within the United States.[32]

Bombay missionaries ultimately found this plan to be impossible in their area; they in fact seemed quite surprised in their unpublished correspondence to the Board that anyone had imagined it could be supported on such a scale. In its place, missionaries established boarding schools, also staffed by native teachers, but with more oversight than in the free schools.[33] When possible, they did take children into their own homes, beginning in the mid-1820s. These children would commonly be orphans or children of parents who were willing to have their children educated by the missionaries. They were called the "charity children" in the mission letters.[34]

The Bombay missionaries were reluctant to change the names of these children, reminding the Board in Boston that the children's names were "as much fixed under this government in a civil point of view as those of persons in any Christian country." Finding no scriptural argument for changing the names, they continued to use their "original names" in daily life, though they would use the American names in their correspondence with donors. This was one of the ways that we can see the missionary experience changing the missionaries. Supporters in the United States were consistently frustrated that the missionaries could not obtain more children, and the missionaries had to remind them that "Hindoo customs are dearer to many than life itself," and so to have an orphan "fed and clothed and taught in the family of another religion would be, in the eyes of this people, an utter disgust." The missionaries were glad that they were "permitted to proceed so quietly" with their work.

The permission they spoke of here was not from the government, but from Indians themselves. Experience in the field had taught them that they could not demand too much too quickly, and that they had to respect at least some aspects of native culture. At the very least, they had to let the children whom they adopted retain their own names.[35] Their concerns about domestic education highlighted the distance between Boston and Bombay, and the ways that working in the mission field could itself shift American ideas about what was required. If missionaries demanded transformation, supporters in the United States wanted to see even starker changes. Christian imperialism, then, could sound different depending on who was speaking.

Missionaries in Bombay also voiced an interesting critique of the domestic education project. As much as missionaries wanted to transform South Asian society, they worried that too stark a separation of their students from their culture would render them unfit to return to their communities as adults. In order for these children to be useful to the mission, they were expected to serve as missionaries to their own people as adults. If they were too thoroughly assimilated to American Christianity, missionaries worried, they would not be accepted by their own people and thus could not perform this important work. In places where this form of education was more successful, precisely such a problem could occur. The missionaries' reservations about this effect reflect the tensions within their plans to transform foreign society in their own image. While there were many things that the Americans hoped to change about life and culture in India, they expected this to be a gradual process, and one that would need the participation of Indians themselves. Consciously or not, they adapted the British imperial policy of working through Indian institutions as they planned their long-term strategy for the conversion of India.

The ways that missionaries hoped to bring about profound cultural transformation is perhaps best seen in the ways that the mission related to women. As evangelical Americans looked at India, they saw profound problems with gender relations. They expected this before they left: missionary wives were told about the seclusion of Indian women and the particular duty of missionary women to seek out indigenous women and deliver the message of the Gospel to them. Missionaries used women's status as a measure of the civilization of a community. They were particularly concerned with the role of women in raising the next generation. In their explanations for how difficult it was to convert Hindus to Christianity, they frequently described how children had learned supposedly backward beliefs "with their mother's milk." Religion and culture were imbibed from infancy, and mothers were central to this transfer.[36] Accordingly, making Christian women was a central task for American missionaries. As the Gospel message in general was linked to culture in the missionary mind, the message to women was particularly so.

The missionaries' attempts to change many aspects of Indian culture could be seen in the ways that they talked about women's schools. Female education was an early and continued priority of the Bombay mission. The goal of these schools was the transformation of Indian culture, and the missionaries recorded this as a major source of opposition they faced. It was not just the preaching of the Gospel, but the female schools that "called forth some of the enmity of their hearts" and led at least some local people to throw stones at the missionaries. The missionaries always attributed this resistance to first a general opposition to mission work, and then to a more specific opposition to their work with women. The schools for boys were never mentioned as possible causes for creating anger amongst native people.[37]

Perhaps the missionary interpretation here was the result of their own different goals for girls' and boys' schools. Missionaries were in fact explicit that in educating girls they hoped to change Indian society at large. Their goal was to transform the ways that Indian parents thought about their daughters as well as the possibilities for those young women as they grew up. They wanted to train Indian women to be like American women in their skills and priorities, and they wanted to prepare them to be good wives to the young men they were educating as well. Although it was largely focused on cultural and labor issues, missionary women's education was not secular. In the missionary formulation, these issues were deeply entwined with religious ones. As missionary Hollis Read explained, it was clear that education alone could not make a difference in the lives of Indian women. They could easily enough, he wrote, come to appreciate "how fine and comfortable a thing it is, to have a neat, pretty house, with clean furniture, to sleep on a bed, to sit on a chair, to eat from a table with plate, knife, fork and spoon—to sew, knit, spin, etc." Yet to make it so that they could have and enjoy such things, a missionary would need "to change the whole constitution of society, to change custom and to destroy caste—to exchange Hindooism for Christianity." The social and domestic habits of Hindus were "inseparably intwined" with their religion, he wrote; to change the one would require the conversion of the other.[38]

For all of the missionaries' hopes that education would be the key to introducing Christianity to India, none of the students came to the mission requesting baptism. They could require students to attend chapel, they could assign missionary tracts and scripture as reading assignments, and they could catechize their students regularly, but the students were not empty vessels waiting to receive this information passively. They were educated by mission-sponsored schools, but they did not join the mission churches themselves.

Babajee, the Christian Brahmin

With so few conversions, the missionaries worried that American Christians would conclude that the people of India could not be converted. To assure them that this was not the case, Hollis Read, one of the Board missionaries in Bombay, published a memoir of one of the earlier converts for American audiences. *The Christian Brahmun* was the story of Babajee, a Hindu convert to Christianity in Bombay who went on to work at the mission's station in Ahmednuggur. Published in two volumes, the book is both a relation of Babajee's life and journey of faith and also a lengthy (largely critical) description of the culture and customs of India. As Read describes India to his readers, he hopes that they will come away with two conclusions. First, readers should be impressed by Babajee himself and hold him in high esteem for overcoming what Read defined as the difficulties of his native culture. It is part of a tradition of evangelical life stories that could inspire readers in their own devotion. Second, those difficulties helped to explain for Read why the missionaries had had so little success thus far with conversions. Babajee, Read explained, would not have been remarkable had he been born in a Christian country. Warning readers not to "expect too much," he explained that Babajee's faith and character would not have been out of the ordinary in America. He exemplified both faith and doubt, "ardent devotion" as well as "neglect of duty." Were he to be "weighted in the balance of Christian diligence in America," he "would be found wanting; but when tried by the heathen standard, or when compared with any thing [Read had] seen among native converts, he was truly an example worthy of imitation." As a Christian, Babajee was quite normal. He only rose to importance because he was an Indian Christian. Conversion, then, could effect "wonderful changes" in native men and women, even if it did not result in their complete transformation into exemplary Christians by American standards.[39]

Babajee first came to the Bombay mission in 1823, when he was thirty-four years old. He had spent three years working at the Scottish mission as a teacher of the Mahratta language, and he continued this work for the Americans. At times, Read reflected, Babajee seemed to be thinking about Christianity, but it was not until 1831 that he requested baptism. In the intervening years, Read described him as going back and forth between showing signs of Christian piety and turning back to "infidelity and idolatry." Before his conversion, Read informed his readers, Babajee was no different from any other Brahmins. As a member of that high caste, Babajee had been educated, hence his importance to the missionaries. He also exhibited the arrogance, pride, and dishonesty that Read believed to be inherent to this group. "He was as learned and as ignorant, as false and as subtle as his brethren," Read wrote. "He was as devoid of moral rectitude, and as reckless of the happiness and of the natural rights of his fellow-beings, as any Brahmin in India." He had, in fact, been briefly fired for profligacy and unfaithfulness in his work on the mission's business. This behavior and character would later be held in dramatic contrast to what Babajee was like after his conversion.[40]

The missionaries had reason to hope in 1828 that perhaps Babajee would convert. That was the year of a conflict in the Bombay schools, when teachers objected to the missionaries' insistence that all employees of the mission must stand during the recitation of prayer during the required Sunday worship service. When a group of teachers came together to express their unwillingness to conform to the mission's rules, Babajee would not join them. He did not see anything improper in standing during Christian prayers, and even when he was threatened with losing his caste status, he remained firm. Multiple meetings were held among the Brahmins to condemn him, Read reported, some of which included a thousand people or more demanding that Babajee take a stand against the missionaries. Yet Babajee would not do so and instead criticized other Brahmins for eating beef, drinking brandy, and asked why they were not being condemned. The atonement that the Brahmins demanded of Babajee was "of so humiliating a nature" that the missionaries sent him out of Bombay until tempers could cool. Read assumed that the event must have taught Babajee "a disgust for many of the fooleries of caste" as well as "the shameless corruption of the [Brahmin] priesthood," and yet Babajee showed no signs of a change in "his heart." He was not yet a Christian.[41]

Such a change, Read reported, did not come until three years later, and then it came quite suddenly. Babajee came to Allen Graves, another of the Bombay missionaries, expressing an interest in becoming a Christian. Graves delivered a speech that he seemed to have delivered many times earlier to others who seemed similarly interested but unsure. This was a decision about eternity, Graves warned. Now Babajee must make a choice that would affect not only the rest of his life, but the state of his soul after his death as well. There was a right choice and a wrong choice, and it was up to Babajee to decide the correct path. That night, Babajee later told the missionaries, he could not sleep. He was convinced that Christianity was the true religion and resolved to change his life from then on. The next morning, he arrived at the mission door with a drinking cup in his hand, the only possession that he took with him when he left his former life behind and resolved to begin anew. Graves was shocked. They prayed together on their knees, and Babajee in his own words acknowledged "that he was worthy to be utterly and eternally rejected" and asked God "to receive him on the ground of grace in Christ alone, and to purify and accept him for ever."[42]

As Graves described this scene to Read, he wrote about how utterly surprised he was to see such an apparently genuine transformation. "Such a solemn self-dedication and confession astonished me," he wrote, "as totally beyond my anticipation and such as I had scarcely, if ever witnessed. I could not but think it sincere." Graves "dared not long defer his baptism," waiving the usual period of delay to test the sincerity of conversions, and Babajee was soon baptized and welcomed into Christian fellowship. He took communion that same day. This was an extraordinary story of conversion. As Graves's surprised reactions to Babajee's arrival on his doorstep suggest, this was not a common occurrence at the American mission. His willingness to renounce caste and "all his connections" alone was surprising, as was the apparent quickness of his change of heart. It was difficult, Read reminded his readers, for a "native convert to divest himself entirely of all those ten thousand superstitions and absurdities which he imbibed with his mother's milk." And yet here was Babajee, apparently doing just this. Here was evidence of the works of grace, Read wrote. Against all odds, this Brahmin had become a Christian.[43]

The transformation affected not only his faith, but also his character. In contrast to his earlier similarity to other Brahmins, Read explained in great detail the many ways that Babajee was now very different. He now exhibited an inquisitiveness and desire to "search after the truth," which did not typify most of the Brahmins of Read's acquaintance. Unlike the Brahmins, he could distinguish good from evil and was anxious to help the "welfare of his countrymen." "Disinterestednes," Read noted, had no direct translation into the Mahratta language, so alien was it from what he saw in their culture. Yet after his conversion, Babajee exemplified this virtue, putting the needs of his community above his own. Babajee, further, came to reject prejudice against those of lower caste, inviting the poor to eat with him at his own table, and generally renouncing any "usage of caste" that would have placed him above others earlier in his life. Babajee now was honest in his speech and in his business, with a character that was simple and not duplicitous. For Read and his audience, this change could suggest the kind of large-scale transformation that might happen if others converted. Mass conversions could lead to a complete regeneration of Indian culture, or so they hoped.[44]

When Babajee wrote the story of his conversion in his own words, though, this process seems less immediate and more gradual. As he wrote his own story, Babajee described the series of questions that he asked himself that eventually resulted in his becoming a Christian. The process he describes suggests a man who was not unsurprisingly affected by his proximity to missionaries for a decade before his conversion, but had spent years attempting to reconcile the questions that the missionaries raised for him with his own tradition and culture. The first question that Babajee asked himself was whether he was a sinner. This, he answered in the affirmative. He next asked what the punishment for sin was and determined that it was eternal damnation. In this, the influence of the missionaries could be felt. Babajee next turned to examine his own behavior to see what he might do to improve. Conversion was not his first step. Before this, he measured his life against the teachings of Hinduism and determined that he was not living correctly according to its teachings. He found a guru to teach him mantras and repeated them "at least three thousand times," he wrote. Still, he felt doubts. Hinduism, he had come to believe, was idolatry. The idols were not themselves gods, and yet they were worshipped as if they had power in and of themselves. It was at this point that he began to think explicitly about what the missionaries had told him about Jesus, and only then did he begin to consider becoming a Christian. As Read acknowledged, by the time of his conversion, Babajee was already well educated about scripture and sacred history. He had spent almost a decade in the employ of the mission, teaching the missionaries the Mahratta language and working in the schools. He had attended the required weekly services for years and had gradually begun to incorporate the missionaries' teaching into his own worldview. What seemed to the missionaries to be a sudden and dramatic act of God appears, in Babajee's own telling, to be a much slower and more dynamic process in which a convert was in conversation with the missionaries' message.[45]

After his conversion, Babajee was an incredible asset to the mission. Shortly after his baptism, he moved to Ahmednuggur with Hollis Read to help begin a new mission station there. He helped to lead the daily worship services that were required for native converts and dependents on the mission (including the inmates of the poor asylum), and accompanied Read every day in his trips into town to distribute tracts and preach to whoever would provide the missionary with an audience. Read praised Babajee's preaching for its reliance on nature and the "little things" to illustrate the nature of God. When preaching to Brahmins, for example, Babajee would point to a flower or a tree and ask them who had created it, and thus opened a discussion comparing the Christian God with Shiva, Vishnu, and the pantheon on Hindu deities. He would also address people in private when they visited him at home.[46]

It was probably no coincidence that it was after Babajee began helping the mission in preaching that the numbers of converts began to rise. In the six months before his death, seven converts were baptized in Ahmednuggur, bringing the total number of former Hindus that had joined the American mission's churches to ten. When the station there organized its church in 1833, Babajee was elected its first elder. His ministry was effective enough that after his death, Read reflected that the mission had become too dependent on him, and his death was a sign from God that the missionaries needed to remember to rely on God alone, and not any individual human, for the advancement of the church.[47]

Read provided translations of Babajee's sermons and religious writings in the memoir, allowing his American readers to hear for themselves what Christian preaching sounded like from the voice of a former Brahmin. In one of these, Babajee wrote a letter to his fellow converts in Bombay after Appa, a convert at the Scottish mission, had apostatized. His letter warned against following in Appa's footsteps and caring too much about worldly possessions and attainments. "Brethren," he exhorted, "if you love the world, you cannot love God." They needed instead to "cast away fear and unbelief, and adultery, and sorcery, and idolatry, and lying, and theft, and every abominable practice; and flee from the abominations of the heathen; and arm yourselves against the devices of the devil." He advocated a renunciation not just of "the world," but of a specific formulation of the world that resembled the missionary description of India.[48] When he helped to write the rules of order for the congregation at Ahmednuggur in 1833, he provided some idea of how he thought converts could do this. The list of twenty-four directives for church members was almost entirely phrased in the negative. They were to refrain from ardent spirits (except as medicines) and drugs, from gambling, from "buffoonery," idleness, and obscene, abusive, or unkind language. They were to avoid participation in certain aspects of Hindu culture, including anything that was opposed to Christianity, in addition to "heathen festivals," "heathen sports, shows, juggler feats, etc.," and "heathen practices" for births, weddings, and funerals. When sick, they should not turn to mystic incantations. The only positive instructions that church members were called to do were to administer to the sick, and to wash, clothe, and bury the dead.[49]

It is difficult to discern the ways in which the "Christian Brahmin's" faith may have differed from that of the American missionaries, largely because his words come to us filtered through their archive and their translation. What they celebrated, though, is worth noting. Babajee took their message and put it in a new, Indian package. This was particularly the case when Read discussed Babajee's *abhungu*, or metric poems in a style commonly used by Brahmins. These were recited in a "sing-song" style, Read informed his American readers, and were extremely popular. Usually they praised the gods and instructed listeners. Read noted that because of the poems' ubiquity, they were sure to become a problem for potential converts, who would listen to the Hindu poems and lose their way. Accordingly, this was an important genre for the missionaries to use; Christian versions needed to be written. Composing them seemed to be beyond the missionaries' power. "It is not, however, likely to be done with effect," he wrote, "except by a learned native. The foreigner's *imitation* of it would be so remote and barbarous, that the people would scarcely recognize it." Luckily, Babajee was just the person to take on this task, composing verses titled "Who Is Jesus," "Confession," "The Savior," and "Christ a Father and a Friend." The last of these ended with an appeal to all listeners to follow Jesus:

Let all the people worship and adore Him! How vain, how vile to worship other gods, the creatures of His hand!

Behold the man consumed by a hundred desires! Can gold, or pride, or lust procure him peace and pardon? But I will cling to Jesus.

Tell me, O! ye people, how a man can be clean in the sight of God! I have searched your shastras; I have tried your gods; but, alas! In vain! Come ye to Jesus; He is the fountain.[50]

Taking the missionaries' teachings and shaping them into a new form was precisely what missionaries hoped that their native helpers would be able to do for them. Babajee was so celebrated because he was able to balance the transformative power of conversion with remaining understandable to his own people.

Even as the missionaries praised Babajee's ability to speak to other Indians in ways that they could not, they insisted that it was only through them that Babajee would be heard by Hindus. Because he had lost caste, they explained, people would not listen to him on his own if he tried to preach in public. He could not, accordingly, itinerate alone or even distribute tracts without the presence of an American missionary. Read described their daily trips to town, where he would begin to preach and then indicate Babajee and tell his audience that Babajee would finish what he had begun. Only then would the audience listen to Babajee, giving him the respect that they had previously given to Read. As Read understood it, Babajee was now able to gain the respect of his people only through the authority of the American. At the same time, though, the missionaries understood that they were reliant on Babajee and others like him for spreading their message. Alone, the missionaries' emphasis on the harsh discipline of their faith attracted few new adherents. Even Babajee had long resisted conversion because of his understanding that it was a strict and severe religion.[51]

One of the most profound changes that occurred with Babajee's conversion had to do with his private life. When Babajee discussed his own sins, adultery was the only one he named individually.[52] Before he could be baptized, Babajee needed to reconsider his relationship with a woman named Audee. They had been living together for many years, and yet were not married. When she was a girl, Audee had been betrothed to an older man. When he died, the laws of caste prevented her from marrying again. She was to spend the rest of her life as a widow. Yet she, like many other women in similar positions, found this an unattractive or impossible option. She and Babajee lived as man and wife. The missionaries criticized this taboo against widow remarriage, explaining that it could have very negative effects on morality. While some women like Audee were treated "in every respect as wives," they could also "become common prostitutes" to the extent that, Read surmised, "the terms widow, and prostitute, are synonymous." "Immediately" after his conversion, Babajee became convinced that their relationship was improper. Living with a woman who was not one's wife was out of the question for American missionaries. They would need to have their marriage solemnized in the American church, and he asked the missionaries to perform this service. They did so at the mission chapel in 1831. Audee, for her part, did not adopt the religion of her husband. She did agree to give up the worship of idols, but did not become a Christian. Or at least, not yet.[53]

It was not uncommon for difficulties to arise when one spouse underwent a conversion and the other did not. This marriage was no exception. In the year following their wedding, according to the missionaries, Audee was a thorn in Babajee's side, not understanding the cultural transformations that he was going through or why he felt compelled to change their lives so dramatically. In July 1832, though, she too joined the church, having experienced a change in her heart after watching the death of Mr. Harvey, one of the American missionaries. The experience of watching a good Christian death and seeing Harvey's concern for her spiritual well-being apparently was sufficient to convince her to embrace the church. Audee's conversion created the first native Christian couple within the American mission.[54]

If mission wives were important for modeling Christian marriage to potential converts, Audee and Babajee were far more so. They were founding members of a native church in Ahmednuggur. While Audee was mostly mentioned in the mission records as "Babajee's wife," and later as "Babajee's widow," the stories about her that the missionaries recorded suggest the importance of this native Christian woman to their work. Her story was supposed to make American readers particularly aware of the backwardness of Indian culture. The prohibition against widows being remarried should have made American women "see a reason why Hindoo wives so readily submit to the Suttee," as Babajee's biographer explained. The Anglo-American missionary fascination with *sati* generally focused on the horror of women burning themselves on the funeral pyre of their husbands. Audee's story told of one woman rescued from such a fate through Christianity. The message here was clear: "Never do we feel more forcibly than when contemplating such exhibitions of idolatry," the biographer explained, "that nothing but the gospel can raise the degraded females of India, and assign to woman her appropriate place among intelligent and happy beings."[55]

Audee was not only important as Babajee's wife; she became an important symbol for both American and Indian audiences of what a native Christian family might look like. In addition to her conversion, the missionaries described her second marriage for American audiences. After Babajee died of cholera, Audee married another native assistant to the missionaries, Dajeeba. This marriage, too, took place at the mission house, and it followed Anglo-American Christian traditions. "The novelty of the occasion," the missionaries noted, attracted some attention. Those Hindus in attendance, the missionaries were sure, were provided the opportunity to compare "the simplicity and quietness of a Christian marriage with the confusion and parade of a Hindoo wedding."[56] Hindu wedding traditions had earlier been the subject of some of the missionaries' writings about India. American evangelical readers would have understood from the mission's early reports that Hindu weddings were very different from those to which Americans were accustomed. The Bombay mission journal of 1816, for example, described Hindu marriage customs as involving the negotiation between fathers, the consultation of astronomers, and the parade of the young bride and groom. It was important that girls be married before they turned eleven, missionaries informed their American readers, and they described the newly married Hindu couples they saw as "little children now become husband and wife."[57] With this as the norm, in the eyes of missionaries, the example of the American-style wedding of Indian converts was a striking contrast for Indians to behold.

It was late in the summer of 1833 that Audee was married for the second time. Both of her husbands were Christian converts, and both of them worked as assistants to the missionaries in Bombay. Her story disappears from the American records, though, after her marriage to Dajeeba. She had served her purpose. Embodying a native version of Christian marriage and a rejection of caste and tradition, she could stand for the mission as the example they could hold up for those who thought that India was too different to be changed. She and her husbands showed the ways that even those with high status, like Babajee, could become Christians—and Christians not only in what they said they believed about Jesus, but Christians in how they lived their lives and structured their families.

Babajee and Audee's story was important to the Bombay mission mainly because there were so few converts like them. The Bombay mission was entirely unimpressive to the Board in terms of the numbers of people it was able to convert. The attendees at regular worship services tended to be students and Europeans. Few native Indians were interested enough in what the mission was preaching to change their own religion. The missionaries blamed this on caste. Particularly, they believed that Brahmins were reluctant to give up their caste by becoming Christians. Accordingly, Babajee's transformation into the "Christian Brahmin" was remarkable. The missionaries assumed that if they did not have such high standards for baptism, they would probably have had more applicants for it. Yet they never altered their conception of what was needed for true Christianity: the adoption of civilization as they defined it, alongside a belief in Jesus. At other mission locations, too, missionaries shared this conviction that Christianity was more than a creed: it was a way of life, and a particular set of behaviors that Americans, like the British, were uniquely able to spread to the rest of the world.

Once Babajee had converted and was helping to lead worship services, it did not follow that the missionaries felt they were no longer needed. Their ultimate goal was to end the mission and turn it into a native church, to be led by native Christians. The time for that, though, was far in the future, they were sure. In the meantime, they needed more missionaries to help transform India. Before his death, Babajee wrote a letter to Rufus Anderson. In it, Babajee echoed the missionaries' constant appeals for more helpers at the mission and thanked Anderson for sending the missionaries that had been able to come. "These have made known to us the true shastras," he wrote, "the true savior and the true way of atonement for sin. Through them we have a great joy and happiness in Christ." Many more like them needed to come, Babajee believed.[58]

If the missionaries in 1818 had expected that they would be able to convert India, and the whole world, simply by preaching the Gospel, they found that in practice it was much more difficult than this. The particular nature of the Protestantism that they preached and the demands that it placed on its adherents made its attractions difficult for many others to identify with. The Christian imperialism that motivated them shaped their understanding of the cultural and political demands of their faith, and these created difficulties for them in finding converts. The mission schools, which were supposed to reveal the connections between Christianity and civilization, could be used selectively by families to provide a new kind of education for children without necessarily agreeing to a transformation of faith and culture. Indeed, when missionaries pushed too hard on the religious aspects of their schools, they tended to find that parents and teachers pushed back, insisting on using these institutions in the ways that they wanted to.

Those few converts who did join the Bombay mission in the 1820s and 1830s found themselves in an in-between position, transformed too much to fit fully into their original culture, but not enough to be fully equal with the missionaries themselves. Nearly all of the converts worked in the employ of the mission after their conversion, revealing in part the difficulty that many would face outside of their small Christian community. The persecution that they faced was very real: Dajeeba, for example, was physically assaulted on at least one occasion after his conversion. Read saw this as an explanation for Dajeeba's seeming lack of zeal in evangelism but hardly saw it as a valid excuse for not standing and preaching in public. Read and the other missionaries had high expectations of their converts, and few chose to join them.[59]

Missionaries took great pride in the high demands of their faith. It was these demands that had the potential to transform Indian society and make it a properly civilized part of the kingdom of God. In their interactions with native Indians, however, missionaries had difficulty controlling the conversion experience to make this kind of change possible. Though they were able to bring thousands of students into their schools, they were unable to ultimately convert them. In dramatic contrast to the Bombay mission's small number of converts in these decades was the tremendous success that the Board's missionaries in the Cherokee nation and the Sandwich Islands experienced. There, a different approach to the ways that missions were organized combined with different political and cultural realities to result in a very different picture of the work of American missions in both Christianization and civilization.

Chapter 4

Missions as Settler Colonies

Alijah Conger was a thirty-five-year-old carpenter and farmer in Rockaway, New Jersey, when he made his public profession of faith in April 1818
and joined his local Presbyterian church. As he read the *Boston Recorder* the
following winter, he was taken with a discussion of the difficulty that the
Board's Brainerd Mission to the Cherokee was having in finding mechanics.
Thinking this over, he later recalled, "the thought struck me that I ought
to go to their assistance." The decision was probably more involved than
Conger made it seem. About the same time, Peter Kanouse, a church elder,
returned to Rockaway. Kanouse had recently served as an assistant missionary at the Board's Eliot station among the Choctaw. As Kanouse was not
a minister, he did not spend his time in preaching, or even in translating
scriptures as the missionaries in India were doing. Instead, much of his work
consisted of touring the missions among the Cherokee and the Choctaw
to determine what sorts of people were needed to help bring about the
conversion of the American Indians. Overwhelmingly, he saw those needs
as lying within the agricultural and mechanical programs of these missions.
The Board ought to set up a "domestic establishment," he insisted, complete with a farm, mechanic shop, and boarding schools where they might
"receive Indian Children as apprentices to the several arts, withal to be

More of a mindset of meeting
their needs.

taught reading, writing, and Arithmetic." The Board agreed with him, and Kanouse began to search for individuals ready to do the work.[1] Conger was just the sort of man he was looking for.

Within the year, Conger, too, had become an assistant missionary, moving his wife and five children with him to Brainerd, the Board's main mission station in the Cherokee Nation. He was valued for a different sort of skill set than the Bombay missionaries had been. He had spent six years teaching in a common school, was skilled at making furniture, and was "a very good farmer," according to his minister. He was also, apparently, a good evangelist: shortly after he had determined to work for the mission, he had convinced six of his neighbors—farmers, blacksmiths, and shoemakers "burning with zeal for the cause of Christ"—to come to the mission as well, and bring their families with them, too. Only two of these, John Talmage and John Vail, were selected by the Board to serve as assistant missionaries alongside Conger. Kanouse, too, prepared to return to the missions when his health allowed, along with his brother, another John, who was a carpenter. Vail was an "understanding and intelligent Christian" who ran his own farm and was especially skilled with livestock. Talmage was described as a "great acquisition" to the mission for he was "a Blacksmith and Tool maker of the first grade, and also understands Farming in all its various modes, as practiced here; is remarkably healthy, industrious, and oeconomical, and possesses an uncommon pleasant and obliging disposition." His wife, too, would be a useful addition to the mission, as she was, like the other Rockaway women, "very zealous . . . for the Christianization of the poor pagans of the wilderness." Except for this description of Mrs. Talmage, the Board almost seemed to be looking for good colonists more than for good missionaries.[2]

This Rockaway party made up only part of the large establishment in the Cherokee Nation. They joined other lay assistants like themselves from elsewhere in the Northeast, along with a group of ordained ministers. Altogether, the Board's Cherokee mission would employ a large number of assistant missionaries in the years before 1860: twenty-two married couples (including twenty-two men and twenty-five women over the years), in addition to four single men and twenty-six single women. The ordained missionary staff in the Cherokee Nation consisted of eighteen men and their wives. The missions to the Choctaw were similar, with twenty-nine married couples (twenty-nine men and thirty-one women), seven single men, and forty-seven single women serving as assistants to the eighteen ordained missionaries and their wives. In comparison to the Bombay missions, which employed only four married couples and one single woman in the same years as missionary assistants, it is clear that the Board had some-thing different in mind for its Cherokee and Choctaw missions.[3] These mission stations had a distinct style marked by the settlement of a sizeable group of American evangelicals. These were not missions primarily con-cerned with planting native churches and moving on. They were staying put, and teaching others how to live like them.

This style of mission, with its large settlement of ordained and lay mis-sionaries and assistants, was also adopted in a few other locations, most nota-bly the Sandwich Islands (Hawaii), which employed a full staff of well over a hundred missionaries and assistants before 1860, including twenty couples serving as missionary assistants. As the Board was learning about how mis-sions worked in various imperial contexts, the missions they established on this model attempted to replicate their ideal form of Christian imperialism. By tweaking the model of settler colonialism, missionaries hoped that they might be able to successfully convert large populations.

Among the many forms of empire, settler colonialism is unique in that it is not primarily interested in obtaining labor or commodities from a foreign people, but rather in claiming land for expatriates to populate and change.[4] Usually, this process included the removal of native peoples from that land, often with the justification that the settlers would be better able to use the space productively. Missionaries, too, were sending out farmers and the like to settle and transform foreign space, but they would do it differently. Missionaries who supported the settler model were clearly not interested in removing native people; it was those people who brought them to the new land in the first place. They were, however, very invested in transforming those people into something new through conversion.

If settler colonies hoped to repopulate colonial spaces with civilized peo-ple, settler missions had similar goals. But the missionaries expected that the new civilized population would consist of the same people who had always lived there, now converted to Christianity and civilization. They would be transformed by following the example and teachings of the missionary establishments that had settled among them. Lay Christians would lead by example and through teaching. They would reveal to the unconverted what it meant to be a Christian civilization. The "heathen" would be awed not only by the Gospel but by the technology and order of American agriculture and mechanics, and would eventually adopt the whole parcel together. Or at least, that was what the Board and its missionaries imagined would happen.

The settler missions were on a scale unlike what the Board attempted anywhere else. They stand out for the large number of missionary assistants at each station and the wide range of work that those assistants performed. These missions employed single women before they were a common sight at any of the other missions. Here those women could be more easily incorporated into the mission family and perform important work as teachers in the large schools. Farmers and their families, too, were needed to teach the art of husbandry, showing their pupils how civilized people farmed, from the tools they used to the way they divided their tasks according to sex. Missionaries also helped with governance, encouraging the restructuring of these communities as much as they could on the model of the United States. These missions brought the secular in with the sacred, clearly showing how the missionaries envisioned civilization to be enmeshed with Christianity. Saving souls was not just a matter of preaching: it needed to also incorporate the complete alteration of non-Christian cultures from a state of savagery or barbarism.

The distinctiveness of the settler missions should not distract us, though, from what they shared with the Board's other missions. For there were many things in common across the Board's global reach. Education, of course, was a central part of mission work everywhere, and the logic governing the large educational enterprises of the settler missions shaped the smaller schools elsewhere. Most American missionaries, wherever they were stationed, agreed with the idea that separating "heathen" children from their families and communities was ideal, in order to inculcate religious beliefs and cultural behaviors most effectively. Most agreed, too, that the world would be a better place if more places looked like America (or at least the New England that they believed stood in for America as a whole). What marked the settlement missions as decidedly different was not a matter of ideals or goals; it was a matter of opportunity.

In the Cherokee Nation and the Sandwich Islands, the Board's missions were able to expand in scale not because of any particular idea about the needs and abilities of the peoples there, or any special enthusiasm of the missionaries. They were able to look like colonies because in these places, to an extent not experienced elsewhere, the missionaries found themselves in the favor of the government. Within the Cherokee Nation, this meant that the U.S. government, and often the leadership among the Cherokee as well, valued the mission's work and sought to help it, rather than hinder it. In the Sandwich Islands, the missionaries quite early gained the trust of the royal family and were thus encouraged to work within Hawaii. This was what the missionaries had in mind when they critiqued the East India Company for failing to do its duty to the "heathen." When governments and missionaries worked together, the missionary enterprise could be grand indeed. Christian imperialism would look like this, with Christian settlements converting the world one station at a time.

Missions and the War Department

The Board's missions to the Cherokee and Choctaw in the 1810s and 1820s were unique in that they received much of their funding through the Civilization Fund of the US government. While the other missions depended entirely on donations from the "Christian public," North American missions received thousands of dollars from the government in exchange for their efforts in not only converting American Indians to Christianity but also spreading civilization throughout the continent. The Board would later be famous for its opposition to the Jackson administration's policy of Indian removal, but they earlier benefited from certain aspects of the government's relations with Native Americans. In the decades before the late-1820s, the civilization of Native Americans was as much a political goal as their removal from the land east of the Mississippi.

From Washington's presidency through Jackson's election, the government endorsed a program of introducing civilization among American Indians. It was Henry Knox, the first secretary of war, who had suggested that Indian civilization ought to be a concern of the federal government, and that missionary societies should work with government officials to bring it about. The federal government was interested in Indian civilization for two reasons. The first concerned foreign relations: the government hoped that civilized and Christian Indians could act as allies or a buffer between the United States and other foreign powers in the continent. This was a pressing interest in the decades preceding the Board's missions, and would only begin to shift with the conclusion of the War of 1812. The resolution of that war meant that the American government had less concern about European powers in North America, and this would have important effects on the relationship between the government and Native Americans. Importantly, this was when the government began to shift away from dealing with Indian tribes as independent and sovereign nations through treaties.

The other reason for the government's support of civilizing Native Americans was economic. Central to the government's understanding of civilization was the individual ownership of land. The collective ownership of property within the Cherokee Nation for use in hunting seemed to define them as "savages" and prevented that land from being used for white agriculture. Part of the civilizing program involved not only changing the Cherokee people, but converting their land into individual plots that could be cultivated by Cherokees or bought up by white purchasers. The government and other white observers assumed that the Cherokee claimed more land than they could possibly farm. Civilizing the Cherokee, then, would open up large swaths of land for settlement by white farmers.

As Knox and others outlined the civilization policy, they explained that the only alternative was the extermination of all Indians east of the Mississippi. These stark choices were not unique to Knox; they were a popular understanding of Indian affairs in the late eighteenth and early nineteenth centuries. From the perspective of Americans in the Northeast, in particular, where Indian tribes had largely died out as the white American population expanded, it seemed that incorporation or migration were the only alternatives to death. As these bleak alternatives suggest, civilization was hardly the only component of federal Indian policy. Along with the efforts to transform Native Americans into potential republican citizens was another, more draconian policy, to remove American Indians from the land to the east of the Mississippi. By the time that Cyrus Kingsbury, the Board's first missionary to the Cherokee, sent his first report of the early progress of the mission, the federal government had begun the process of removing some of the Cherokee from Tennessee into the Arkansas Territory. The government offered to pay for the transport across the Mississippi of any families willing to relocate, in addition to providing a musket, blanket, kettle, and steel trap. Those who remained would be allowed to retain a square mile of land each. These stark options were a sign of what was to come: as those Cherokee who opposed these efforts for voluntary removal pointed out, the United States was asserting sovereignty over their land and attempting to make the alternative to removal so unpleasant that everyone would choose to leave.[5]

It was only with the American Board's entry into the Cherokee Nation in 1816 that Knox's vision of a partnership between the government and missionary societies in this work was undertaken.[6] From the earliest stages of the planning of the Cherokee mission, it was clear that the mission would have a close relationship with the federal government. Accordingly, when Kingsbury began to prepare for his mission, he traveled to Washington, DC, to meet with John C. Calhoun, the secretary of war, and President Monroe. There he also met Indian Agent Return Meigs, along with some Cherokee men who had accompanied him to the capital. Kingsbury urged Calhoun and Monroe to support his mission. Doing so, he urged, would give the government a "noble and lasting monument" to their "enlightened and generous policy" to the Indians.[7] These appeals were successful: the Board received funding and support from the secretary of war through the Indian Affairs office under the government's civilization policy.[8] While not necessarily a Christianizing project, the government's civilizing policy toward Indians worked well with missionary endeavors. As the Board reminded their supporters in the 1818 *Annual Report*, civilization needed to "prepare the way" before conversions or the birth of a strong and vibrant church could be expected. Because of this, the Board happily contributed to the government policy of civilization, seeing no particular conflict that ought to keep them from accepting government money.[9]

Starting in 1820, Congress established a special Civilization Fund, an annual appropriation of ten thousand dollars for the purposes of the "civilization of the Indian tribes" throughout the United States. Secretary of War Calhoun distributed these funds to the various missionary societies working with Native Americans, though the majority of the money went to the ABCFM for its multiple missions to Native American groups. This money could go a long way within the Board's missions. In 1820, the entire budget of the Cherokee missions was $9,967.34.[10] The portion of the Civilization Fund that would go to the Cherokee missions would make a real difference in the sorts of programs that the mission could undertake. As had been the case earlier, government support of missions were contingent on the inclusion of certain "indispensible" subjects in the schools' curriculum. In addition to the basics of reading, writing, and arithmetic, Calhoun wrote, the boys needed to learn "the practical knowledge of the mode of agriculture, and of such of the mechanic arts as are suited to the condition of the Indians," and the girls would have to learn "spinning, weaving, and sewing."[11] By 1822, the federal government supported fourteen schools throughout the country under this plan, with a total of 508 students (230 of whom were Cherokees). Religious and secular supporters alike commented on the seeming success of this program: over the course of the mission, the Cherokee Nation did indeed seem to become more civilized, by which observers meant that they looked and acted more like the white Americans around them.[12]

This apparent gain in civilization was not only attributable to the actions of the missionaries, however. In the face of enormous pressure from the

Why Cherokee was so apt to become civilized.

U.S. government, Cherokee leaders had to find ways to protect their land, people, and way of life. The rhetoric and policy of civilization seemed to offer them an opportunity to remain on their land. A limited assimilation could benefit the Cherokee, some nationalist leaders came to believe. From the turn of the nineteenth century, then, internal Cherokee politics focused on these questions of whether and how much the Cherokee ought to become civilized, with some leaders encouraging cooperation and assimilation as the best path for survival. Individual Cherokee farmers had begun experimenting with plantation agriculture since at least the time of the Revolution. Political movements to make the Cherokee government more republican in its style predated the missionary arrival. Cherokee leaders were able to take advantage of the help offered by the missions to demonstrate their commitment to civilization to the United States in the hopes that it would allow them to be taken more seriously as an independent and sovereign power. For American observers, though, the missionary program received the credit for these demonstrations of the seeming possibilities for Indian progress.[13]

As they taught the superiority of a civilized way of life, missionaries became embroiled in these conflicts among the Cherokee about acculturation and politics. In the late 1820s, some on the Cherokee Council hoped that their nation would make a new, written constitution. They planned to adopt it on July 4, 1827. The date was no accident: the constitution was designed in part out of an effort to show Americans that the Cherokees were similar to themselves. Political reform had been supported within the nation from the 1810s, as leaders hoped that creating a clearer, solidified, and institutional center of the nation would help them to fight American efforts to claim Cherokee land. In order to claim sovereignty, some of the Cherokee believed, they ought to become a state in the way that the United States was a state. For many Cherokee, however, this looked like acculturation and giving up a traditional way of life. By the mid–1820s, the Cherokee had experienced new social divisions along class, race, and educational lines. While earlier divisions within the Nation had been regional, now the society seemed fractured in part according to the standards of white Americans, including the missionaries. New laws encouraged monogamy, prohibited gambling, card playing, and theatrical performances. Dances were discouraged, as was ball playing. Missionaries were an important force behind these and other regulations, and that position was well recognized by the Cherokees. One law from 1820 even required attendance in mission schools once a student had enrolled.[14] Those who opposed these political reforms often also expressed an opposition to the missions, as the two issues of religion and politics had become so closely entwined through the Board's missions.

As a condition of the government's financial support, the Board was responsible for sending regular reports on the mission to the secretary of war, who was charged with overseeing the relations between the United States and Native American groups before the creation of the Department of the Interior in 1849. The Board's reports to the War Department stressed the progress in the schools and in particular, the number of students, and enumerated the property of the mission, presumably to show how previous disbursements had been spent. By 1820, the Board mission at Brainerd owned considerable livestock, acres of cleared land, agricultural implements, tools for carpentry, blacksmithing, and masonry, in addition to their buildings and mills. In that year, almost two hundred children were taught by the Board at their three schools in the Cherokee Nation. Only the Brainerd school included an extensive agricultural program; the other schools, called the "local schools" were smaller in scale, and the students there generally lived at home with their parents. The missionaries could point to some success. Even those students who did not stay enrolled at the schools went back to their communities able to read and write in English, which was an important marker of their acculturation for the missionaries and the secretary of war.[15]

The remarkable thing about these government reports was that they were identical to those that the missionaries provided to the Board and to their religious supporters. Missionaries did not apparently feel the need to reframe their reports for religious and governmental audiences. Indeed, there is little distinction between the civilization and educational efforts of the Board and their more explicit Christianization work. The 1823 report to Calhoun, for example, included a numeration of the students who were felt to be "under the influence of divine truth" and a description of the Cherokee church members.[16] The reports to the Christian public, similarly, include much of what you would expect in the annual reports of any New England school of the early nineteenth century. The Board appointed a visiting committee to the Brainerd School, including Agent Meigs, and their descriptions evaluated the secular as well as the religious concerns of the school. Among the first items discussed in their report was a description of the buildings and property of the mission station, with the conclusion that the space was "fit for agriculture," and that as many as fifty acres would soon be cleared, enclosed by fences, and under cultivation, all with the labor of the Cherokee students.[17]

By and large, successive secretaries of war seem to have been pleased by what they read in these reports. John C. Calhoun, for example, shared the Board's definition of their goals, and called the reports "very satisfactory," said they gave a "most cheering prospect of complete success," and assured the Board of the continual aid that they could expect from the government.[18] The Cherokee mission, then, did what the Board wanted it to do: it united the goals of governance and religion, revealing the similar interests that the Board assumed the government had with the Christian public in general. Not until the administration of Andrew Jackson dramatically changed federal Indian policy did the mission receive any critique of what they were doing in the Cherokee Nation. These reports are accordingly a useful window into the goals that the missionaries, the Board, and the government had for the Cherokee mission.

Cherokee Missions and the Settlement Model

A rudimentary form of the settler mission model dated to the beginning of missionary interest in the Cherokee Nation. When Gideon Blackburn, a Presbyterian minister, established his mission to the Cherokee in the first decade of the century, he had relied on a lay Christian family to run the mission school and take care of the day-to-day operations of the mission. The family taught their Cherokee students the basics of a common English education, in addition to the trappings of "civilized life." The mission oversaw the clothes they wore, the food they ate, and finally the beds and blankets on which they slept. Importantly, the transformations that were happening in Blackburn's school were decidedly not about students converting to Christian faith. Its supporters hardly minded. They saw the projects of civilization and Christianization as linked and assumed that the one would lead to the other.[19] This basic premise would guide the later Cherokee mission of the American Board and indeed all of its missions that took on the settler model. As missionary Lorrin Andrews would explain it in 1834, just as it was clearly a missionaries' duty to preach the word of God, it was "just as obvious" that missionaries should provide instruction in "every thing which will open their minds, which will enable them to understand the word of God and their relations to their fellow-men—in short, everything pertaining to civilized society."[20] These missions were typified most importantly by the types of schools they established, and the wide range of lay women and men that the missions required to staff them.

Establishing mission schools was an important part of all of the Board's missions, and the Cherokee schools were no different. Given the Board's emphasis on civilization in North America, it is not surprising that they explicitly modeled their plan on Blackburn's earlier establishment. Teaching Cherokee students English at boarding schools located within the nation seemed to strike the ideal balance between removing Cherokee children from the influence of their parents without setting them up for failure on their return home after graduation. English seemed to be the best language for their education for several reasons, not least because the Cherokee language had not yet been committed to writing. Additionally, missionaries insisted, English would give the students the greatest possible access not only to the Bible but also to "every other book, which may instruct them." English was the key not only to their conversion, but to their civilization.[21] Above all, the students were to be introduced to American ways of doing things and broken from their Cherokee traditions. "These children," the Board reminded its supporters, had been "collected from the wilderness, and placed under the direction of Christian benevolence." It was the duty of the mission to do everything that they could for their students. After all, they wrote, "Soon they will be mingling with their countrymen, and imparting their acquired character to others, and they to others still, in a wider and still wider range. No time is to be lost." It was essential to give their students the right "acquired character"—both to defend them against the presumed tendency to backslide when they returned to their homes and also to make those pupils into walking advertisements of the benefits of Christian civilization and education.[22]

The Cherokee schools differed from most of the Board's overseas schools in a few important respects. First, missionaries here were able to actually implement the project of domestic education that had so excited American supporters of the Bombay mission. If children there were difficult to "obtain," the missionaries did not have similar problems in the Cherokee Nation. Here, children were brought into the mission family, sponsored by American donors, and given Christian names in honor of their patrons and other well-known New Englanders. Elias Boudinot, the famous graduate of the Board's schools in the Cherokee Nation and in Connecticut, named for the New Jersey statesman, is only one example of this trend.[23]

In addition, the content of the missionary education differed in Native American missions, and this had everything to do with the connection to the government and the predominance of civilization in guiding the work of the missionaries. When Cyrus Kingsbury was planning the curriculum for the schools, he explained to Samuel Worcester that his goal was "to make them useful citizens and pious Christians." In order to do this, they needed a common English education to give them "habits of industry" and a "competent knowledge of the economy of civilized life."[24] This second emphasis had profound implications for the structure of the Cherokee mission. It meant that the missionaries would try to obtain as much land as they could cultivate, in addition to horses and farming implements, and teach the students how to farm and live like white Americans. And so in the mission, farming for the male and needle arts for the female students were emphasized by the missionaries as important in training their pupils for life as citizens and civilized Christians.[25]

This emphasis on agriculture and other "arts of civilization" was explicitly outlined in the government's agreement to aid the mission's endeavors. When Henry Clay promised to supply the mission with some of its needs, he focused on these goals in particular. The government would build the mission's school buildings, as well as supply agricultural tools including plows, hoes, axes, looms, and spinning wheels. Once the school had female students enrolled, the government would supply spinning wheels and looms for them.[26] This arrangement worked out well for the Board, and led Samuel Worcester to reflect with satisfaction that "the views of our Board are very fully in accordance with those of the Government on this general subject of Indian civilization." Both groups agreed on the importance that Indians would come to live in "contracted limits—into fixed and compact settlements," and further that they needed to have everything done to "conciliate these uncultivated people to the measures necessary for their good." This was precisely what the Cherokee mission sought to do through its union with the government for Indian education and civilization.[27]

In practice, the mission's schools sought to train students in the branches of common education while introducing civilized habits among both boys and girls. The male students would do this through working on the mission farm, the female students would do this through learning the "domestic arts" and particularly the use of the needle. Missionaries saw their farms as a particularly useful means of reaching their male students. Clearing and cultivating the land, they insisted, would be the best way to teach them "the habits of industry and good management." The girls would be trained by female teachers, either wives of the missionaries or single women, who would introduce both "the common domestic employments of women, and . . . those studies, which are taught in the common schools of our country." Missionaries were delighted to see the progress of their female students, who were "remarkable for their obedience, and aptness to learn." They reported to their supporters that these students were performing at a level that could be expected of white American girls, accustomed to attending school from early in their childhood.[28] In both cases, the missionaries were attempting to instill what they saw as the proper gender roles for men and women. One of the major critiques missionaries had expressed about native cultures was, indeed, the "laziness" of men and the female control of agriculture. For Northeastern missionaries, this looked like an oppressive situation for Cherokee women, who were being forced to perform labor that was not appropriate to their sex. Accordingly, as missionaries instructed their students in the "arts of civilization," they were quite clear that these corresponded with particular gender roles. Part of becoming civilized was creating a domestic role for women and an agricultural role for men.

As they taught children formally in schools, the mission's civilization program was also designed to teach adults in less formal ways. In particular, through the creation of saw- and grist-mills, and through the employment of blacksmiths, the missionaries expected to do great things, not only for their own comfort, but "to the progress of civilization among the natives." As the missionaries explained in their 1822 *Annual Report*, these aspects of the mission "tend much to introduce civilization. Whenever, for instance, a Cherokee begins to enjoy the advantage of a grist mill, he abandons the practice of pounding his corn; and the same may be said, with respect to many other improvements of society."[29] Just as the students were trained in the correct ways to go about doing things through American technology, so too were their parents to be convinced of the backwardness of their own methods, and the superiority of American style.

An educational program on this scale could not rely on native teachers, as missionaries from other stations around the world had to do. Board missionaries around the world constantly complained about the quality of the teachers that they could hire. In many places, missionaries insisted that it was impossible to find teachers who were themselves well-educated. When learned teachers could be hired, as was the case in Bombay, missionaries instead complained that the teachers undercut their attempts at evangelism in the classroom. In the settler missions, however, schools would be largely staffed by teachers who were committed to the mission and its joint projects of Christianization and civilization. Certainly, ordained missionaries were essential, but lay assistant missionaries took on a new importance. The different educational establishments at the Cherokee mission meant that the mission needed a different sort of staff than the Bombay mission had.

The Cherokee mission needed farmers, shoemakers, and single women to help train the students and provide examples of civilized living. The Board regularly advertised their need for new assistants in the Annual Reports of the mission, as when Cherokee missionaries wrote of their "despair" for the farm unless they could find "one or two pious men to labor with them [the students] and direct this important branch of their education."[30] Potential teachers eagerly responded. These teachers would be men and women like the Congers, Talmages, and Vails: pious Christians, moved by the supposed plight of the American Indians and called to take their part in bringing about their salvation.

Like the assistant missionaries from New Jersey, many of those who came to the Cherokee were from farming backgrounds. Most of these were expected to do that same type of work on the Cherokee farms, showing those who came to the mission what it would look like to farm in a civilized manner. John and Eliza Elsworth, of Greensboro, Vermont, for example, came to the Cherokee mission as a farm couple. They were in their twenties when they first inquired about mission work in 1820. John was educated well enough to allow him "to teach reading, writing, and common arithmetic very well." One of the women recommended for the mission was heralded for her work as "a teacher of little children" as well as her good understanding of "the use of her needle."[31] Ainsworth Blunt was a twenty-one-year-old church member of "approved piety" who had been discouraged from the ministry by his pastor. Blunt was advised, instead, to devote himself to God through his work as a farmer and a cooper, and was eventually recommended for mission work in that capacity in 1822 along with his wife Harriet.[32] Erastus Dean, a blacksmith, went with his wife Sarah to the Cherokee in the same year.[33] In their lay capacities, they would be an important part of the mission settlement.

Even those who served as full (ordained) missionaries among the Cherokee had backgrounds in fields beyond preaching. William Potter, of Clinton, New York, had worked as a school teacher, a weaver, and a farmer before he became a missionary to the Cherokee. He had felt called to work "among the heathen in our country" for three years before he reached out to the Board to inquire whether he might "rejoice to spend [his] days among the Indians in the capacity of a school teacher." It was only after he was commissioned by the Board that he set out to become a licensed preacher. A local minister reported that he had made impressive "improvement in Christian knowledge,' and had become "a very acceptable preacher" who, if he hadn't engaged to serve as a missionary, would have received requests to serve congregations within Connecticut. Accompanied by his wife Laura, Potter left for the Brainerd mission in 1820.[34] John Thomson, too, was appointed a Cherokee missionary after spending his life working with his hands and learning "a trade which might render him useful in giving instruction to the Heathen in the arts of civilized life." He eventually became a theological student at Princeton, where he earned "unqualified praise" for his studies.[35]

Single women, too, were welcomed to the settler missions decades before they would be normal sights at other missions. It was by no means clear to the women themselves, their friends at home, or the Board whether this was a good idea at first. All of the women's letters begin with a note of apology or position of supplication to the Board. Frequently, ministers and male family members would write on behalf of young women, asking the Board for their advice on the matter. Hannah Kelly, for example, had both her minister and her younger brother write on her behalf in 1826, when she offered herself for missionary service. Her brother had been "slow in giving her encouragement," but gradually came to feel that it would be best for her to go.[36] Others were more enthusiastic about single women in the mission field from the beginning. William Potter, for example, enthusiastically recommended that his sister accompany his family to the Cherokee mission. She had for years "felt a desire to go among the heathen, but the object being delicate she had never before opened her mind to any person about it." It was only the occasion of her brother's appointment as a missionary that she asked whether "it would be expedient for a female to go out unmarried as a missionary" and whether "such a person [might] be useful in any degree?" Potter, a thirty-year-old woman, with an education that was "common for females," had worked with children and was believed to have "a very good talent for government."[37] Such qualifications were typical for the single women whom the Board allowed to serve as assistant missionaries. They were all expected to work as teachers among the young children who would come to the mission and were valued for their teaching as well as domestic skills.

American women in the mission field were supposed to be able to reach "heathen" women in ways that their husbands could not and they were supposed to demonstrate to any who might observe them how a Christian family was organized. It is striking, then, to hear the story of Ann Paine, an assistant missionary who went against all of these general rules. In many ways, Paine resembled the other women of the Brainerd mission. She was a woman of deep faith, who would help to found her church and a women's prayer group in Pennsylvania. She had a background in teaching and felt called to use those skills to help the "heathen" whom she believed could be the Lost Tribes of Israel. How "honored" she would be, if she could find herself in any way "instrumental of any good to them." She had seriously considered her situation and had decided to dedicate her life to mission work. "Not without mature, and I trust, not without prayerful consideration," she wrote, "would I thus devote myself, as far as my power extends, and whatever *is, or hereafter shall be mine*; nor like the wretched Saphira, would I make the sacrifice."[38] These sorts of promises were typical of the missionaries, who delighted in sacrificing their homes and comforts for the glory of a missionary life. What set Paine apart, though, was just what she would be giving up. Ann Paine was married, and she hoped to work among the Cherokee without her husband.

Instead of fulfilling her calling through such conventional means as joining a local auxiliary and making regular contributions to the mission cause, Ann Paine joined the ranks of the assistant missionaries at Brainerd in the early 1820s. She left her husband in Pennsylvania, bringing her children with her as she worked as a teacher at the mission. In 1819, Paine wrote to Samuel Worcester about her "peculiar" situation and the possibility of her undertaking the superintendence of the female school at Brainerd. At Worcester's suggestion, Paine obtained a written document clarifying her relationship with her husband. This written separation from bed and board was signed by witnesses and largely concerned the practical and economic terms of their separation. It allowed her to take her children and leave her husband behind. While the mission was not mentioned, it was this arrangement that allowed for Ann Paine to join the mission family without her husband the following year. Even as she remained married, she was to consider herself a missionary for life, as all the Board missionaries were instructed.[39] This was a unique situation in the Board's missions, and it is the exception that proves the rule about their understanding of the proper relationship between men and women in the mission, and indeed, in civilized societies.

The Paines' separation document was completed within a month and was a basic statement of terms for the separation of bed and board. It was explicitly Ann Paine's "choice and option" to either continue within the household of Clement Paine or separate from him. The document outlined the specifics of Ann Paine's support if she left, clarified that she could not make any debts in Clement's name, and explained that they were not released from the bonds of marriage and were legally still husband and wife. Such arrangements were not unheard of in the early nineteenth century, though they were done only in situations where there were real differences in interests between husband and wife. What is remarkable about the Paines' separation is the approval it received from evangelical observers. Though this may have been an unhappy or abusive marriage as well, the contrast in Ann and Clement's religious beliefs seemed sufficient to the Board to justify the breaking of the marriage covenant and the establishment of a new arrangement. More than this, the separation would be the event that would allow Ann Paine to come forward to a new and more public role within American Christianity as a missionary.

While for most missionary couples, the duties of marriage and of mission were yoked, Ann Paine's situation put the two at odds with each other. Neither she nor the Board was unaware of, or unconcerned about, this fact. Worcester, for example, was very concerned that they "must not do wrong; we must take prudent care, that our good be not evil spoken of, we must as far as possible '*shun the appearance of evil.*'" In the discussions about this situation, it becomes clear that part of this issue for Worcester was family governance, and the relationship between the mission and the families that comprised it. As had been clear in the situation of the Notts in Bombay, who left the mission over a conflict with their unmarried brethren, it was extremely difficult for there to be families at the mission station who tried to live outside of missionary control. When Clement Paine suggested that he could accompany his family to Brainerd, without himself becoming connected to the mission, he was met with the firm opposition of the Board. Worcester insisted that "it will be obvious to every one, that no person, especially no master of a family, should make his residence at a missionary station, unless he is really friendly to the object, and disposed to promote it." There was some distinction between the role of a family head in Pennsylvania, and the role of a family head within a mission family. Worcester simply could not imagine what it might look like at the mission to have Clement Paine acting as a nonmissionary husband to his assistant missionary wife. In order for Ann Paine to be a part of the mission, either her husband had to be a missionary too, or she had to be, for practical purposes, single. She could not have split allegiances to the mission and to her spouse. Since religious differences between the Paines meant that Clement could not be affiliated with the mission himself, if Ann wanted to serve as superintendent of the school, she had to do so without her husband.[40]

At Brainerd, Paine joined the mission family, who seemed surprisingly unconcerned about her marital state. Four months after her arrival, however, Paine's husband sent for her, as his health had taken a turn for the worse.

At this point, the question of duty again came to the fore, and Ann and the missionaries, now without input from the Board, debated whether it would be proper for her to remain at the mission, or to return to her husband; what was at issue was which role, wife or missionary, had stronger claims to her. The discussion about whether she should stay or go was not a simple one, but spoke to the missionaries' sense of the role of women in the world and of the centrality of marriage, even with a document of separation, to religious life. While Paine felt that her duty lay with the mission, the other members of the mission family were less convinced, and ultimately decided that her place was at home with her husband. As a result, in late April 1821, Ann Paine and her children returned to Pennsylvania.[41] Paine's story is remarkable, and shows that even as the Board was committed to endorsing a traditional model of family governance, it recognized the individual calling that women could feel to serve as missionaries. Paine's departure and the support she received from both the missionaries and the Board highlights the persistence of these values even in this unique case.

After her return to Pennsylvania, Ann Paine disappears from the historic record. It is unclear from census records whether she remained in Clement Paine's household, though he survived for several decades. In 1860, an article was published in the *New York Evangelist* that seems to have been an obituary of sorts for her. The author described her Christian character but did not mention her time as a missionary, and recorded her final reflections on the vanity of the world and her hopes for heaven. Her only deathbed anxiety, the author reported, was the hope that her "husband and children may come to Christ."[42]

Writing about their passion for this work, the missionaries frequently used the word "zeal." William Mamaring was said to weep during the night, so intense was his desire to work among the Indians.[43] Missionaries around the world emphasized the ways that their emotions drove them to their work, of course. What was different about these individuals was that in places where the Board was unable to establish a settler-style mission, they would have had no options to live out their sense of calling. If they were single women, they could perhaps marry a man who was planning on becoming a missionary himself, but laymen and unmarried women had no place in most of the Board's missions. The pious farmers and mechanics of New England instead had to be satisfied with reading about the work of missions and contributing to the Board's efforts. These settlements offered new and direct ways of participation for those who felt particularly called to mission work but who lacked the theological training or marital status to bring them into other aspects of foreign mission work. The settlement missions worked, in other words, not only because they did work toward civilization that the Board found valuable, but because they tapped into a network of white American Christians who hoped to do more for the mission movement and eagerly seized the opportunity to do what they were doing in New England—farming, teaching, blacksmithing, among other things—in a new place and with a new purpose.

Settlement Missions on the Sandwich Islands

The Sandwich Islands mission had much in common with the Cherokee mission, but because the political context was different, so too was the way that missionaries embraced the settlement model. The unexpected level of support that missionaries received from the Hawaiian government changed the way that the mission would operate. Initially, it seemed that Hawaii would be very similar to the Cherokee project. Twenty-two men, women, and children made up the initial mission family that departed Boston in October 1820. Two of these were ordained ministers, who were accompanied by their wives and families, in addition to a farmer, a doctor, two catechists, and a printer. They all "went forth desirous of carrying the arts of civilized communities, as well as the blessings of the Gospel."[44] Over the years, the Sandwich Islands continued to see an unusually high number of missionaries and assistant missionaries, and employed single women as teachers in the same way that the Cherokee mission had done. Some of these continued to serve in roles outside of evangelization: at least one shoemaker was sent as an assistant missionary, and the Board eventually appointed an assistant missionary for "secular affairs" to take care of the business affairs of the mission so that the ordained missionaries could focus their attention more fully on the churches and schools. But the missionaries did not establish a farm as part of their schools. They did not seek to begin a program of boarding education on a large scale in order to separate children from the bad examples of their parents. They were deeply invested in the project of civilization and in teaching by example, but their type of settlement was distinct from that in the Cherokee Nation.

Indeed, the educational program at the Sandwich Islands was completely unique among the Board's missions globally. It was extensive, with thousands of students studying every year. By 1831, the mission oversaw nine hundred schools, and as many Hawaiian teachers to staff them. One individual mission station examined five thousand students the year before, and another had ten thousand students in its domain.[45] Beyond its scale though, what set the Hawaiian schools apart was that the students were mostly adults. For the missions were the beneficiaries of the conversion of the island's leadership and their wholehearted embrace of education. As much as missionaries around the world spoke about the eager reception that their schools and books received, no other mission experienced numbers like this in the early nineteenth century. The Hawaiian missionaries found themselves part of an actual transformation of local culture. They bonded with government leaders, helped to implement laws based on the Ten Commandments, and engaged in a print war against American commercial and naval ship captains about the course of Hawaii and the place of morality within its government. Here, as in Bombay and in the Cherokee Nation, missionaries would debate those with more commercial interests in the land and the people over what the proper American relationship to a foreign people ought to be. If the Cherokee missionaries had cooperated with the American government in order to bring about the transformation of Cherokee culture on the model of the United States, the Sandwich Island missionaries cooperated with Hawaiian governments to bring about that same conversion.[46]

Before the missionaries left for the Sandwich Islands, American observers knew enough about Hawaii from commercial connections to be convinced that these were a people in need of civilization. The Hawaiians were described as people who had "plunged in the lowest depths of sensuality and sin" and were in need not only of the word of God, but also of a transformation of their way of life. Like the Cherokee, they inhabited a rich land that could produce wonderful things if only it was properly used. As one of the mission's supporters explained, even though Hawaiians "dwell in one of the finest climates, and own one of the richest soils, in the world," as yet they knew "little or nothing of those social, intellectual and moral enjoyments which we prize as among our highest privileges." The missionaries needed to "promote improvement and civilization," "introduce husbandry and manufacture," encourage "conjugal fidelity" and familial concord, "educate the rising generation," and "meliorate the condition of the female sex." To do all of this, they would need "at the same time," to introduce Christianity. Only that religion would give individuals and nations at large the sense of a future world that could influence their conduct in this one. At the time that the mission was begun, then, civilization and Christianity went hand in hand. The missionaries, further, expected to introduce husbandry alongside "the still more important knowledge of the oracles of Divine Truth." The instructions to the first group of Sandwich Islands missionaries described their ultimate goal in visual terms. They were to "aim at nothing short of covering those Islands with fruitful fields, and pleasant dwellings, and schools and churches; of raising up the whole people to an elevated state of Christian Civilization; of bringing, or preparing the means of bringing, thousands and millions of the present and succeeding generations to the mansions of eternal blessedness."[47]

No one was quite prepared for what happened when the missionaries actually arrived. As they always did, the Prudential Committee of the Board instructed its missionaries to keep out of politics. They were to avoid "all interference, and intermeddling with political affairs and party concerns" upon their arrival in the Sandwich Islands, though such instructions did not bar the missionaries from cooperating with a willing government. In Hawaii, the limits of such cooperation would be seen. Upon their arrival, the missionaries received a promise of protection and patronage from the government and were delighted to find themselves arriving at a "most interesting period where the Islands were actually without any religion and emphatically waiting for the law of Christ." Hiram Bingham, one of the ordained missionaries, wrote to Boston that "tho' you may not be prepared to hear it, and though the Christian public in America will hardly be persuaded to believe it," the traditional religion of Hawaii was dead. The "taboo system which has been founded in ignorance and superstition, and cemented with human blood, and supported for ages by unhallowed and misguided passions" no longer stood in the way of the progress of Christianity. What was more, the new king and high priest had seemed to embrace Christianity. The missionaries reported that the king had renounced idol worship, had declared "that there is but one God that can serve and do us good, and that he is in heaven," and that the two had issued public orders to abolish idolatry. From the time of their first letter from Hawaii, the missionaries were confident that the Sandwich Islands would soon be filled with preachers and schoolmasters from the United States, with a civilized and Christian population.[48]

The missionaries' timing could not have been better to suit their purposes. The year 1819 marked a significant transformation for Hawaii. The king died, and in the wake of his death, the Hawaiian people began important transitions. Only months after the king's son was crowned, the *kapu* (or taboo) system was abolished in Hawaii, at least partially in response to the criticism that the practice had received from foreign traders. This was a major change for Hawaiian society, as the *kapu* system organized not only religious life but also the social order. It was the *kapu* system that had enforced the boundaries of class and gender, and in its absence, there were many possibilities for new developments. It was at this moment that the American missionaries entered Hawaii as representatives of not only Christianity but of the American culture that Hawaiians had come to know through trade and commercial connections. They were quickly welcomed.[49]

Further easing the entry of the American missionaries into Hawaii was the fact that they entered with preexisting connections to the royal family. George Humehume, the king's son, had studied at the Cornwall School, and when the missionaries accompanied him home to Kauai, his father received him with joy and surprise: he had believed his son to be dead. For eight weeks, two missionaries remained with the king, instructing him and his family. Already the king could "read intelligently in the new Testament, desirous to outstrip all his subjects in the acquisition of useful knowledge." The missionaries counted the head chief of Oahu and his wife among their other students, in addition to the daughter of another chief.[50] The relationships between the chiefs and the missionaries approached friendship at times. When Hiram Bingham had a son, the king and queen attended the baptism, and paid their condolences when the baby died shortly thereafter.[51]

By 1827, the missionaries could report a complete revolution among the chiefs of the Sandwich Islands and their wives. When two of the missionary wives held a tea party for the chiefs, their families, and the missionaries, twenty-one chiefs attended. Almost all of them had either joined the church or were preparing to do so. The mission was delighted at the rapid changes that they had seen among the Hawaiian elite and described the scene in great detail for their American readers. Look around the room, they wrote, and "you would have seen the regent, once haughty, heathen Kaahumanu, now condescending and kind and grateful to her Christian teachers, with her two royal sisters Kalokua and Opiia all members of the church, bearing the Christian names of Elisabeth, Maria, and Lydia." All three of these now were "exerting a great influence over the people in favor of reformation, and rejoicing in the mercy of God in giving them the gospel." As the missionaries made their round of the tea party attendees, their descriptions continued in this vein. The governor of Hawaii was "dignified, sociable, and friendly" and had built a church at Kailua. One couple had recently brought their infant son for baptism. Several of the chiefs worked for the mission, aiding in translation efforts and overseeing schools;

one even went on an itinerating tour around Hawaii in 1826, "exhorting the people to obey the word of God and the voice of the chiefs." It was amazing to the missionaries that these two things, the word of God and of the Hawaiian government, had become analogous. These men and women had "laid aside their vices and excesses, and their love of noise and war." Instead of singing "the roaring hula" they joined the missionaries "in a song of Zion." From the example of this elite, the effects were remarkable: huge numbers attended worship regularly and came for education in the mission's schools.[52]

Simply educating the Hawaiian kings, chiefs, and their families would hardly be cause for finding the missionaries interfering with local government. This was precisely what a group of merchants and sea captains would accuse the missionaries of in the mid-1820s. Indeed, the missionaries went beyond simply teaching the leaders of the Sandwich Islands. They helped the regent Kaahumanu to bring about a series of legal reforms in the 1820s. This was the idea of the governor of Hawaii, but the inspiration seemed to come from the mission. The laws, the missionaries explained, were based on the Ten Commandments. When asked to defend them, the missionaries and Kaahumanu repeatedly explained that they were required by the law of God. These laws outlawed murder, theft, and adultery. Additional laws prohibited gambling, fornication, and the sale of alcohol. These were celebrated by the mission as a major step toward the civilization of the islands. When Kaahumanu invited Bingham to say a prayer at the ceremony announcing these laws to the people, he happily accepted her offer, even though she warned that it might anger some of the foreigners on the islands. It certainly did so. The seeming connection between the mission and the government was certainly noticed and not always celebrated. For many of the sailors who stopped in Hawaii on their way to other Pacific or Asian ports, the islands offered the possibility to find new supplies and entertainments. They did not appreciate the moralizing influence of the missionaries. Soon they were publishing complaints in American papers that the missionaries were "*interfering* with the affairs of the government."[53]

The most controversial of the new laws among the Americans on the Hawaiian Islands concerned prostitution. Among other things, this law prevented Hawaiian women from boarding visiting ships "on an infamous errand." Echoing the concerns of antiprostitution reformers in American cities, these missionaries worried about the effects of prostitution on individual women and on society in general. The crews and captains of

American ships strongly opposed such a law, while the missionaries strongly endorsed it. Soon the annual reports of the Sandwich Islands missions were filled with details of the threats that missionaries received not only from commercial captains but also from Lieutenant Percival of the U.S. Navy. According to the missionaries, they had received death threats, and chiefs had been forced into making these laws unenforceable. These "men of peculiarly depraved habits" necessitated laws such as these, the missionaries insisted.[54]

It would not have been lost on anyone that the story the missionaries told was one of corruption of the Hawaiians by unscrupulous Americans and Europeans. The missionaries had made enough progress in the Sandwich Islands, they said, that the kings had now adopted the Ten Commandments for the basis of the criminal code. Some ten thousand Hawaiians had joined together to form "moral societies" to encourage religious training and moral conduct. Hundreds of Hawaiian couples had begun to solemnize their marriages in the Christian church every year. They were on the road to civilization. In the face of this, it was Americans who attempted to maintain prostitution. The effect of not enforcing this law, missionaries claimed was disastrous: the female schools were broken up, and many of their students "immediately became victims" to prostitution. As they had earlier critiqued the East India Company, here they critiqued the emblem of American commercial power overseas. Although they had been able to exert unprecedented influence over their converts, they worried that the U.S. Navy and American commercial interest could interfere with their implementation of Christian imperialism.[55]

The missionaries had struggled with American merchants and captains since the time of their arrival in Hawaii. In 1821, they accused unnamed "citizens of a civilized and Christian country, who stand as high in the affections of a wife at home and in the confidence of their employers, as the commanders of the Cleopatras Barge, or even of the Thaddeus" of bringing some of the girls who lived at the mission into "disgrace." For the missionaries, this was a fight of power against grace: their opponents were "men who glory in their shame, and threaten 'prosecution and vengeance if their names are mentioned in America,'" but the missionaries had right on their side. While the missionaries claimed the authority of "Humanity, Benevolence, and the Authority of God," they described the riot that seamen caused in February 1826 as they threatened to do violence to the homes and persons of the missionaries and chiefs if the *kapu* against women was not lifted. As the missionaries informed their supporters at home again and again, it was the duty of the mission, and of Christians in America and abroad, to oppose such issues. Lieutenant John Percival became the face of their frustration at the role of nonmissionary Americans in the Sandwich Islands. What angered the missionaries so much about the behavior of Percival was not just what he had done in Hawaii, but that he had done so from such an important position. As a result of the missionaries' reports, the navy opened an inquiry into Percival's behavior. This was essential, the Board explained to its supporters, because not only had he been charged with interfering with local laws that were intended to preserve public morals and "lived publicly in vice," but he had done so while standing as "the representative of his country." From the perspective of the mission, such behavior was deplorable both in itself and because it gave the wrong idea of what civilization was really like.[56]

The unique circumstances at Hawaii led to a close examination of the relationship between civilization and Christianity. When the missionaries arrived in Hawaii, they had the good fortune and incredible challenge of coming into a population that eagerly embraced Christianity even as it had not yet reached the status of a civilized nation. This flew in the face of everything that the missionaries had expected to find. The idea that civilization and Christianity went hand in hand was a truism of the early missions. By 1832, though, the Sandwich Islands missionaries had to face the complicated question whether the Sandwich Islands were "a Christian nation." The answer to this was surprising. "Obviously they are not a nation of idolaters," the Board began, noting that Christianity was "nominally the religion of the nation." The rulers were almost all church members, the government sponsored the erection of church buildings with public support, the Sabbath was widely respected, polygamy was abandoned in favor of Christian marriages, and the people were anxious to receive the Scriptures. Quite simply, the Board explained, "They *are* a Christian people. Christianity has *preceded* civilization, and is leading the way to it." If the obvious question facing the missionaries was whether Hawaii was a Christian nation, the next question was just as clear. If the Sandwich Islands were now a Christian nation, what was left for the missionary to do? The answer, again, lay in that connection between civilization and Christianity. Even if the latter preceded the former in this case, the two needed to go together. Too easily, the people might "relapse into idolatry." The field, the Board warned, was not "actually secured." More preaching was needed, and more teaching. Until the whole of the people were educated, until they lived in a civilized style, the missionary's work would not be done. The missionaries would not be done until it could no longer be asked whether or not this was a Christian nation: until the answer was obvious to any who looked on the people and their culture, more needed to be done.[57]

Though they did not do so in the systematic way that was implemented among American Indians, the missionaries in the Hawaiian Islands did attempt "to set an example of industry." The Board was happy to report that many of the islanders had learned "the use of tools" through watching the missionaries, and as a result had created doors, chairs, chests, tables, bedsteads, and cupboards. Their list of furniture was not only designed to show how skilled these people had become with the American tools; it also revealed the extent to which these tools in turn introduced them to entirely new household items. For, as the Board had explained to its supporters, traditional Hawaiian homes lacked the sort of domestic comforts that were required in American homes. "The great mass of the natives," they explained, "are yet necessarily ignorant of the arts of domestic life in use among civilized nations." Life, for them, was "a round of indolence, with barely enough labor to keep them from starvation." They lived in "small and filthy" homes of one room that provided little space for individual family members and little protection from the weather. They dressed, further, inappropriately: only a "cloth about the loins, and another thrown carelessly over the shoulders," if even that much. Clothing, the missionaries explained, was understood to be "rather as an ornament, than a covering—to be worn only on special occasions for display." Missionaries, then, felt that they had much work to do, and were anxious to have more assistance from the United States. In particular, they needed more teachers, male and female, who could oversee the schools and train native students to be teachers.[58]

For the missionaries of the Sandwich Islands, this was a lesson learned through experience. By the early 1830s, the missionaries had been active in Hawaii for a decade and had seen some remarkable changes in many respects. The chiefs had embraced them, their preaching attracted thousands of worshipers weekly, and the people seemed eager to learn from them. Yet, as they explained in 1832, the actual effects of their work were less impressive than numbers suggested. Yes, they had been able to distribute large numbers of religious texts, and yes, the "mass of the people" had come to some understanding of who God was and what God's laws were. Both of these were true because they had been able to institute a large network of "native schools," taught by Hawaiians, not missionaries, where literacy and religious training were emphasized. All the same, they were convinced that they had not done much in reality toward turning Hawaii into the "elevated state of Christian civilization" that they had been instructed to create. This, they explained, was due to their reliance on native schools to take care of the bulk of their educational program. The only people who seemed to really have been changed, who had learned not just to read, but to think about what they had read, and to try and improve themselves more generally, had been taught by the missionaries themselves. Native teachers, they insisted, "failed to do what their name implies in a civilized country." Missionaries had to take more direct charge of the educational program if they wanted to see Hawaii become truly civilized.[59]

From the beginning, the agricultural ambitions of the mission were unsuccessful and so were quickly given up. The missionaries could not gain access to cattle or horses, and worried that if they worked too hard to "cultivate the soil, [or] to change the mode of agriculture," they would lose some of the support they had received from the government for their literacy training. Accordingly, the missionaries decided in 1823 that it was "the design of Providence to diminish the proportion of laymen and increase the number of preachers" at their station, even though "schoolmasters, physicians, and mechanics" were still desired. Mechanics were less necessary than they might have been in other places, though, based on the importance of the Sandwich Islands for international commerce at this time. Mechanics "of different kinds, from different countries" already visited Hawaii, and so the missionaries stressed that any assistant sent to the mission needed to be "competent to teach a good school, and conduct profitably, a prayer meeting, or religious conference among the natives, should the exigencies of the mission and of this yet unstable nation demand it, and were all duly qualified to preach it would doubtless be still better, so that every tentmaker should be a Paul, and every fisherman a Peter, in the great work of gathering these gentiles."[60]

Large numbers of men and women answered this call. When the fourth group of missionaries arrived in Hawaii in 1832, there were thirty-two of them able to come before the king and seek his welcome. This was "a formidable array of missionaries, such as probably never before sat together in the court of an earthly prince," as Hiram Bingham described the scene. By 1837, an additional thirty-two were sent to join the mission family.[61] Married couples and single women alike came to the Sandwich Islands, eager to spread the word of God and the culture of their home country among this apparently eager population. Missionaries were called on to create special schools for the children of the chiefs, and did so. They were explicitly charged, then, with the task of training the future leaders of the Hawaiian kingdom. Over the years, several missionaries left the work of the Board to run secular schools or serve as chaplains to naval ships coming through the region. Their role as representatives of American Christian civilization in the rapidly Christianizing Sandwich Islands placed them in a unique position between religion and governance. In significant numbers, the American missionaries at Hawaii worked to transform not only the faith of the people but also—directly as well as indirectly—their culture and even their government.[62]

The missions on the settlement style were what the Board meant when it envisioned a Christian imperialism. Here governments worked with the missions to spread religion and civilization. They wanted to bring the blessings of God alongside any commercial benefits that the United States might enjoy from its dealings with the outside world. In the Cherokee and Sandwich Islands missions, the Board's missionaries had peculiar advantages in the support of governments, both imperial and indigenous. Such support allowed them to operate on an unusually extensive scale in order to bring about their joint goals of Christianization and civilization. Both missions employed large numbers of lay men and women as part of the mission family with the explicit instructions that such assistants were to serve as examples of the Christian lifestyle. In matters large and small—from the arrangement of their families to the style of their homes and their use of tools—these missions were to be something like living dioramas of Christian civilization. Once they gained the support of the local leadership, they were able to take more active roles in reforming the cultures that they encountered.

Among those educated at the Cherokee missions were the people who would go on to become important leaders in the Cherokee Nation in the coming years. It was through these connections that the missionaries were able to influence John Ross and Elias Boudinot, who would be among the most vocal opponents of the removal of their people from the land east of the Mississippi River. The missionaries, that is, were involved with both governments in the Cherokee case—American and Cherokee—and this would be the cause of much confusion over the next decade. For this period of seeing the relation of the United States to the Cherokee as ideal for missions would not last. The Age of Jackson would bring the missionaries into conflict with a new type of American empire.

Chapter 5

American Politics and the Cherokee Mission

After a decade of work among the Cherokee, the Board's attempts at a settlement mission seemed to have paid off well. The Cherokee seemed to be adopting the civilization that the missionaries had been urging, and there were tangible signs of these developments. In the 1820s, the Cherokee committed their language to writing and adopted a written constitution. For excited missionary supporters, these were clear indications of civilization and assimilation. While the numbers of Christian converts were never overwhelming, Cherokee missionaries saw a regular stream of several conversions a year, more than most other Board missions did in this era. Hundreds of students attended the Cherokee schools. By 1826, the Board could inform its supporters that their experience there showed that "the transforming efficacy of the Christian religion, both upon individuals and upon neighborhoods, is now seen in different parts of the Cherokee nation."[1] All of these signs seemed to indicate divine favor over their endeavors. Yet the 1820s was not a decade of unmitigated success or optimism for the Cherokee mission. These years also saw a major shift in the government's approach to mission work among American Indians, which would in turn have profound effects on the ways that missionaries approached their work not only in North America, but around the world.

When Elias Cornelius visited the Cherokee in 1817 as an agent of the Board, he assured the chiefs with whom he met that the Board would only send "good men" to them, and that they would "never seek to deprive them of any of their lands."[2] From the beginning, then, the mission had operated against a background of American incursions on Cherokee soil. So long as the relationship of the U.S. government with the Cherokees seemed defined by the Civilization Fund, the Board's supporters felt that they could make such a commitment to the Indians. This approach, further, seemed to be successful not only in bringing civilization to the Cherokees but in uniting the interests of the Indians with white Americans. For example, Cornelius informed his readers that Slafecha Barnett, a Creek Indian, had been quoted in a Georgia paper at the time as telling his countrymen that "God made us all both red and white Americans, to live in one Island," and that it was God's will that "we should live together." In the passage Cornelius quoted, Barnett went on to criticize the earlier connections between the Creeks and the British against the Americans; it was to the United States, instead, that the Indians' interests were aligned, he said. Barnett's statement seemed proof to Cornelius of the importance of sending mission schools to the Indians, for it was through this kind of connection that the Indians could be assimilated and come to find their interests united with the Americans.[3]

Though the Cherokee mission had begun in a relationship of cooperation between the American Board and the federal government, the changing government relationship to the Cherokee would come to demand a dramatic response on the part of the missionaries and the Board. The state of Georgia's refusal to recognize Cherokee sovereignty and the Jackson administration's pursuit of Indian removal met firm opposition from the mission and its supporters. Over the late 1820s and into the 1830s, the missionaries and the Board came to be among the most vocal opponents of removal. The abandonment of the civilization program, and the denial of what the Board had considered promises to the Cherokee who had become civilized, led the Board to reconsider the proper relationship of missions to the federal government. The crisis of Indian removal resulted in a sharp missionary critique of this style of American imperialism.

The debates around Indian removal brought the missionaries into American politics to an unprecedented extent. While missionaries and their supporters had earlier been content to assert their own role as the embodiment of American values and culture abroad, they now had to face the realization that they represented only one of many American cultures, and that other groups of Americans disagreed with them profoundly. At first, this brought the Board into a new position as a major opponent of government policy. Led by Jeremiah Evarts and Samuel A. Worcester, the Board publicly opposed removal and organized petition campaigns both within the Cherokee Nation and among American citizens against it. These were ineffective, as was the Supreme Court case that the missionaries eventually brought against the state of Georgia. The missionaries' foray into federal politics left them scarred. Here, in a most dramatic fashion, they contended for their vision of American relations with the outside world. They had been fighting for their vision of Christians imperialism and of a global America that was interested in the religious and moral state of foreign peoples. This vision was ultimately challenged by a continental one that saw the destiny of America in westward expansion and the seizure of native lands.

From Civilization to Removal

When the Board established its mission among the Cherokee, there was an easy agreement between their settler-style mission and the government's policy of civilization toward Native Americans. Both had a goal of assimilating others into American norms, although the missions emphasized religious themes more heavily than the government did. The expectation of those missionaries and their assistants was that the Cherokee would eventually alter their lifestyles and beliefs on seeing the superiority of the American style. Before the removal crisis, these missionary settlements seemed to be ideal from the perspective of the Board. This was what it looked like when a Christian government acted as it ought toward foreign peoples. By supporting the missions, the Board felt, the United States was doing what the British should have been doing in India: they were joining their national power with religious duty, using their superiority and authority to bring about changes that would have positive effects not only on the temporal, but also on the spiritual, lives of others. The removal crisis would challenge this understanding of how the United States related to its colonial subjects, for this was how the government soon came to see the American Indians.

In the early writings of both Board members and government officials, there was an expectation that the mission could help to create not only Christians but "citizens," and that the uneasy relationship that existed between local whites and the Cherokees could only be repaired through the elevation of the latter to the ranks of the civilized. The precise meaning of this citizenship was not defined by either missionaries or government officials, though both used the term. At the very least, they were referring to an informal participation in civic life, though at times both groups seemed to be pointing toward something more formal. This was why one visitor to Blackburn's mission could describe the Cherokee as necessarily becoming a "branch of the Union" in the near future. Meigs, too, felt that the Cherokee would eventually become "a valuable part of our extensive population." Calhoun, for his part, talked of the value of civilizing to be the preparation "for a complete extension of our laws and authority over them [the Cherokees]." All of these observers seemed to have been imagining a future time when the Cherokees would be civilized, assimilated into American social and perhaps even political life, and stripped of their Cherokee identity.[4]

Not everyone shared this vision of a future incorporation of the Cherokee into American life. Competing with civilization as a federal policy was the idea of Indian removal. These were two sides of the same coin, and had been so since the administration of George Washington. Government officials assumed that if Native Americans would not choose to become civilized and to assimilate to American norms, they would need to be removed from their ancestral lands to make room for white American expansion. By the late 1820s, Indian removal was becoming much more popular among many American voters eager to settle the land currently occupied by native groups. The position of civilization was becoming less politically tenable over the course of the decade, even as the missionaries and their supporters embraced it.

Expand the empire

The debates between these two groups of Americans over civilization or removal would become most heated in the areas where the Cherokee lived. As Cyrus Kingsbury noticed on his travels through Tennessee and Georgia, local whites were frustrated by the federal commitment to civilization in the years after the War of 1812. Conflicts over land titles and frustration about money paid to the Cherokee for damage to their property by the American army led many of the whites Kingsbury met to feel hostile to the presence of the Cherokees and to the project of Indian civilization. They wanted the federal government to rid the region of the Cherokees and other native groups, and to open their land for white cultivation.[5] The Board was well aware of this situation. Indeed, when the missionaries first established their Cherokee mission, they also established an Arkansas mission for those Cherokee and Choctaw who had voluntarily moved west in the 1810s in response to government incentives. By the time the missionaries arrived in the Cherokee Nation, there had already been years of negotiations between the United States and Cherokee governments about the land and who had the right to live on it. The decade between the missionary

They had to
pick a side.

arrival in the Cherokee Nation and the passage of the Indian Removal
Act was marked by continued attempts by the American government to
encourage migration, and by many others within the Cherokee Nation to
assert their sovereignty over their own land.

It was not long before the missionaries were brought into the middle
of these conflicts. When the Cherokee National Council sent delegates to
Washington, DC, to address government officials in February 1819 about
the policy of removal to Arkansas, they requested that a representative of
the mission accompany them. Samuel Worcester did so, taking part in the
discussions about the position of the Cherokee and their desire to remain
where they were. He reported that the delegates' argument focused on the
theme of civilization. In the East, the Cherokees argued, they had "begun
to cultivate the land, and made considerable advances in civilizing arts," and
had a system of education, while removal would take them to "a boundless
wilderness, where everything would invite and impel them to revert to the
hunting, and wandering and savage life," in spite of the "prevalent" desire
for civilization and improvement across the nation. In other words, the
Cherokee were adopting the same language used by the missionaries and
by the supporters of the government's civilization policy as they explained
why they had the right to remain on their own land.[6]

At issue in 1819 were the relative definitions of land ownership among
the Cherokee and the Americans. The aspects of the treaty under discussion that seemed like a compromise to Americans—the provision for some
to remain in the East while those who did not want to assimilate moved
West—were entirely problematic for the Cherokee. Aside from the fact that
those who did not want to assimilate did not necessarily want to abandon
their homeland, the way that Americans understood land use to work was
very different from the Cherokee, which became clear in this treaty. For each
household that moved West, a certain number of acres would be ceded to the
United States, raising complications for both groups in terms of the borders
of the Cherokee Nation. Because the Cherokee did not hold land privately,
but communally, they disagreed with the central premise that in moving
west, Cherokee families could give up "their" portion of the Cherokee land.

Big Culture
Clash

＊

With Worcester in Washington, the missionaries found themselves
brought into the middle of these political negotiations. Arguments about
the legality and practicality of land exchange for removal would continue
between the Cherokee and American governments for the next decade,
but in 1819, as a sign of good faith the Cherokee were prepared to cede
4 million acres in exchange for the creation of a permanent school fund,

They liked it because they wanted them to become civilized. [handwritten margin note]

with proceeds from the land sale going to the creation of schools for Cherokee education. For his part, Worcester found this to be "auspicious," as it revealed a government that had "not only a favorable disposition towards the Indians, but also a conviction that they can be, and must be, civilized." This interpretation of the treaty was likely not shared by the bulk of the Cherokee Nation, but it does reveal a great deal about the Board's perceptions of Indian policy and their position on the issue of the connection between the political and the missionary.[7]

Did not hold up their bargin [handwritten margin note]

The optimism of the Cherokee about the school fund was not to be rewarded. Even after the Cherokee transferred their land to the United States, the American government did not set up a school fund, and no money was ever exchanged to benefit Cherokee education or any other purpose. This was a clear indication of what was to come. The missionaries' involvement at this point was marked by optimism about their government's commitment to their cause. Based on the funding that the missions received from the government and the positive correspondence they held with certain government officials, the Board was sure that their commitment to civilization and Christianization as a national project was shared.[8]

The election of Andrew Jackson in 1828 profoundly shifted the tone of Cherokee relations to the United States. Jackson had, since his negotiations with the Cherokees in 1817 after the War of 1812, been a vocal proponent of Indian removal. The Board, on the other hand, was at the fore of the attacks on this policy by groups throughout the North that argued that removal violated Indians' treaty rights, and was a partisan policy that was attempting to placate the South at the cost of national honor. Removal also had very real impacts on the Board's ability to evangelize within North America. Jackson's move away from the earlier policy of civilization can be seen in the cuts to the Board's appropriations for Indian education from 1830 forward. To justify this shift, Jackson explained that his interpretation of the law was that the Civilization Fund only required work west of the Mississippi to be supported by the federal government. Civilizing Native Americans to the east of the Mississippi was simply not a priority.[9]

Importantly, the Board and its missionaries were not uniformly opposed to Indian removal. Jedidiah Morse, for example, had advocated removal after his 1820 tour of the Indian tribes in North America. Morse and others thought that removal and what they termed "colonization" would allow some Native American groups, particularly smaller ones from the Northeast, to protect themselves from being overtaken by whites and establish towns where they could become civilized.[10] Removal, in this framework,

It was best to remove them.

was supposed to be benevolent in the same way that the colonization movement at the time discussed the removal of African Americans from the
United States. Nonwhites, in both cases, could not be expected to thrive
among white American settlement, and so should go to a separate place
where they might be able to make lives for themselves.

The Cherokee, though, seemed to be a different case for the Board. The
reason for this special status of the Cherokees in the minds of the Board, and
indeed many of those opposed to removal throughout the country, was the
success they seemed to have had in becoming civilized. The experience of
the Cherokee missionaries belied the argument that American Indians could
not assimilate. In addition to missionary reports of success in education and
Christianization, by the 1820s, the creation of Sequoya's Syllabary was a
celebrated development that made it possible for the Cherokee language to
become a written language. Because literacy was such an important part of
the definition of civilization, this was an important step in Cherokee history
as viewed by white Americans. Within a few short years, the literacy rates
in the nation expanded exponentially.[11] In addition, the Cherokee Nation
was becoming a republic, and one modeled on the United States. From the
series of laws passed earlier in the decade, the nation had progressed to the
creation of a formal written constitution, signed on July 4, 1827. The Board
saw this as a sign of great progress and described the constitution as being
"on the most approved model among civilized nations."[12]

even written language

While many hailed this as a clear sign of the progress of the Cherokees
toward civilization, officials in Georgia were incensed by these claims of
tribal sovereignty within their state boundaries. The state of Georgia had
for years been engaged in a struggle with the Cherokee over the territory
that both claimed to be within their legal boundaries. In 1802, Georgia
had ceded her western land claims to the United States in exchange for a
promise that the federal government would extinguish Indian titles to land
within the chartered limits of the state. As president, Jefferson had promised
to convince the Indians to leave the area that was within the chartered
limits of Georgia, and by the late 1820s, the people of Georgia were tired
of waiting. In 1819, the state demanded the complete extinction of Cherokee title to land within the chartered boundaries of Georgia, but to no
avail. The Cherokee Constitution, with its assertion of sovereignty over the
contested land, seemed to be the final straw pushing the state to pass a resolution declaring its own jurisdiction over the land in December 1827. The
Georgians had been waiting for President John Quincy Adams to denounce
the Cherokee Constitution; Adams eventually declared that it would not

change the relationship between the U.S. government and the Cherokees. In response, the Georgia legislature required all white residents of the Cherokee territory to declare their allegiance to the state government and its laws by 1830, under threat of arrest. The implications for the missionaries became clearer the next year, when the state legislature responded to the election of Andrew Jackson by declaring that all state laws extended over the Cherokee territory.[13] While the Board and its missionaries had earlier been connected with the federal government, it was this law that fully brought them into American politics.

At first, the correspondence of the Cherokee missionaries was unchanged in the lead up to and the aftermath of this law. From his position in Boston, the Board's corresponding secretary David Green had advised the missionaries to avoid taking a "partisan" stance in spite of the deep feelings that both the Indians and the missionaries had on the subject of removal.[14] The missionaries' letters continued to focus on the progress of the schools, the membership in the churches, and the erection of new buildings. Gradually, however, more and more of their letters came to focus on the state of the Cherokees, their opposition to removal, and what the missionaries called the "oppressive measures of Georgia." Soon the missionary correspondence was almost entirely political, with only brief passages mentioning mission operations.[15] Samuel A. Worcester, the most outspoken of the missionaries, went so far as to include a discussion of the relative rights of the states and the federal government under the Articles of Confederation and the Constitution in his correspondence with the Board.[16]

In late December 1830, the Board missionaries met with a group of Moravian missionaries to the Cherokees to prepare a statement in support of the Cherokees against Georgia. Worcester reported that "perfect unanimity prevailed" at the meeting, which was to be the most bold and direct statement of missionary politics yet. While Worcester had at first felt some "hesitancy in regard to the expediency of *speaking out*," he reported that no one else had. The missionaries in both groups were united in their sense that "justice and truth" were on their side. In making their arguments, the missionaries spoke on behalf of the Cherokee. They argued that the Georgia laws were unconstitutional, and that they went against the treaties previously existing between the United States and the Cherokee Nation. Though the missionaries were guided by their faith, their arguments focused on these secular and political issues.[17]

As the missionaries living among the Cherokees were entering into political activism out of what they saw as a moral imperative, so too were the members of the Board in New England. Board leaders in Boston were convinced that Indian removal was the central political issue of the age, and that it was their duty to raise public consciousness about it and to defend the rights of the Indians. They corresponded with Senator Theodore Frelinghuysen of New Jersey, a former director of the Board, about the situation in Georgia. One of his letters described this situation as "one of the most embarrassing and difficult, that has ever been presented." When the federal government began seriously considering an Indian Removal Bill that would force the involuntary removal of Native Americans from the land east of the Mississippi, the Board prepared memorials for Congress opposing it.[18]

Jeremiah Evarts in particular, former editor of the *Panoplist* and *Missionary Herald*, former treasurer of the Board, and by 1829, one of its corresponding secretaries, came to take a prominent role in the national anti-removal campaign. In that year, he visited Washington, DC, on the Board's behalf to discuss the condition of the Indians and the missionaries' success among them with the Committee on Indian Affairs and the secretary of war. Evarts also became the instigator of petition campaigns against removal and wrote a series of essays titled "On the Present Crisis in the Condition of the American Indian," under the pseudonym William Penn.[19] Like the missionaries, he claimed to be motivated by religious and moral feelings instead of partisanship. Despite his assertions that he was not focused on politics, the argumentation he adopted was explicitly political, with an emphasis on the treaty history between the United States and Indian tribes and the international ramifications of unjust behavior by the United States. Only in the twenty-second of twenty-four letters does Evarts turn his focus to the morality of the laws, asking whether "the reasoning or the morality" of the law was more remarkable. The minds of benevolent Americans, he argued, were united against Indian removal. Evarts insisted that information was needed by the mass of Americans to be able to understand the situation, and that this was an eminently important issue for the nation, which would ultimately be judged both "by the whole civilized world," as well as by "the Great Arbiter of Nations."[20]

Evarts took on this leadership in the anti-removal movement while continuing his duties for the Board, furthering the sense of a link between the Board and political activism on this issue. Speaking on behalf of the "friends of the Indians," Evarts outlined the actions that he thought the Cherokee should take, and in so doing, he continued a major shift in the understanding of the proper relationship between the missionaries and politics. Not only did Evarts travel to Washington to speak in defense of the work that his missionaries were doing among the Cherokees, he also advised the Cherokee leadership on the course that they should take in dealing with the U.S. government. First, he wrote, they ought to prepare a petition that would detail the land that the Cherokee owned and had not ceded. Evarts went so far as to outline the arguments that they ought to take in this petition. He also encouraged the Cherokees to send a deputation to Washington that should insist on being heard before the Committee on Indian Affairs. If they did not find success in Congress, he wrote, they ought then to bring suit in front of the Supreme Court.[21] By 1830, Evarts was writing regularly to Worcester about Indian rights, proposing speeches, commenting on the progress of treaties, and suggesting that Worcester write a statement of facts about the Cherokees for publication. Although he told Worcester not to advise the Cherokees on their political activities, he encouraged him to "at their request" review their petitions to "see that the words are right to express their meaning." The lines between missionary labor and political activism were blurry throughout this crisis.[22]

The Moral Politics of the Cherokee Mission

The missionaries and the Board were thus becoming remarkably more directly involved in politics than ever before. The passage of the 1830 Georgia laws made staying out of politics no longer an option. When the state required an oath of allegiance from all white residents in the Cherokee Nation, the missionaries were forced to take a political action, either in support of Georgia's attempts to gain sovereignty over the land and people of that territory, or against it. The Board interpreted the law as the state's attempt to rid the region of missionaries who had been such vocal opponents of removal. Whether it was specifically aimed at missionaries or not, they were the only white men who would eventually be arrested under the new regulations.[23]

The missionaries did not feel that they could sign the oath of allegiance, because doing so would be to grant the jurisdiction of the state of Georgia over lands that they knew to be within the domain of the Cherokee Nation. It was a moral as much as a political issue, and they would not sign. Explaining his decision to the governor, Elizur Butler wrote that he was governed by his conscience. "My principles of action are founded on the word of God," he expanded, "and if adhering to the 'law and the testimony,' and endeavoring to follow the examples of Holy Writ, my conduct be construed into an undefinable interference with political transaction, I cannot help it. I cannot change my religious views or general religious conduct with the various political changes of the time." At issue here, Butler insisted, was a contest between his "religious views" and mere "exigences [*sic*] of political affairs," and before Butler would compromise the former, he would "sacrifice [his] life." The Prudential Committee in Boston fully supported them in this, and Jeremiah Evarts in his correspondence with the missionaries indeed depicted it as impossible that any of the Board's missionaries could sign such an oath. He and the rest of the Prudential Committee vowed to support the missionaries even if they were arrested for refusing to comply.[24] *Federal funding*

The missionaries did not want to be arrested, however, and so they tried to use their links to the federal government as protection against that of the state. Initially, the missionaries' argued that they were in the Cherokee Nation "under the sanction and protection of the U.S. Government," since the ABCFM had received funding from the federal government for their missions. Earlier in Butler's letter to the governor, he claimed that the "sole object" of his residence among the Cherokee was "to assist the Government of the United States in promoting the civilization and Christianization of the Cherokees." This was, to say the least, disingenuous. In his application to serve as a missionary, Butler had written about his calling to be "employed wholly in the service of Christ." It was the sense of "the perishing of new of millions of heathen" that brought him to mission work, not service of the government. Up until this point, however, Butler and the Board had felt it possible to combine these two goals. It was only when the government changed its course that the missionaries had to really think about their relationship to politics and, indeed, to national identity. The missionaries certainly did not really believe that they were agents of the government. Yet their claims reveal a certain amount of wishful thinking. They did think that their goals coincided with those of the federal government, and they thought that this was as it should be.

The Georgia courts initially accepted the argument that the missionaries were "authorized agents" of the U.S. government. Worcester, as postmaster of New Echota, had an even more secure position as a government agent who was not subject to the Georgia law. In response to this decision of the state court, officials in Georgia soon petitioned the president to learn whether he in fact considered the missionaries to be agents of the federal government. Unsurprisingly, Jackson said they were not. Worcester was removed from his position as postmaster. The missionaries would again be liable for arrest.[25]

Since none of the Board missionaries in Georgia signed the oath, they were left with two options for how to proceed. They could remain where they were and be arrested and imprisoned, or they could leave their stations to take up residence at one of the Board's stations in Tennessee instead. The Board left this up to the individual missionary's discretion. Some, including William Thompson, Daniel Butrick and Isaac Proctor, felt that it was "inexpedient to expose [themselves] to the penalty of the law," and so moved to missionary stations outside of Georgia.[26] Two of the Board's other missionaries, Samuel A. Worcester and Elizur Butler, ultimately decided to remain and challenge the law directly. Worcester asserted that he felt it was his duty to "remain and quietly pursue my labors for the spiritual welfare of the Cherokee people, until I am forcibly removed."[27] Worcester was arrested in July. Now that he was no longer postmaster of New Echota and the president refused to acknowledge the Board missionaries as government agents, the missionaries had no defenses. The only course of action was to challenge the authority of Georgia directly.

The Cherokee Nation itself had already tried to challenge Georgia's claims over its land in the U.S. Supreme Court case *Cherokee Nation v. Georgia*. Indeed, after they had been unsuccessful in their efforts in Congress, they had done so at the recommendation of Jeremiah Evarts and others. The case sought an injunction against the state of Georgia to prevent it from passing further laws that would infringe on the rights of the Cherokee. Relying on the long history of treaties between the United States and Indian nations, the lawyers for the Cherokee Nation insisted that the court recognize that the Cherokee possessed sovereignty over its own land and people. The court, however, did not agree with this assertion. Nor did the court grant that the Cherokee had no independence from Georgia's laws. Instead, Justice John Marshall defined the Cherokee as a "domestic dependent nation" in a state of "pupilage" toward the United States. Marshall's decision rejected the argument of the Cherokees on the grounds that since it was not a foreign state, it had had no standing to bring suit against Georgia.[28] In light of this, opponents of Indian removal decided that another test case would be necessary to establish the unconstitutionality of the Georgia laws and the sovereignty of the Cherokee Nation over its territory. The missionaries seemed to be ideal candidates for such a case. Worcester enlisted the help of William Wirt, the Baltimore lawyer who had argued for the

Cherokee in their case, to determine what the conduct of the missionaries ought to be and what the likelihood of their success would be if they brought a case before the Supreme Court. Wirt wrote to Worcester that it was Worcester's decision whether he would effectively martyr himself by choosing "to become the victim by whose sufferings this question is to be raised." The missionaries, then, understood themselves to be setting aside their own self-interest in favor of a decidedly political issue: Cherokee sovereignty.[29] By September 1831, Wirt was sure that if Worcester proceeded according to his instructions, the U.S. Supreme Court would soon strike down the Georgia laws.[30]

Over the summer and early fall of 1831, Worcester prepared for his arrest and imprisonment, writing to the Board about what the best course of action would be and what should happen to his family during his time in jail.[31] On September 15, Worcester, Butler, and nine other men, including some Methodist missionaries, stood trial in Georgia for breaking this law and all were found guilty. The missionaries requested that the *Missionary Herald* and the Boston *Recorder* be sent to them in prison, and they prepared themselves for a lengthy imprisonment. By January 1832, the missionaries and the Board had reached a plan of action: they would appeal the decision of the Georgia court and bring their case to the U.S. Supreme Court. If it decided against them, they would submit to such a decision and appeal to the governor for clemency, satisfied that they had taken a stand on principle, even if they were not successful. This, to the Board, seemed to be the path of duty for the missionaries in the context of the current political climate. They were visited in jail by local ministers who urged them to seek clemency from the governor and to stop pursuing the rights of the Cherokee in court, but they remained firm in their determination to bring their case before the Supreme Court. Some of these visitors, such as Dr. Church, were convinced that the Supreme Court would never decide in the missionaries' favor, but that the issue could soon bring the country to civil war if the court did decide in their favor and if the federal government tried to execute such a decision.[32]

The U.S. Supreme Court heard their case in February 1832. *Worcester v. Georgia* considered the constitutionality of the Georgia law, and this time reached a different decision about the status of the Cherokee Nation. Because the plaintiff was a U.S. citizen who was challenging the constitutionality of a state law, the court could consider the case. Now the court, again led by Chief Justice Marshall, proclaimed that the Cherokee were "a distinct community occupying its own territory in which the laws of Georgia can have no force." It was the federal government, and not the states, that could regulate relations with the Cherokees, and so the Georgia laws were voided. Marshall ordered the state to reverse its conviction of the missionaries and release them from prison.[33] The Board's entry into politics thus seemed vindicated, since the Supreme Court decided in their favor.

This vindication was short lived, however. It very quickly became clear to observers that whatever the opinion of the court, the authorities in Georgia would not enforce the decision. It was in response to this case that Jackson famously quipped that Marshall had made his decision and now could see about enforcing it. Worcester and Butler remained imprisoned. They hoped to petition the Supreme Court to force the compliance of the state with the decision. Before they could do so, however, the political context in the country shifted, and the Board's supporters began to doubt the propriety of a mission society taking such an explicitly political stance.

The Risks of Political Missions

This shift in public opinion about the mission's opposition to removal came from an unexpected source: the Nullification Crisis. The crisis is well known to students of the American Civil War for its importance in the development of states' rights rhetoric, and its connection to the history of foreign missions should serve as a reminder of the impossibility of separating religion from politics. The crisis began when South Carolinians, displeased with the so-called "tariff of abominations" declared that the state had the right to nullify federal law. The public discussion of these issues happened simultaneously to those about the aftermath of *Worcester v. Georgia*, and the Board's supporters throughout the country noticed that both issues dealt with the question of the relative authority of the federal and state governments. For those who feared that the Nullification Crisis could lead to the fracture of the Union, it appeared that Georgia might come to South Carolina's aid if the federal government attempted to enforce the U.S. Supreme Court's decision about Cherokee sovereignty. By April 1832, evangelicals in Georgia approached the imprisoned missionaries, convinced that if they pushed the case any further, it could lead to civil war. They urged the missionaries to give up and insisted that they could gain their freedom through a pardon from the governor of Georgia if they would only promise not to appeal to the federal government for help in enforcing the decision. One particularly concerned observer wrote to the missionaries that they were at risk of being seen not as "martyrs, if things come to the worst—[but] as political preachers." This was a profound difference. The political actions of

the missionaries would be understood, even celebrated, if they were martyrs; "political preachers," on the other hand, were criticized for stepping
out of their appropriate sphere of action. The missionaries had previously
explained their political involvement as being a moral imperative. By the
mid-1830s they were starting to lose support for this stance.[34]

Letters came to the Board in Boston as well, as prominent Board members such as Stephen Van Rensselaer suggested that the Board had gone far
enough in supporting the case and that the missionaries ought to accept
a pardon. One visitor from Georgia explained more fully the political climate in Georgia and the growing sentiment that the situation in Georgia
was a "common cause" with that in South Carolina and nullification, and
of the resulting importance of diminishing support for South Carolina by
dropping the challenge to removal. The leadership of the Board became
convinced by the end of 1832 that there were pressing "considerations
of a public nature" that called on them to end their case against Georgia,
especially since they were now convinced that even if they were successful,
"Georgia [will] have the triumph at last." In the words of one of their correspondents, it had become clear that appeal to the Supreme Court to take
action in enforcing their earlier decision "*cannot benefit the Indians*. Neither
will the *missionaries benefit by it*." The proper course of action, it appeared,
was to remove themselves from the political fray and try to secure the best
possible outcome for the missionaries and for the Cherokees.[35]

Guided by the summaries of the opinions of the individual members of
the Prudential Committee as well as those ministers who had approached
them in prison, Worcester and Butler ultimately decided to petition the
Georgia governor for release from prison, though not before standing for
several months on the principle that they should not do anything that
would "prevent the effect of the decision of the Supreme Court, in establishing the principles of justice for which we have contended, and protecting the oppressed." They worried what the aftermath of such a course
would be for the authority of the court in political life; if they did not force
the recognition of the decision, then who afterward could "place any reliance on the Supreme Court of the United States for protection against laws
however unconstitutional," they wondered.[36] By December, though, their
concerns for "the peace of the country" outweighed these other worries,
and the missionaries had appealed for a pardon from the governor. They had
become convinced that if they tested the court's authority, they would fail,
and that they could do nothing to prevent the removal of the Cherokees
and the seizure of their lands. They chose to submit and to return to their

work of evangelizing the Cherokees, even as they were forced to migrate westward. In January 1833, they were released from prison.[37]

A large part of the reason for the missionaries' decision to cease their efforts to oppose the Georgia law was the growing sense that such opposition was futile. The missionaries and the Board had become convinced that nothing could be done to prevent the seizure of Cherokee land from surrounding whites. Some of the missionaries began listing reasons why the Cherokee should make a treaty with the United States for their emigration.[38] When the Prudential Committee of the Board held a special meeting in December 1832 to decide how to advise Worcester and Butler to proceed, its members were nearly unanimous in their conviction that the situation had become hopeless, and the Cherokees ought to be convinced to leave their lands and move west. Rufus Anderson, who would come to lead the Board by midcentury and was ever conscious of the importance of separating the work of Christianization from civilization, was particularly emphatic on this point. As a "purely religious question," he found, it was for the better good of the Cherokees that they go, and so the missionaries should urge such a move.[39] The Board's correspondents in Washington had reached similar opinions; Senator Theodore Frelinghuysen wrote the Board's corresponding secretary, Benjamin Wisner, that he was convinced that the Cherokees "will have to remove," as Congress and the president were so far set against them. Although all of these earlier champions of Cherokee rights remained convinced that the tribe retained the right of possession of the land, it now seemed futile. Yet even with this shift in the opinion of their supporters, the Cherokee delegation to Washington in January 1833 refused to back down. Even with the knowledge that the Board had changed its views, the Cherokees refused to make a treaty with the United States.[40]

Support for a treaty was by no means universal among the missionaries. Elizur Butler, for example, doubted that the Cherokees could be expected to trust Indian Affairs officers to protect them in their new location, and Daniel Butrick was an outspoken critic. The return of Butler and Worcester to the Cherokees had produced some mistrust among the Cherokees; Butler reported that while John Ross, a leader of the Cherokee antitreaty party, understood their conduct, some "less informed" Cherokees did not. Butler refused to back out of political matters fully. When Georgians tried to claim the mission property at Haweis and charged rent, he refused to pay and briefly considered challenging the law and bringing a case to the Supreme Court if he was evicted. Butler also wrote about the possibility of

Jackson's impeachment if he refused to uphold Indian treaties. These were not serious plans—he never explained the legal strategy of how he would get such a case to the U.S. Supreme Court—but his enthusiasm for the idea suggests the extent of his frustration at the way things worked out. Through 1834, he was writing to the secretary of war about the missionaries' position in the Cherokee lands "by permission and under the protection of the United States government."[41]

Yet Samuel A. Worcester believed, along with the Board in Boston, that it was now necessary for the Cherokee to reach an agreement with the United States. He was accordingly an active participant in the creation of what would become the controversial New Echota Treaty of 1835.[42] This treaty was the ultimate resolution of the Indian removal crisis and was made between the U.S. government and the so-called Treaty Party within the Cherokee Nation. Led by friends of the mission including Elias Boudinot, the Treaty Party shared the Board's sense that there was no hope for the Cherokee to remain on their ancestral lands. Accordingly, under the treaty they relinquished their lands east of the Mississippi River in exchange for provisions in the West. Sixteen thousand of the seventeen thousand Cherokees living in the East objected to this treaty, and yet it was ratified and upheld by the United States. The treaty provided for two years preparation for removal, after which point the Cherokees were forcibly removed from their ancestral lands in what has been known as the Trail of Tears.[43] Board missionaries followed them to their new homes west of the Mississippi, though many of the Cherokees had lost faith in the missionaries after the involvement of the Board in the treaty.[44]

Worcester and Butler are the usual faces of the Board's relation to the politics of Cherokee removal, as their outspoken opposition to removal and arrest drew attention to the cause. Yet theirs is not the only missionary story of the removal era. Daniel Butrick, another of the Cherokee missionaries, took a different course during the removal crisis. The contrast between his story and that of Worcester and Butler highlights the difficulties that the Board faced during this time when it became clear that their vision of Christian imperialism would not survive. Unlike his colleagues, Butrick decided that it was not his duty to challenge the laws of Georgia in pursuit of his missionary work. Instead, he withdrew from his mission station when forced out by the Georgia Guard and relocated it within the boundaries of Tennessee. As a missionary, he felt, his duty lay only in bringing the Gospel and education, not in political interference. From 1829, Butrick was, like the other missionaries, focused on political issues, but his stance was more removed. He enclosed in a letter to the Board, for example, the "Memorial of the Cherokees" from December 1829 that was published in the *Phoenix*. This Memorial to the U.S. Congress included a history of U.S.-Cherokee relations and a list of grievances, including the issues with Georgia. In it, the Cherokees appealed to Congress after the refusal of the president and the secretary of war to provide protection against Georgia. Echoing the arguments in the William Penn essays, they explained that through the right of inheritance and through treaties, the Cherokees had the right to the land in question.[45] "Whether they are to be speedily removed or to continue here a few years longer," he wrote, "we cannot tell. God knows, and he will let us know as soon as it shall be necessary." Unlike Evarts, Worcester, and others, Butrick believed that the missionaries could not do anything either "to retard or hasten their removal." He trusted that if the U.S. government removed them, it would continue to support their education in the West by funding the missionaries.[46]

While Worcester and Butler were in prison, Butrick continued to work among the Cherokees, some of whom traveled from Georgia to his new location just over the border in Tennessee, and he eventually became distressed by the tone of the Board's public approval of the imprisoned missionaries. In 1833, he wrote a letter to the Board that he described as "self-justification" in the face of what he had taken as the lack of support from the Board of his course of action. In particular, he was upset by the coverage of the issue in the *Missionary Herald*. The *Herald* had reprinted a letter from Butler, for example, which had described any attempts to escape imprisonment as cowardice and idolatry. The secretary of the ABCFM denied that the American had actually censured the missionaries' behavior as Butrick had interpreted.[47] Butrick insisted that it was not a part of a missionary's duties to defend the "temporal and political rights" of his charges, nor to "regulate the conduct of Presidents, governors, judges, &c or to take any part of the responsibilities of civil authorities upon myself." Operating under the assumption that the Board disagreed with him on this point, he insisted that the guide to his conduct was the Bible and not the Board, and that the Prudential Committee could not make him act "contrary to my own sense of duty."[48] In 1840, after the removal controversy had concluded with the Treaty of New Echota and the forced removal of the missionaries from the East, Butrick assembled a summary of the controversy with Georgia for the Board's records, consisting of transcribed letters and Butrick's commentary on the proceedings. What emerges from this document is a sort of manifesto for missionaries to stay out of politics. It is a statement of the dangers of missionaries pushing a vision of Christian imperialism even when the government was unwilling to cooperate. In Butrick's telling of the events of 1833 through 1840, the course that he took is the more successful one. His withdrawal from Georgia allowed for continued work among the Cherokees and prevented the sense of betrayal that many Cherokees came to feel in response to Worcester and Butler's eventual capitulation. In the midst of a very bad political situation, Butrick insisted, the missionaries ought to have remained out of politics.[49]

During the aftermath of *Worcester v. Georgia* and the release of Worcester and Butler from jail, Butrick was eager to contrast the very different states of his mission station to that of Worcester. While Worcester had been celebrated by the Cherokees when he was imprisoned for his defense of their rights, he emerged from jail as a traitor and was met with distrust by the Cherokees. His support of the Treaty of New Echota, and his rumored role in convincing Boudinot and others to make that treaty in the first place, left many Cherokees feeling betrayed. His emigration to Arkansas in 1835 suggested that he felt that all the Cherokee ought to migrate. And this was the story that the Prudential Committee's annual reports told about the entire Cherokee mission in these years. Their reports painted a picture of failure and stagnation in the midst of the removal crisis.

This was not Butrick's experience, however. For him, these years were marked by increasing church and school attendance. His stance against the treaty as "antinational" and "antichristian" won some support from the Cherokees at his station, and he, like Worcester in earlier years, was quick to say that this was not a political stance, but a moral one. Butrick painted the "controversy with Georgia," as he described it, as having been largely created by Worcester's actions and the inappropriate insertion of the Prudential Committee in these politics, and their final backing down from a moral stance for what were clearly political reasons.[50] The lesson from all of this seemed to be that the role of the missionary was not to get involved in politics, but when necessary, to take a moral stance. This is what Butrick thought he had done by refusing to sign his allegiance to the state of Georgia without going so far as to be imprisoned and challenge the laws in the Supreme Court. It is what he thought he had done by opposing the treaty and waiting for the mass of Cherokees to decide for themselves what steps they ought to take in relation to the question of removal. As the letters from the representatives of the Board to Butrick in the late 1830s suggests, they too had come to feel cautious about taking too political a position in relation to the Cherokee. The experiences of the Cherokee missionaries through two decades had left the Board struggling with the question of how to connect themselves with, or remain aloof from, secular governments.

To a degree unheard of in any of their other missions, the Board had been cooperating with a colonial governing power at these stations among the Cherokee. As their criticism of the British Empire's reluctance to aid mission work reveals, this was precisely the sort of relationship that the Board thought governments and missions ought to have. They certainly would have liked to have governments around the world act in a manner that they considered Christian, supporting evangelization efforts among the "heathen." The reason that the missionaries became as politically engaged as they did during the removal crisis was precisely because it was a contest over the role of their government and nation conducted on a continental and even a global stage.[51]

As had been the case in India, it was the extension of imperial authority that gave the missionaries access to the "heathen" they hoped to convert, but the position of the United States here was different from that of the East India Company in Bombay. The extension of American settlements into Cherokee territory defined the relationship of the two nations; over the course of the period that the Board missionaries worked with the Cherokees, that relationship became increasingly antagonistic. As American citizens and Cherokee missionaries, the priorities of the missionaries were tested and they found their religious work marked by the political context in which they worked. With the election of Jackson and the shift to a more vigorous removal policy, the Board missionaries found themselves placed at the nexus of one of the most controversial political issues of the day, and both the Board and the majority of the missionaries threw themselves into the political fray.

In political activism, the Board had to balance its interest in the moral standing of the country and that of their mission. They were against Cherokee removal because they supported Cherokee sovereignty and the treaty rights of the tribe. They were, further, proud of the progress that the Cherokees had made under the civilization program and saw this as a better governmental policy more in line with their vision of Christian imperialism. The Board felt that the Cherokee deserved to remain where they were and should not be relocated to a place that might encourage them to revert to "heathenish" behaviors. Only after leading a petition campaign and challenging the authority of Georgia in the Supreme Court did the Board and the majority of its missionaries recognize that the tide of white southerners was irrepressible, and that the case of the Cherokees was hopeless. This decision was made in large part as a result of concerns about the stability of the Union in the context of the Nullification Crisis. At that point, the Board abandoned its earlier arguments on principle and urged the Cherokees to retreat and get the best deal that they could. This turnabout was seen as a major betrayal by many in the Cherokee Nation, damaging the credibility of the mission project. The counterexample of Daniel Butrick, who had avoided arrest in Georgia and attempted to stay out of politics during this time, pointed to the possibilities for the missionaries to have continued success in evangelization by avoiding political conflict through retreat.

Indian removal represented a major transition in the history of American Indian policy; it also represented a major shift in the ways that American missionaries viewed government cooperation. In the aftermath of this contest over the way that the United States would act as an imperial power, the Board lost its hope for a benevolent American empire. If the early republic was a period marked by a debate about what the role of the United States would be within the world, the failure of the opposition to Cherokee removal marked a victory for a continental vision of American empire, as well as a failure of the mission movement's vision of a global Christian imperialism. Unable to rally sufficient support for their alternate vision of the United States, the Board would gradually shift its approach, at home and abroad, over the next decade.

Chapter 6

Missionaries and Colonies

In 1839, the American Board received an unusual letter from one of its missionaries. John Leighton Wilson had decided that the time had come to close his mission and move out of Liberia. Wilson had begun the Board's mission to Cape Palmas in Liberia less than a decade before. Up to this point, none of the Board's missions had been closed. Even when Indian removal forced the Cherokee off of their land, the missionaries followed them, and the missions continued. Missions were not supposed to close until the population had become Christianized and churches were able to continue under local leadership. This had not happened in Liberia; instead, conflicts between the mission and the colonial government in Cape Palmas led Wilson to this decision.

Like most of the Board's missions, the one in Cape Palmas was located on land governed by an imperial power. Just as they had done elsewhere, missionaries negotiated with a colonial government over their relationship with, and access to, native populations. The Christian imperialism of the missionaries had frequently drawn missionaries into debates about the proper role of Anglo-Americans in foreign spaces. Around the world, the Board had confronted difficulties when missions and governments differed in their ideas about what their goals ought to be. Wilson understood his work in this global context. His letters would compare his mission to other missions of the Board and the American colonial presence in Liberia with other colonization schemes around the world, including the European colonization of South Africa. What he saw in Liberia did not strike him as divergent from that history, and it was this that led him to want to close his mission.

Wilson summarized the "history of colonization in every other age of the world" as one marked "at every step by oppression and bloodshed." Wilson's writings would be some of the most anticolonial that the Board's missionaries yet produced, even as he continued to think with the framework of Christian imperialism. He insisted that missionaries' greatest concern was with those whom colonial governments oppressed. It was to them that the missionaries wanted to bring the Gospel, and it was with them that the missionaries ought to stand in solidarity. If colonial governments failed to help native peoples, then those colonial governments ought to be resisted. Such a strong anti-imperial stance sounds odd coming out of one of the Board missionaries. After all, the Board could hardly have been considered anti-imperial before this point. Whatever its conflicts with empires in particular times and places, the Board had never consistently opposed imperialism as such. The mission movement itself depended on imperialism and espoused a particular vision of how imperialism ought to work.

Wilson's experience in Liberia was different than what missionaries in India had faced. In Liberia, the colonists were Americans, not British. Of course, the Board had encountered American imperialism before. The experience with the Cherokees was profoundly important for the missionaries in Liberia. Cherokee removal shaped their interpretation of what they saw in West Africa, as well as how they related to the colonial government in Cape Palmas. In contrast to the Cherokee experience, the Board was not dealing with the U.S. government. Instead, its missionaries encountered the Maryland Colonization Society, an American voluntary society that had purchased land in West Africa for the settlement of former slaves and free blacks from the United States. The Colonization Society shared many of the goals of the Board, including bearing civilization to Africa, but this did not prevent Wilson from critiquing it for failing to meet his standard of Christian imperialism. If anything, it increased his frustration. In West Africa, the Board missionaries again worked to embody their ideal of the American presence overseas, civilizing and Christianizing in turn. The conflicts that emerged here were more fraught than elsewhere on the Board's map, though, for when the Board confronted the question of what an American presence ought to look like in Liberia, it was arguing with other Americans.

It had taken Wilson almost a decade to reach his opposition to the American colony in Cape Palmas. Like the Board, he had at first believed that the Colonization Society might be a perfect partner for a missionary organization. Here was a group that seemed to seek the same kind of Christian imperialism that animated the Board. In practice, however, the groups found that they had different ideas of what the relationship between America and Africa ought to be. Both groups claimed that their goals included the Christianization and the civilization of Africa, but they had very different ideas about the way that this should be done and the prioritization of these and other goals. Ultimately, the missionaries would abandon Liberia in favor of a new mission station that was far from any colonial power, American or European.

For modern readers, who have been trained to think of the American imperial age as beginning at the very end of the nineteenth century, the American experience in Liberia has seemed to be an exception: a foreign solution to the domestic problem of slavery, not an imperialist movement. Yet thinking about this story from the perspective of those Americans in Africa, rather than from those in the United States, reveals the ways in which Liberia was not so different from other settler colonies. The history of the Liberian mission and its conflicts with the Cape Palmas government reveals the range of opinions that Americans held about American imperialism in the early nineteenth century.

Colonization and Missions

The colonization of Liberia by African Americans was the realization of long-held goals by a group of American reformers who had searched for a way to end slavery in the United States without having to incorporate free blacks into the population. Shortly after the Revolution, some Americans began talking about the possibility of colonizing free African Americans somewhere outside of the United States. For some of these early proponents, one of the major reasons for supporting the colonization of Africa by free African Americans had to do with religion. Samuel Hopkins and Ezra Stiles, both New England ministers in the 1770s, approached Massachusetts and Connecticut churches with a proposal to send the Gospel to Africa through educated and pious Christian African Americans. Hopkins and Stiles were motivated by their concern about the poor conditions of blacks in America. They imagined that immigrating to Africa, which they described in terms of a "return" even though the vast majority of those who would settle in Liberia had been born in the United States, would improve the lives of these African Americans. In turn, the settlers would help Africans by spreading Christianity and civilization. Though many colonizationists were motivated more by fears about blacks in America than by concerns for the spiritual welfare of Africa, these sorts of arguments remained important. For evangelical Protestants in New England, these religious claims about colonization were quite convincing.[1]

In 1816, many of those interested in colonization formed the American Colonization Society (ACS) in order to open a colony of African Americans in Liberia, some two hundred miles south of the British settlement at Sierra Leone. Politicians numbered among the members of the ACS, and one of these, Charles Fenton Mercer, used his position in the House of Representatives to push through legislation in 1819 that provided federal support for colonization. The stated goals of Mercer's Slave Trade Act were to aid in the prevention of the Atlantic slave trade. Effectively, the act gave the president the ability to buy land in Africa and move African Americans onto that land. Until the Jackson administration, the federal government was a major financial sponsor of the ACS's work under the provisions of this law.[2] The ACS first acquired land in Liberia in 1821, and African American colonists began arriving shortly after. The first colonists were free blacks from the South, though by the mid-1830s, when the Board began its mission there, most colonists were manumitted slaves who gained their freedom on the condition of their removal to Africa.[3]

Supporters of the Colonization Society came from a range of backgrounds and were motivated by multiple interests, but all were concerned about race relations in the United States. As colonizationists urged former slaves and freemen to "return" to Africa, they claimed to be providing for the gradual end of slavery in America while removing the troublesome dynamics of a multiracial society. For some colonizationists, those dynamics included the potential for race war if free blacks were allowed to live side by side with free whites. Some also worried that the presence of free blacks living near enslaved women and men would lead to uprisings against the white population. Colonization accordingly seemed to be a way to avoid violence, and perhaps even to protect slavery where it existed.

Other colonizationists focused on a different kind of dynamic. For them, slavery needed to end. In the 1820s, benevolent-minded New Englanders saw colonization as an appropriate method for dealing with the problems of slavery and race in America. It seemed to be a legitimate way to end slavery while causing the least possible disruption within the United States. Especially in the years before 1831, when William Lloyd Garrison repudiated colonization as a racist movement and instead endorsed immediate abolitionism, efforts for the removal of free blacks and emancipated slaves to a colony outside of the boundaries of the United States were widely supported among white reform circles.[4] African Americans had long voiced similar critiques of colonization. Yet even among those who recognized the problems of claiming that whites and blacks could not live safely and productively together in the United States, the racism of the United States seemed impossible to overcome.

For these colonizationists, it seemed hopeless that African Americans could ever achieve equality or respect within the United States. Only in Africa, this reasoning went, could African American men be seen as "men."[5] The colonizers were likened to, and depicted themselves as, "latter-day Pilgrims," and the American colony in Liberia was likened to Jamestown and Plymouth. Only in a foreign context, it seemed, could African Americans become fully American. For colonists, Liberia offered a chance to start again in a place without color prejudice (though not, as they would discover, without conflict between colonists and officers of the Colonization Society or between black colonists and native Africans). For supporters of colonization, it provided a convenient means of removing a major challenge to the idea of America as a land of equality and opportunity, as well as a population that some feared could be dangerous. This is the central irony of the colonization movement: it demanded the removal of African Americans from the United States because of the dangers they supposedly posed to American society, even as those colonizers were to act as the bearers of American civilization to a benighted Africa. The apparent contradiction that this population who supposedly could not participate in American republican society would, once in Africa, become the bearers of that very culture seems to have been lost on many contemporaries.[6]

As the Colonization Society imagined the relationship between its colony and Africa, it emphasized the ways that the colonists would be able to help Africans by providing a model of American civilization. Accordingly, in addition to the benefits to the United States and colonists, colonization supporters could point to its supposed benefits to Africa. Colonists would bring with them the seeds of American culture and civilization, including its political and religious institutions. Through colonization, they claimed, Africa could become civilized. This promise of the "redemption" of Africa through colonization was critical for many colonization supporters and would be extremely attractive to supporters of foreign missions. After all, colonization could theoretically have taken African Americans just about anywhere. Africa was chosen as the proper destination in part for its symbolism as both an ancestral home and as a place that Americans were indebted to for the slave trade. African American colonists could bring the benefits of America to Africa, and in so doing, repair some of the damage of slavery. Colonization Society publications emphasized some of these benefits that the colony supposedly provided Africans. The colony officials seemed to have taken these goals to heart. By 1831, the journal reported, Liberians were coming to the colony asking to be made "Americans" with colony protection. Governor Mechlin of Liberia found this to be "the most effectual [means] of civilizing them, for as soon as they consider themselves as subjects of Liberia, they visit us more freely, and by associating with the colonists, insensibly adopt our manners and customs, and gradually, from being ignorant pagans, become civilized and Christians."[7]

It was this type of argument that the American Board found most exciting in the colonization movement. From the time of Colonization Society's founding, the Board was friendly to its project. When the ACS emphasized its work for civilization, it could seem to Board members that the two organizations shared many of the same goals, in addition to a similar perspective on slavery. The Board's periodicals frequently included articles covering the Colonization Society and its work in Liberia. These articles emphasized the ways that colonization worked for the "redemption" of Africa. In 1830, for example, readers of the *Missionary Herald* learned of the "great blessing" that the colony was for Liberia and its people. Through the example of the colonists, the natives were "ashamed to go without clothing as they once did, and to wear their gregrees, to which they ascribe supernatural power; they learn to value time and labor; they are taught to observe week and Sabbath days, and to feel a sense of duty." In other words, they were beginning to look and act more like civilized people, embracing the virtues of industriousness and modesty, and rejecting the religious practices of their ancestors. In addition to this, mission supporters could read about how the colony would be able to help bring a "final stop" to the slave trade, both on the Atlantic and within Africa.[8] For all their enthusiasm about what the Colonization Society was doing in Liberia, missionary supporters did not expect the colony to do all the work of bringing civilization and Christianity to Africa. This would take the dedicated focus of missionaries whose sole priority was working with native Africans.

Mission supporters came to this conclusion because as they came to learn more about the colony, they began to realize that they had different ideas about how to go about the work of "redeeming" Africa. Their main critique of the colony was that for all of the talk about how the colonists would help Africans, in practice most of the colonists' energy was spent on establishing their own homes, farms, and businesses. If the African American colonists were bearers of American civilization, they did so through example, not explicit instruction. Evangelization of native Africans was not a priority of the colony. Early on, the colonists included Baptist, Episcopal, Methodist, Presbyterian, Lutheran, and African Methodist Episcopal ministers, but they generally focused their attentions within the colony itself and did not seem interested in working with native Africans. Lott Carey, for example, was a black Baptist missionary who was one of the first immigrants to Africa. Like many colonists, he hoped to find a place to live in a place without color prejudice. Much of his time in Liberia was consumed by colonial politics, and so his mission came to be mostly oriented toward the colonists themselves, though he did work with some African natives as well. John Pinney, a white Presbyterian missionary, also saw his work consumed by colonial politics once in Liberia. Both men served as colonial officials in addition to their religious roles and found their focus shifting away from conversion.[9]

For those interested in evangelizing to African natives, Carey and Pinney's work was an important first step, but also revealed the limitations of relying on the colony to do the work of converting Africans. The colony's focus would always be on the colony. If the conversion of Africa was the goal, then a new group of Americans was needed to focus purely on evangelization. The Board insisted that the colonists were simply not interested in this work, and that they were too intent on becoming commercially successful both as individuals and as a colony. Even those colonists whom missionaries thought might have the qualifications to "redeem" Africa were too busy working to build their wealth in their new home to work for the Christianization of Africa. Especially after the Board's difficulties with political involvement in the Cherokee Nation, it was reluctant to trust ministers associated with the colony to do the important work of converting the indigenous population. This was where the foreign mission movement could augment the work of colonization by providing missionaries dedicated to the work of bringing Christian civilization to Africa. Mission supporters were frustrated with the extent to which the colony was focusing on trade and commercial pursuits over what they saw as the more important work of conversion.[10] Starting in 1824, the Board began to work on opening a mission in Liberia that would minister to Africans, not African Americans, and bring about the conversion of Africa.

In Liberia, the Board hoped to open a mission that would be able to rely on the colony for some support, just as its missions had turned to imperial governments for support elsewhere in the world. The Colonization Society would be a partner in the work, the Board hoped. This partnership did not imply, however, that the Board expected the two institutions to be fully united. Even as the mission relied on the colony, the Board stressed the importance of keeping the two projects separate. The mission and the colony, it insisted, had distinct purposes and interests. If both groups hoped to bring civilization to Africa, they planned to do so in different ways. While the colony was to be permanent, the mission would be temporary. As the Board expected everywhere, it would only remain in Liberia until a native church could survive in its place. While the colony was primarily focused on the needs of African American settlers, the mission would focus on the needs of Liberians. Only when this was made clear would native kings and chiefs welcome the presence of the missionaries among their people. By insisting on this separation, the Board clearly attempted to apply the lessons it had learned elsewhere to Liberia. Indigenous people frequently mistrusted colonial governments, and so it made sense for missionaries to distance themselves.

More than this, though, the Board had learned that missionaries, too, should be distrustful of the promises of colonial protection and cooperation. The Cherokee example would loom in the background throughout the missionary experience in Liberia. Rather than reminding supporters of that example, the Board again looked to British precedent, in particular the South African mission's uneasy relationship with the English colony at the Cape of Good Hope. Hinting at the future tensions between the mission and colonists, the Board missionaries saw no reason why "a colony of coloured people from Am. constituted as it must necessarily be of all sorts of men, will give any less cause of complaint to missionaries" than colonists anywhere else. Accordingly, the mission would be primarily working with native Africans, not American colonists.[11]

The Beginning of the Mission to Cape Palmas

In 1833, the Board sent John Leighton Wilson to West Africa on an exploring tour. Wilson was charged with deciding where to establish the American mission and toured the Liberian coast, gathering information for the Board. As their earlier questions to Ashmun suggested, they were still concerned about local "superstitions" and the hold that these had over the people, what their culture was like, and how successful the missionaries thought they could be in converting them. While the Board was grateful for the information gained through the colony, and expected even more information to come through colonial channels in the future, it still felt that little was known about Africa and its people. "Concerning most of them," Rufus Anderson wrote, "our knowledge is exceedingly vague and general." It was time, he wrote, for "mere curiosity [to] subside" and "Christian benevolence [to] awake, and investigate the intellectual and moral conditions of the whole people."[12]

In March of the next year, Wilson wrote his reports to the Board on the state of the colony and on the prospects of the mission. In spite of discordant reports in the United States about Liberia, Wilson found that it had the potential to be "one of the most flourishing [settlements] in the world" in time. He found the colonists to be for the most part "industrious, active, and enterprising—comfortable in their circumstances and altogether contented and happy in their situation," though others he found to be "destitute" and unsatisfied with their ability to change their situation. While he felt that the colonists neglected agriculture, he noted that the colony's commercial interests progressed well. In his report on the colony, he discussed the relationship between the colonists and the native Liberians, noting that the natives performed most of the manual labor and domestic work of the colony. Wilson thought that the colonists treated them well. The mission could expect "nothing *direct*" from the colony in their support of evangelization. He trusted, though, "that this colony will not always withhold its aid," but would in time lend support to missionaries seeking to evangelize the native population. This was a generally positive picture of the colony, but Wilson still felt that it was essential for the mission and the colony to remain "as distinct as possible."[13]

Wilson suggested Cape Palmas for the destination of his mission. Cape Palmas was south of the main settlement at Monrovia, but was to be the site of a new colony from the Maryland Colonization Society (MCS). Citizens of that state had recently founded the MCS when they worried that sectional differences within the colonization movement had weakened the national association. The Maryland Society's goal was to relocate Maryland free blacks, and it was sponsored by the state legislature for this purpose. The Maryland Society had only been founded in 1831, and the mission began very close to the same time as the colony itself. In fact, Wilson's exploring tour coincided with the beginning of the colony. In this way, Cape Palmas

Figure 5. In this engraving of the Cape Palmas mission circulated in the missionary press, viewers were meant to notice the differences in architectural styles between the American framed houses of the mission and the round thatched huts of the Grebo, pictured at the bottom of the hill. The mission buildings, complete with grazing livestock, were emblems of the civilization that missionaries hoped their converts could achieve. Courtesy of the Wider Church Ministries of the United Church of Christ, ABC 79, Box 1, Folder 2.

made for a very different space from Monrovia. The mission and the colony were both new, and the local native people, the Grebo, would learn about the two groups at the same time.

It was in a healthy location, and the Grebo people expressed a desire for the mission to start new schools for their children. Wilson described the Grebo as having a population of about three thousand and being "much more intelligent and numerous" than the groups who lived closer to Monrovia. Wilson worried about the distance of Cape Palmas from Monrovia, revealing again the importance that missionaries placed on proximity to imperial governments. He hoped, though, that the apparent enthusiasm of the native population for schools would ally them to the mission more generally and provide some protection. In addition to this, Wilson could depend on help from the white governor of Cape Palmas, Dr. James Hall. Wilson had initially toured the land with Hall, and the two men became friendly.

From the beginning of the American presence at Cape Palmas, despite Wilson's insistence on separation, the two projects were linked. While Wilson reported that he had made it clear to the Grebo that the mission was separate from the colony and allied with the Grebo, the mission was only able to operate with the approval of the colony. The arrangement for establishing Cape Palmas further entwined the two projects. Hall could only procure land for the colony from the Grebo if he promised to provide schools for Grebo children. These schools were to be provided by the mission in exchange for the use of the colony's land for the mission buildings. The Grebo kings in particular were described as being desirous of schools. Wilson wrote that they had "a universal desire, nay an imperious demand" for Christian schools.[14]

Wilson's descriptions of Cape Palmas and its people expressed his sense of optimism at the outset of his mission. He would be working among a population of three to four thousand native Africans, with fifteen hundred children of school age. He found the Grebo to be somewhat civilized already, describing the king as a "fine looking man" who was "dignified, modest, and sensible in his appearance." The claim of modesty was particularly significant, given the Board's association of heathenism with lasciviousness. Wilson also did not think that religious "superstitions" would be a significant obstacle to his work. In fact, he believed that "the truth concerning them is they possess little or no religion, and in this respect they are peculiarly ready for the reception of the Gospel." The main problems he identified were cultural, not religious: theft, lying, cheating, stealing, quarreling, swearing, and polygamy. These, he thought, could be resolved through the mission. The important thing, he found, was that the people were clearly, in his mind, showing a desire to gain the "advantages of civilization." At the beginning of his work in Liberia, Wilson was convinced that "there is no pagan people on the face of the earth who will more readily embrace the Gospel than the native African."[15]

The place to test this idea was in the mission schools. It was here that the missionaries hoped to bring about the transformation of the Grebo from a "pagan" to a civilized people. These schools resembled other mission schools in many ways, revealing the essential overlap in what the evangelical mission community thought the entire rest of the world ought to look like. Inside the classrooms, students were taught reading, writing, arithmetic, and geography. The teaching did not just occur in the classrooms, however; missionaries assumed that their students would go on to have a relationship with the mission outside of simply being pupils.[16] As at other missions, students boarded whenever possible, out of the missionary concern for separating native children from their families in order to change the children's behavior. It was common sense to the missionaries that if the children were allowed to remain with their families, the mission would not be able to have the sort of influence that they sought in nonacademic matters: prayer, dress, and industry. As was the case elsewhere, these students would receive new names in return for support from American Protestants. One hint of the complicated connections between mission and colony can be seen in the presence of one child in the mission school named for John Latrobe, director of the Maryland Colonization Society. To Latrobe, Wilson would send reports of the progress of "your name sake" in the school, hoping that the child would soon be able to write a letter himself.[17]

The Liberian schools were different from the Board's other schools in one important way. In Liberia, the mission welcomed both native children and the children of African American colonists. At first, the Board did not know what to make of African American children being accepted into the mission schools, though the missionaries insisted. Rufus Anderson urged Wilson not to make the mission schools into institutions serving mainly the colonial population, though colonial children who would agree to eventually become teachers or assistants to the mission could be enrolled.[18] For the missionaries, though, this mixed student body was important as a way both to counter some of the tensions that arose between the colonial and native populations and to aid the civilizing of the colonists themselves. They taught indigenous boarding students English, and more remarkably, taught American boarding students the indigenous languages. Every evening, the students came to the mission house to speak to each other in the foreign language. This served the dual purposes of training the native students in the civilized language of English and also preparing the colonial students to assist the mission among the native population after they completed their schooling. In this sense, the mission was claiming the children of the colony for its own project of transforming Africa. By asserting that the needs of the colonists for missionary education was similar to those of the native children, the missionaries equated the colonists with the natives in the scale of civilization. The colony itself was not yet fully civilized, they asserted; the mission was required to elevate this imperial project.[19]

The Mission and the Colony

Even as the mission critiqued the colonists, at first the mission and the colony seemed able to exist side by side. Wilson worked well with James Hall, the first governor of Cape Palmas. The two supplied each other with news and information about the region, and traveled together on tours to the surrounding villages. During his first years in Liberia, Wilson reported that the colony was in a good condition. Like other observers of the African American settlements in West Africa, Wilson focused on markers of civilization, such as agricultural practices and the style of homes being built, and he was generally positive in his depictions at first. Additionally, he found that the colonists got along with the indigenous population "much better" than he had initially feared. While he had worried about the "spirited" nature of the Grebo, he found upon his return to the colony in late 1834 that they were "very materially improved" since the arrival of the American emigrants. In some ways, then, Wilson believed that the colony was contributing to the civilizing of Africa. During Hall's government of Cape Palmas, which would last through 1836, the colony attempted to incorporate the Grebo into the colony, and Wilson approved of this. With education, he believed, many of the Grebo would be beneficial members of any society.

Even as Wilson depicted the early years of the colony in a positive light, there were signs of trouble ahead. In the same letter in which he spoke of Hall's good effects on the colonists, Wilson advised the Board against sending African American teachers to work in the Cape Palmas mission. Revealing his racial prejudice, Wilson described African Americans as "proverbially degraded." In the colonists, he saw "a bigoted and self important spirit." A more generous interpretation would notice that the behaviors that Wilson interpreted as bigoted and self-important were in fact the attempts of African Americans to make lives for themselves in Liberia. The goal of colonization that had most appealed to African American colonists, after all, had been the opportunities that the colony could provide for them to set up their own homes, raise their families, and make money away from the racism of American society. For those who survived the difficult climate, this did in fact become a possibility, and many African American families asserted their independence accordingly. Wilson struggled with the reality that in Liberia, he had an equal status to African Americans. In the first several years of his mission, however, the white government of the colony led by Dr. Hall tempered this.[20]

Three groups of people lived in Cape Palmas: the colony, the mission, and the Grebo. As missionaries throughout the world negotiated their position relative to imperial governing powers and native populations, so too did Wilson and his fellow missionaries need to determine how to relate to the colonial and the native populations. For their part, the colonists, too, attempted to determine how they ought to relate to the native population and the mission. Both groups of Americans, as it turned out, had different answers to this question, shaped by their different understandings of what the purpose of America in Africa ought to be. Very quickly, relations between the colonists and the Grebo soured. In particular, the colonists complained about theft. Initially, the mission attempted to remain out of the political realm in Cape Palmas. Before 1837, Wilson's correspondence frequently sympathized with the white government and criticized the black colonists, whom he found lazy. Yet Wilson's role was to work with the native population; colonial politics were not his primary concern.

In spite of this, Wilson's connections to the Grebo, and particularly his friendship with King Freeman, meant that he frequently acted as a mediator between the colony and the Grebo. In 1836, for example, the colony took a major step forward in its work of civilizing Africa by composing a code of laws for the governance of the Grebo. These laws were composed in Baltimore by the leaders of the Maryland Society, advised by Dr. Hall and Simleh Ballah, a Grebo man with close ties to both the mission and the colony. When Ballah returned to Cape Palmas, Freeman asked Wilson to read the new laws aloud to the Grebo. The laws included provisions for trials in front of judges, and put the colonial governor in the position of ultimate authority in cases of dispute between the Grebo and the African Americans. Wilson read the laws to the Grebo without commentary, but it is telling that it was Wilson, and not a colonial official, whom Freeman asked to explain the new code of laws. Wilson was frequently in the middle of relations between the colony and the Grebo. For all his insistence about the separation between the mission and the colony, the fact remained that both were American institutions, and so were inherently linked in the minds of the Grebo.[21]

While Wilson does not seem to have approved of the ways that the colony went about providing a legal system for the Grebo, he certainly shared a desire to change the ways that disputes were settled. In one of Wilson's earliest letters published in the *Missionary Herald*, he focused on the "manner of trying criminals" among the Grebo as a matter of particular interest to supporters of the missions. For Wilson, these came down not only to questions of law and order, but also of religious practice. When someone died, he explained, it was almost always accompanied by suspicion of poisoning, a kind of witchcraft. To determine if an individual was guilty, the "*doctors*, or as they are more frequently called, 'devil-men,'" Wilson wrote, would force the accused to go through some sort of painful ordeal. They might have to plunge their hands into boiling oil, or be forced to drink a large quantity of sasswood tea. Wilson reported that the tea resulted in death or "violent and distressing vomiting," and he was determined to stop these practices. When one man was accused of poisoning a neighbor, his friends asked Wilson to intervene and save him from the ordeal. Wilson did so, attempting to convince the people that this was an unjust way of trying the man for his crime. His words were not successful, but he did stare down the fetish priest who attempted to make him leave. When Wilson gave the man his hand, he was understood to have taken him under his own protection. Wilson and the colony, then, did continue to share some of the same goals. Wilson's published letter concluded with the news that many Grebo were beginning to tire of these practices, and that Dr. Hall was also working to end them. Wilson entirely approved of this, seeing it as the realization of the civilizing purpose of the American colony in Liberia.[22]

This positive emphasis in Wilson's description of the colonial government changed by 1838, when disagreements between the colony and the mission came to dominate his writing. He reported to Rufus Anderson that his entire opinion about the project of colonization had changed. In fact, he wrote, "the colonization scheme has not only failed to accomplish the good which its friends and patrons expected of it, but that it has been productive of innumerable evils of which they had not the most distant apprehensions." In a five-part letter, Wilson informed Anderson of what he perceived as the failure of colonization in Monrovia and Cape Palmas to bring much benefit to the colonists or to the native Africans. More important, perhaps, Wilson claimed that colonization did active harm to the native Africans he hoped to convert, and that the colonists aided the continuation of the slave trade and in fact attempted to enslave Africans themselves within the colony.[23]

In large part, this change in tone can be attributed to the change in leadership of the Maryland colony. John Russwurm was appointed to be governor of the colony in 1836, after Dr. Hall had urged the Board of Managers in Maryland to choose an African American agent. The reasons for this were twofold. First, Hall and his successor Holmes had been plagued by health problems in West Africa, and they, like the Board, expected that African Americans would not be faced with these difficulties. Second, the Maryland Society wanted the government of the colony eventually to become the responsibility of the colonists themselves, and it felt that white governors would keep the colonists from feeling themselves capable of self-government. In their correspondence with Russwurm, the MCS stressed the importance of his success, and the risk that it was undertaking in such a move. Governor Holmes, whom Russwurm was succeeding, did not seem to share the Maryland Society's guarded optimism in appointing a black governor. Holmes was mortified to be replaced by a black man and only remained in Cape Palmas one day after hearing of the appointment.[24] If the Maryland Society wanted to appoint a respectable African American to the post of governor, it could not have done much better than John Brown Russwurm. A native of Jamaica, Russwurm had been the first black graduate of Bowdoin College. He had served as co-editor of *Freedom's Journal* in the United States before his move to Monrovia, where he edited the *Liberia Herald*. He was a respected member of society there, and settlers in Liberia supported his appointment.[25]

Wilson initially supported the decision, but before long came to have serious problems with the government of Cape Palmas being run by an African American. Unsurprisingly, Wilson's writing about their conflicts placed the blame on Russwurm. He directly linked the appointment of a black governor with the decline of the colony.[26] Wilson focused on the "*irrepressible hatred* which these people (American Africans) have for all white men. The feeling is not seen or observed in America, but it is developed here to a shocking and melancholy extent." Wilson's description of a repressed African American hatred of whites had served as one of the premises of colonization for those who assumed that the two groups could not live safely side-by-side in freedom, because of longstanding resentment. Without the containment of that resentment through white rule, Wilson worried about the functioning of the colony and its relationship to the mission.[27] At work here, then, were the real or imagined prejudices on the part of the black colonists against the white missionaries, in addition to the prejudices of the white missionaries against the black colonists and their leadership.

Additionally, Wilson was convinced that Russwurm's race made it difficult for him to assert authority over the Grebo. His "complexion was a disadvantage so far as it was necessary for him to have an influence over the natives," Wilson wrote to the director of the Maryland Colonization Society. The Grebo, he believed, responded more to whites than to African Americans. In light of this difficulty, Wilson assured the Maryland Society that the colony could expect "my influence" in any case where "your colony will need it." Wilson hoped that in time, if Russwurm pursued "a kind, courteous and firm course of conduct in all of his dealings with them," the Grebo might come to respect Russwurm. Yet Wilson clearly believed that white rule was preferable and perhaps even necessary in Africa.[28]

Like the Board, the Maryland Colonization Society simultaneously stressed the separation between the colony and the mission even as it supported the mission's work. In many ways, it is surprising that the installation of a new governor led to major changes in the relationship between the colony and the mission. The Maryland Society remained committed to the mission and urged Russwurm to pay special attention to it. His instructions included the directive to "promote their [the mission's] interests in all things."[29] This, indeed, had been the relationship that had governed Cape Palmas and Fair Hope since Wilson's arrival. Even as Wilson and Hall stressed separation, they were often together and the mission could count on the colony's support. Russwurm did not plan on changing this dynamic too dramatically. Yet other factors changed under Russwurm's leadership, most importantly the relationship between the colonists and the natives.

Russwurm arrived at the colony during a period of tension. For several years, the colonists and the Grebo had stolen from each other, and the conflicts occasionally turned violent. Observers from Maryland to Liberia began comparing what was happening in Cape Palmas to what had happened in Georgia in the lead up to Cherokee removal. In an attempt to placate the Grebo, the Colonization Society created a government position of native magistrates, who served as constables specifically working within the Grebo community. In appointing Russwurm, as opposed to a white governor, the Maryland Society hoped to ease these problems further. From Maryland, the MCS worried that the situation would deteriorate; it instructed Russwurm to prevent events in Cape Palmas from mirroring what had happened to the Cherokee the decade before. Society secretary John Latrobe had stated that the members of the Maryland Colonization Society "do not wish the History of the United States of America to be repeated in Africa so far as it is connected with the fate of the Aborigines." Within a few years, however, the MCS would urge the Grebo's removal from the cape.[30] The finances of the colony had reduced Russwurm's ability to give "dashes," or gifts, to the indigenous population, which had been so important to maintaining balance and good feelings between the two groups, and a series of thefts on the colonial store had led to fighting between the two groups. Soon, the colonists began to feel the need to be more vigilant in their military exercises, and herein lay the root of much of the conflict between the mission and the colony.[31]

Wilson's depiction of this period marked the beginning of the transition of his opinion about the colony. He expected an outbreak of hostilities any day and was particularly disturbed by what he saw as the bloodlust of the colonists. A prominent member of the colony told him, he reported to Anderson, that "blood must flow and it must flow freely." This, he felt, was the opinion on both sides, and Wilson feared that only the intervention of God would prevent such an outcome. Wilson was convinced that the colonists were set on the extermination of the natives. In a conversation with Dr. Bacon, Wilson asserted that when Bacon had asked, "But what will become of the Natives?" Russwurm had replied, "Oh dear . . . how was it with the poor Cherokees?"[32]

The comparison of the Grebo with the Cherokee was a loaded one. Wilson's relation of this conversation depicted Russwurm as a cruel governor with no respect for indigenous rights. By comparing the Grebo to the Cherokee, Russwurm was able to assert the inevitability of their defeat. When Bacon related this discussion to Anderson, he described his pleasure at Russwurm's frankness about the goals of the colonists. Bacon believed that "they come as conquerors and robbers to acquire by violence where fraud has failed, lands which their laziness will not allow them to cultivate, but on which they hope to live by the labor of the enslaved nations," and this comparison to the case of Cherokee removal seemed to prove this for him. For Wilson and the Board, this metaphor would be particularly poignant in light of the missionary experience during Cherokee removal and would make clear where their sympathies ought to lie. Just as the Board had earlier supported the Cherokee and challenged the governments of Georgia and the United States, Wilson hoped that now the Board would support him in standing by the Grebo and against the colony.[33]

As tensions rose between the Grebo and the colonists, and as violence seemed all the more likely, the differences between the mission and the colony became more stark. One of Russwurm's priorities was to build up the colony's militia power, and this would lead to the mission's clearest rejection of the colony and its leadership. In particular, Wilson and Russwurm would clash over who had to serve in the militia. The colonial constitution specified that all black male residents of the colony were in the general militia and could be called to service at the discretion of the governor. While Russwurm granted that those specifically sent to Liberia by missionary societies were exempt, he maintained that other members of the mission family were required to serve. Because three black colonial assistants were connected with the mission—Stephen James, John Banks, and Josiah Dorsey—this became a major point of contention between Russwurm and Wilson, who refused to grant Russwurm's authority over the matter.[34]

Wilson wrote to Rufus Anderson about the military conflict. The missionary and the governor both asserted authority over the mission and its staff. While Russwurm agreed that James was exempt from military service due to his appointment by the Board, the relationship of Banks and Dorsey to the mission and the colony became the sticking point. John Banks had been one of the original settlers of the colony, and had been put under missionary care by Dr. Hall when he was a boy. Hall and Wilson had agreed that if the mission educated and housed Banks, he would as an adult join the mission as a teacher to the natives. Now that he was ready to begin his work as a teacher, Wilson was furious that the colony sought to take him away and force him to fight. And not only to fight, but to fight those whom he had been trained to educate and whom Wilson had come to Africa to save.[35] Since Banks was residing at the mission school in Cavally, outside of the colony's domain, Wilson had assumed that he would be considered exempt from military duty. Similarly, Josiah Dorsey was at Rocktown, which though it had recently come under colonial control, had given the mission land prior to the arrival of the colonists, giving Wilson the understanding that their school there was outside of the colonial limits.[36]

What had started out as a disagreement about whether two teachers would have to serve in the militia quickly led Wilson to question the ability of missions to survive within the context of settler colonialism. Part of what frustrated him was the question of whether the mission was part of the colony or a separate entity. Wilson insisted that the mission was on grounds over which the colony had no control. This was not the case, as the Maryland Society and even the American Board pointed out. When the missionaries were granted the land for Fair Hope and the mission schools, it was through the colony, with the understanding that the land would revert to the colony when and if the mission left. The missionaries themselves were to be treated as foreigners by the colonial government, exempt from military and civic duties, but subject to the laws and authority of the government. Missionary assistants from areas outside of the colonial jurisdiction would be similarly treated, the Board decided, but those who were from the colony would be eligible for military service, regardless of their relationship to the mission.[37]

The extent of Wilson's anger at the situation surprised the Board; Anderson reproved him for his language in dealing with the governor.[38] The Board felt unable to publish any of Wilson's writings on colonization, lest the Maryland Society decide to publish Wilson's letters to Russwurm to discredit him. Anderson urged him to show more deference in the future, as Russwurm was governor, and whatever Wilson may have thought of him, he deserved respect as a result of his position. Chastened, Wilson promised to behave better, but by no means gave up his objections to the situation. In his response to Anderson's initial answer to his concerns, he laid out an extended explanation of the relationship between the natives and the colonists, proving that the natives "do now and have always regarded themselves just as free and independent of the colony, as the colony does itself of the natives," and that they were not to be understood as being under colonial control. Anderson had in fact never asserted that they were, and Wilson's sensitivity to this issue reveals some of the high stakes of the situation in Cape Palmas.[39]

For Wilson, too, what was happening in Cape Palmas was analogous to what had happened in Georgia to the Cherokee. Wilson reminded Anderson of the missionary stance against Indian removal, finding the same sort of "usurped authority" in the colonial government of Liberia.[40] While no one in either the Maryland Society or the Board claimed that the colonists had authority over the natives at first, Wilson's quickness to jump to that conclusion was the result of the perilous state of affairs that he saw between the colonists and the natives. If, as he insisted, the colonists were prepared to exterminate the natives, it would not be such a leap to assume that they were attempting to claim political authority over them. Wilson insisted at different points in his correspondence that the colonists were effectively crowding out the Grebo, bringing more immigrants to the region than the land could support.[41] While never publicized to the missionaries, within a year the Maryland Colonization Society's policy did shift as Wilson had worried it might. By late 1839, Latrobe asserted that when the Grebo granted the land to the colony, they had rescinded their right to sovereignty over both the land and the people who lived there. The treaties had granted all governing power to Americans, Latrobe insisted, and the colony officially shifted its focus from incorporating the Grebo to removing them from the area.[42]

This question of how the mission related to the colony became a major issue within the Maryland Colonization Society as well. While Wilson wrote to Anderson, Russwurm wrote to John Latrobe. Latrobe was very concerned about the conflicts between the missionaries and the colony. While he was supportive of the missionary presence there, seeing it as an essential part of the colonization movement, he was anxious to assert the sovereignty of the colony. Latrobe wrote to both Anderson and Russwurm explaining that the colony was "the political government" and as such, looked upon all who settled in their territory in the same way that "civilized governments elsewhere look upon their visitors or their people." As he explained further to Russwurm, his concern was that if it were "otherwise, the missionary establishment of Mr. Wilson would be *imperium in imperio.*" Latrobe was worried that if the missionaries were separate from the colony, and if they allied with Africans against the colony, it would not end well for the colonists in Cape Palmas. He instructed Russwurm to obtain all lands where the missionaries hoped to establish new stations, so that the missionaries would not be able to operate in Liberia except with the permission of the colony.[43]

These conflicts led to a complete reversal of Wilson's opinion of colonization generally. His critiques of the colony in large part were that it was not a civilized community. For example, Wilson insisted that the "great majority" of colonists had, "by indolence, improvidence, and activity," suffered from poverty and worse conditions than they would have experienced had they remained in the United States, even under slavery, and that they were further a "mutinous and disorderly community." He also critiqued the colonists for what he saw as their laziness, writing that they "seem[ed] to forget what their own hands were made for, and seem[ed] to have come to the country in the belief that the enjoyment of liberty would consist in entire exemption from manual labor."[44] For one of the Board's missionaries, this was a problematic place to live. If part of the reason for the Board's connections to imperial expansion had been the belief that proximity to a civilized culture was a boon to the transformation of the "heathen world," proximity instead to a community that was indolent or even sinful could be disastrous to the progress of the mission. Instead of providing examples of what the native Africans could aspire to, the colonists were hindering their progress.

Some of Wilson's frustration can be attributed to his understanding of what the goals of colonization were. He had supported colonization because of its claims to promote the civilization of Africa. He had left the United States expecting to be united with the colonists in a missionary endeavor. Colonization, he wrote, had "been dignified by the appellation of a missionary enterprise, and every colonist has been represented as a missionary going forth to carry the bread of life to his perishing fellow men." And yet when he looked at the colonists, he did not see what he expected to see in a missionary. Shocked and upset by the practice of African American families bringing native children into their homes as domestics and then not educating these children, Wilson charged the colony with failing to live up to its promises. He went further, charging the colony with actively oppressing the native people. It was for this reason, he argued, that the natives felt "disgust and hatred for the colony," and looked at Americans "as their enemies and oppressors."[45]

One important leader in the Board had not shared Wilson's expectations of the colony. Rufus Anderson reminded Wilson that the colonization society was a secular institution. Yet Anderson's vision of the sharp distinction between the missions and secular institutions was still rare in this period.[46] Even Anderson, however, was surprised by the extent to which the Cape Palmas government asserted its right of sovereignty over the land and the people. The conflict between the colony and the mission came down to a debate about governance. The Colonization Society, he had believed, was a similar voluntary benevolent organization that aimed to improve Africa. Yet the government of Cape Palmas was claiming sovereignty in the same ways that other colonial states did. In his correspondence with Anderson, Latrobe went so far as to compare his group's claims of political power to those of the East India Company. Both were nonstate organizations with commercial interests. No one, certainly not Anderson, would deny that the East India Company had the right to govern over a foreign land and foreign people. Like the EIC, Latrobe insisted, the Cape Palmas colony had sovereignty over the land it claimed and the people who lived on it.[47]

It was understandable why Wilson and others had invested such hopes in the Liberian colonies in the early 1830s. Not only did the Board have a far closer and friendlier relationship with the Maryland Colonization Society than it had with the institutions that governed its other mission locations, suggesting some sort of alliance, but the colonization movement as a whole had presented one of its probable effects as the redemption of Africa through the colonization of civilized African Americans. Indeed, Latrobe himself was a major supporter of this conception of colonization. His correspondence frequently discussed the missionary benefits of colonization generally. "I am one of those colonizationists," Latrobe explained in a letter to Russwurm, "who look to the plan as a great missionary scheme and if valueless, for other purposes, I would still work in its behalf for the good it will do in christianizing the Heathen." He echoed this goal in his instructions to Russwurm at the time of his appointment, when he wrote that it was the Maryland Colonization Society's goal to "amalgamate the native with the colonist," and "carry both on together to the highest eminences of civilization and the Gospel." Yet Wilson misunderstood this idea of the colony as a missionary enterprise, Latrobe explained to Rufus Anderson in 1838. It was not a matter of every individual being a missionary, but rather that the "planting of a Christian colony on the Western Coast of Africa will promote the spread of religion over the continent." In Latrobe's formulation, colonization, even without explicit missionary exertions, would have the effect of spreading Christianity. It would Christianize Africa through settler colonialism, not missionary work as such.[48]

Wilson, like many others at the Board, came to Liberia as a supporter of colonization, seeing it as an ideal solution to the problem of slavery in the United States. This, then, marked a significant change in worldview on Wilson's part. Colonization, he came to argue, was a relationship of oppression that could not hope to do otherwise than harm the native inhabitants of the land. Wilson anticipated that others might disagree, pointing to the "common origin and sympathetic feelings and interest" between the colonists and natives in Liberia. Wilson insisted, though, that the oppressive nature of the relationship would remain. In fact, the shared African background could lead to further complications when, as Wilson pointed out, native Africans derided the former American slaves who came to Liberia as colonists by taunting them that "his father was once his own or his ancestors bondsman—and that his worth had long since been consumed in tobacco and rum." These complicated dynamics between the colonists and natives cancelled out any "shared interest" between them, Wilson argued.

Possibly the boldest claim that Wilson made against the colony was that it had become engaged in the slave trade. To accuse former slaves and other African Americans of participating in the illegal Atlantic slave trade was a high charge indeed because of the supposed goal of the colonization movement to cancel the debt that America owed Africa due to the slave trade. Wilson insisted that the colonists were financially involved in the work of slave traders and that they aided the traders in their business. In particular, he noted the presence of slavers in the harbors at Monrovia and Cape Palmas, and the occupation of some colonists as agents for the traders. In Wilson's letters to the Board, he claimed that Spanish slave traders had joined the colonists at Grand Bassa in their war against the natives. Wilson implied that the traders took any captives in war for the slave trade.[49] Recognizing that this claim would probably not be accepted at face value in the United States, Wilson supplemented his own writing on the subject with letters from other whites in Liberia attesting to the support that colonists gave to slave traders.[50] Russwurm had allowed a trader named Don Pedro Blanco to dock at Cape Palmas and repair his vessel in 1837. Wilson not only reported this to the Board, but also to the Maryland Society itself, which expressed horror at the events. The MCS worried that reports of the colony aiding a known slave trader would damage its reputation in the United States, and it urged Russwurm to end any aid to slave vessels. Russwurm, for his part, asked the Maryland Society to prevent Wilson's interference in colonial affairs.[51]

The Board never published Wilson's letters on colonization.[52] Yet his critiques prepared the Board for its conflict with the colonial government over the proper relationship between Americans and Africans, and for the mission's eventual removal from Liberia. Because the colony's behavior was "lamentable" in the eyes of the Board, it seemed necessary for the missionaries to work independently of it in order to perform their duties of bringing Christianity and civilization to West Africa. While they had earlier vowed that the mission and the colony would be distinct, this clearly had not worked in practice. Now, the ties needed to be officially broken.

In late 1841, the final step in this break between the mission and the colony occurred when the colony issued an ordinance with deep implications for the native youth in the mission schools and the missionaries themselves. The ordinance required all white and black people (other than those on visiting military or commercial ships) arriving at Cape Palmas to pledge allegiance to the colonial constitution under threat of banishment. It also strengthened the power of the governor in enforcing other colonial laws. This law perhaps reminded the Board of the oath that the state of Georgia attempted to make white residents take a decade earlier. By 1841, Wilson had a number of assistant missionaries at Fair Hope. Some were from Sierra Leone and Cape Coast, and others were native Africans who had graduated from the mission schools and become teachers. Wilson and the American Board considered these all exempt from military duty, but the colony did not recognize the exemption of African teachers and pupils who were living in Cape Palmas. The Maryland Society was firm in its stance that only white missionaries and those from the United States who had registered with the society as assistant missionaries could be exempt from military service.[53]

The position of teachers at the mission schools was an issue that the mission and the colony had disagreed about before, but now the Board joined Wilson in his anger. Earlier, whenever Wilson and Russwurm had disagreements about the ways that the two groups worked together, they would direct the issue to their governing boards in the United States, and Anderson and Latrobe would resolve matters. By this point, however, that course of action was no longer a solution. Anderson, too, was concerned about the colony's attempts to force military labor from native Africans who were students and teachers at the mission. These Africans had no relation to the colony. They were not locals, and if they had not come to the mission, they would not have been under colonial domain. Accordingly, the Board feared that if this law continued, the mission would have a very difficult time convincing African parents to send their children to the mission schools or to work for the mission themselves.[54]

When it became clear that the Maryland Society sanctioned the actions taken in the colony, the Board told the missionaries that it was time to move out of the boundaries of the Liberian colonies.[55] The Board's Prudential Committee passed resolutions critical of the Maryland Society's stance. A brief mention in the *African Repository* assured readers that the "misunderstanding" between the colony and the mission had been resolved. Another article the following year reported that Russwurm had offered his resignation in 1842, but had since rescinded it, just in time for the departure of the Board's missionaries.[56]

Anderson revealed the Board's new sense of the importance of separation from the colony when he advised the missionaries to approach the situation taking the course "proposed by Abraham and Lot." In Genesis, when Abraham and Lot fought with each other about how to divide resources in a new land, they resolved to separate, one going in one direction, and the other in the opposite. Anderson was urging the missionaries to do the same, and move their mission in the opposite direction of the colony. Yet this advice was not without judgment. Anderson and the missionaries would have remembered Lot's eventual fate in Gomorrah, which God destroyed for the sins of that city. The Board thus issued a rather stark critique of the colony and its government. Over the course of the year, the Board became more and more convinced of the propriety of moving the mission entirely.[57]

A New Station in Gabon

Wilson had been hoping to move his mission out of Cape Palmas as early as 1838. Different visions of imperial governance and the ways that Americans ought to relate to Africans had led him to this decision. Accordingly, Wilson asked Anderson and the Board for permission to move the West Africa mission, and he began searching for a new location. Initially, he and the Board had hoped that Rocktown or Fishtown, which were just outside of the colonial territory, and where the mission already had schools, would be eligible sites.[58] Yet concerns that the colony would eventually expand its domain to embrace these locations led Rufus Anderson to urge Wilson to look elsewhere. The Board had come to feel a "great repugnance to extending ourselves towards the Liberian colony," which, Anderson expected, would only expand over time and continue to "interfere with our prosperity and happiness."[59] Over the next four years, Wilson toured the coast of western Africa, looking in particular at the Gold and Ivory Coasts as possible new locations. The Board was particularly excited about the possibility of opening a new mission station somewhere along the Niger.[60]

Wilson and another missionary eventually settled on Gabon, where the mission would evangelize to the Mpongwe. They had received a "cordial reception from the natives," Wilson reported, and he found the local geography to be well suited to their needs. Situated on the banks of a wide river navigable at least thirty miles to the interior, the spot was frequented by ships who traded with the indigenous population and so would have easy access for communication with America. The Mpongwe seemed to Wilson to be excellent candidates for conversion. Not only had they seemed welcoming to the mission, they also were, in his view, "a good deal more advanced in civilization than any natives [he had] before seen or expected to have seen on the Western Coast of Africa." Specifically, the Mpongwe people were active in trade, organized into four villages on the north and south banks of the river, and many of the adults could speak English intelligibly at the time of Wilson's arrival. Describing the people several years later, in his history of West Africa, Wilson would highlight their intelligence, ease of manners, and "real urbanity," which he attributed to their intercourse with Europeans. In the Mpongwe, Wilson found evidence of the "natural capacity of this race for improvement," and he settled his mission among the village of King Glass.[61]

One further thing about Gabon attracted Wilson: it was far distant not only from Liberia, but from any European colonies. That they saw this as a benefit marked a profound shift in the missionary outlook. In all previous missions, the Board valued proximity to Euro-American settlements. Their experiences in Liberia changed this. Despite the frequency of trade, at the time of Wilson's arrival, there was no European settlement on the Gabon River, and this was part of its appeal. The missionaries felt optimistic at the beginning of their Gabon mission and brought some of their assistants from Cape Palmas with them to the new station. Yet this was not to last long; shortly after the missionaries' arrival in Gabon, the French also determined that it was a good candidate for a settlement, tricked the king into signing over the territory while intoxicated, and created a French colony.

With the arrival of the French, the American missionaries once again found themselves forced to confront the question of the missionary relationship to empire, and the position they should assume relative to both the colonists and the groups they had hoped to serve. Wilson again took on the role of mediator, this time between the Mpongwe and the French.

The Mpongwe hoped that Wilson could help them gain assistance from the American or British governments in opposing the presence of the French. When Glass mistakenly signed a treaty ceding sovereignty to the French, thinking it was a letter of friendship, the Mpongwe and the mission both found themselves on French territory. Wilson wrote letters to King Louis Philippe and Queen Victoria on behalf of the Mpongwe in protest of the means by which the French had come to claim the land. Wilson also approached the commander of an American naval ship visiting Gabon. While the American commodore could not interfere in the dispute between the French and the Mpongwe, he did approach the French officers to gain assurances that the American missionaries would not be harmed.

Once the missionaries obtained word from the French that the mission would not be prevented from doing its work, they hoped that they could stay aloof of the matter until the question of the legality of the treaty had been resolved. They found such a position impossible, though, as the cannons that the French ships shot toward the villages passed near the mission premises and eventually broke up a congregation assembled for worship. It was then that the American mission claimed the protection of the U.S. flag, which they flew over the mission house on the advice of the American naval officers in the hopes that the French would recognize it as a statement of neutrality. Explaining his course of action, Wilson insisted that he had seen three possible courses of action: to fly the French flag, to fly the American flag, or to fly no flag at all. For "an institution purely religious" like his mission station, the third option was the most logical, he felt. Yet this had not been effective in protecting the mission from danger. Accordingly, Wilson wrote, he was faced with the decision between flying the French or the American flag. The former, he assumed, would be taken by King Glass and his people as a recognition of French authority in the place. This he felt neither the authority nor the inclination to do. And so he chose to claim the authority of the United States, which angered the French until the American commodore could intercede on the missionaries' behalf.[62]

Wilson had hoped that the U.S. Navy's African Squadron would have taken a stronger stance against the French. He was disappointed that his country stood by and ignored the requests for assistance from the Mpongwe against European imperialism. His anticolonial stance followed him from Liberia to Gabon, but there he continued to believe that Americans ought, in some way, to take an active role in Africa to promote civilization there. As they worked to develop the second stage of their West African mission, the Board's missionaries found that the questions of empire and mission that had driven them from Liberia followed them still. Their hopes for a colonial relationship that would support the cause of mission and bring civilization to Africa were dashed in the face of political reality.

In their mission to West Africa, the Board hoped to cancel the perceived moral debt that America owed Africa and to seize the opportunities presented by an American colony in Liberia.

As in its other missions, the Board realized that it was only because of the colonial presence in West Africa that it could have access to the region and maintain some contact with its missionaries. The Board had always understood Anglo-American empires as Providential in this manner, creating the possibility for missionaries to perform their calling to convert the world. Yet as the Board had earlier learned elsewhere, the real-world experiences of missionaries in an imperial context could be quite complicated, and the relationship between the mission and the local government was very important. Hopes for a comfortable coexistence with the African American colony in Liberia were dashed when it became clear that the colony was not committed to the project of "redeeming" Africa. The colony had its own understanding of the relationship between American and Africa.

Throughout the first decades of the mission movement, the Board had been guided by a vision of Christian imperialism—that the expansion of Western power was a providential sign that the time had come to bring these new spaces into the Kingdom of God. Now the Board was less sure of this providential relationship. By the time he brought his mission out of Liberia, Wilson could write that it was now "forever settled in my own mind, that missionaries and colonization schemes can never and will never go hand in hand."[63] If Cherokee removal had challenged the idea that the United States could serve as an example of benevolent imperialism, the experience in Liberia suggested that even allies in benevolent reform had priorities other than the conversion of the world. In Liberia, American missionaries had claimed authority as Americans and as Christians, still seeing the two categories as linked. The fighting between the mission and the colony made it harder to assert that connection, and so they left. From Gabon, the missionaries hoped to continue their work as servants of God. Their difficulty in working beyond the boundaries of national power was never clearer than when they looked for a symbol of neutrality and turned to the American flag.

Chapter 7

A "Christian Colony" in Singapore

goes ↓

✗

In the mid-1830s, American missionaries again found themselves starting a new mission in the British Empire and attempting to find a balance
between their own goals and those of imperial officials. Ira Tracy, Daniel
Bradley, and Peter Parker had been placed in charge of the Board's mission
to Singapore, with instructions to prepare the way for the evangelization of
China and the rest of East Asia through establishing new education, translation, and publication efforts. These missionaries were not content, though,
to continue in the model that had been laid out for them in Bombay.
Shortly after their arrival, they would propose a new approach to American
evangelism in Asia that would shock the Board in Boston.

In July 1835, these missionaries prepared a lengthy and detailed letter
to the Prudential Committee in which they laid out their plans for what
they called a "Christian colony" of Americans to be located in Singapore.
They had already discussed this plan with British authorities in the East
India Company and could state with some assurance that such a colony would be able to obtain land and become self-sustaining. They asked
the Board to create an American "Missionary Colonization Society" that
would identify and support a group of pious American Protestants who
would become colonists. The missionaries explained that they had met

many farmers, shoemakers, and schoolteachers who were not qualified to serve either as the ministers, printers, or doctors that the Board was currently employing in Asia. Why not, the missionaries suggested, send about twenty families of this description to Singapore, where they might teach Asian women and men by example what it would look like to live within a Christian civilization? Why not have them establish schools, adopt children, and spread American-style arts and industry throughout Asia from this hub of Asian commerce? Why not, they asked, establish an American colony at Singapore?[1]

The Prudential Committee was not supportive of this plan, and there would be no American colony at Singapore. This was not for lack of agreement about some of the basic premises of this plan. Committee members agreed that an American colony might have important benefits to the people of Asia as well as Christians at home. They also did not mention issues of expense or difficulty. It was not a matter of financial possibility. Rather, the problem with the colony had to do with political expediency and terminology. After their experience in the Cherokee Nation and in the midst of their debates about the propriety of the colonies in Liberia, the Board had shifted its understanding of just how its missionaries ought to relate to empire. The Singapore mission was not just about American imperialism though. This was at the time a British colony, and so the Board would once again face international political concerns. After twenty years of at times very tense relations with the British imperial government in South Asia, the American missionary network worried that after this proposal, "the question will be, not whether American *missions* shall be tolerated in the territories of the East India Company, but whether *colonies* of Americans shall be?"[2]

More political matter

The proposed colony was not publicized in the religious press and seems to have been forgotten shortly after it was quashed. Yet it is an important story for the study of American missions in the early republic, for it highlights some of the complex situations that could result when Americans participated in overseas evangelization. Perhaps the most remarkable thing about the proposed American colony at Singapore was not that it was proposed at all, but that it failed. For what the missionaries were actually suggesting was almost identical to what the Board had already done in places like the Sandwich Islands and the Cherokee Nation, and to what they had hoped to do in India. The difference lay in the terminology that they used, the location of the proposed work, and of course, the time that they had proposed it. Here, missionaries spoke in the language of empire and were scolded not because their ideas were problematic, but because their language

Important because

was. After decades of searching for a way to implement Christian imperialism in the Board's missions, Singapore was a final step in shifting the ways that missionaries talked about how American Christians ought to relate to imperialism.[3]

Missionary Expansion in Asia

In the early 1830s, American missionaries attempted to expand their reach in East and Southeast Asia. China had long been the place where American and British evangelicals most hoped to evangelize. Samuel Newell, for example, had explained the importance of potential mission sites in terms of their proximity to China.[4] The extensive population, as well as the perceived civilization of the population, made it seem an ideal location. The Chinese government, however, strictly monitored the access foreigners, especially foreign evangelists, had to its people. Until American and British missionaries would be permitted to enter China, they established new stations in the surrounding region. The Board accordingly established a new mission to Siam and began exploring other options nearby. David Abeel, the Siam missionary, spent several months in Java and Singapore before establishing his mission Bangkok. As many of the Board's missionaries had done before him, he spent this time looking for potential sites for new missions. He found definite possibilities for missionary expansion in the region. He learned, for example, that Java only had two missionaries working among an estimated population of 6 million. The surrounding islands, further, had a healthier climate than previously believed. It was in this report that Singapore first appeared as a possible location for an American mission. The British had recently founded a colony there, and Abeel suggested that it would be a far better place to live than Bengal. Accordingly, in 1832 the Board's *Annual Report* mentioned not only its missionaries to China and Siam, but also the appointment of two new missionaries who would act as explorers, "looking around for scenes of the greatest promise." It was these missionaries who would propose the creation of an American Christian colony in Singapore.[5]

In the 1830s, missionaries were not yet able to enter China to begin a mission on the scale that they would have liked. Americans in those years celebrated the work of two missionaries there, Robert Morrison of the LMS, and Elijah Bridgman of the ABCFM, even as they were frustrated that their work was largely limited to translation. Bridgman insisted that

[handwritten margin note: perfect place but the government wouldn't let them.]

They were the "golden nugget"

this was important work, explaining to American readers that the Chinese were "a reading people" to an extent unheard of among "other heathens."[6] Watching Morrison and Bridgman, the Board waited for the time when the Chinese government would understand that the Americans did "utterly disclaim the right of interfering in the civil governments of nations." All that they wanted to do, they claimed, was to change the religion and the culture of China to welcome it into the kingdom of God. Gradually, it seemed that the way would soon be open to them. Travelers began to report a general sense along the coast, at least, that more in China were beginning to be favorable to the idea of welcoming Westerners into the country. This was largely the result of commerce, but the missionaries saw it as Providence. This was "the elements of human society put in motion and enthralled," the Board wrote. It rejoiced in the "glorious fact, that war, revolution, colonization, commerce, science, art, and a thousand other causes, are bringing every part of the earth within reach of the church, and preparing a high way for her through all nations."[7]

It was with much excitement, then, that the Board sent Ira Tracy and Samuel Williams on a mission to the Chinese in 1833. When the Board issued its instructions to these two, it made clear the immense importance of their work when it described the population they were supposed to serve: "that great community which speaks, and with that still more exterior community which reads, the Chinese language—the language of at least a fourth part of the human race." This was a population of "millions . . . scattered over the neighboring countries and islands." Further, they were not "barbarians: they have arts and sciences, and among them are more persons who are able to read and write, probably, than in Great Britain and America, combined. But the sun of their civilization, which rose four thousand years ago, has never exceeded to the zenith, and it is now stationary, if not retrograde." It was the missionaries' job to begin to address that issue.[8]

Tracy and Williams were asked to stand at the ready, to encourage these developments among the Chinese, and to enable the Board to enter China as soon as possible on a large scale. They would work on translation and printing of tracts and scripture into Chinese for mass distribution. They would help to publish the *Chinese Repository*, an English-language periodical printed at Bridgman's mission in Canton that was designed to spread information about China to the English-speaking world. It was supposed to "acquaint the Christian world with the geography, government, literature, and social and moral condition of China and other nations of southeastern Asia," to help draw American interest to the "spiritual illumination" of the

The hub of trade

rest of the world. The Board expected that soon missionaries would be welcomed in China. They would have access to the interior "long before we are ready to occupy the whole of it." Tracy and Williams were to prepare the way and to gather information about the surrounding area.[9]

From his location in Canton, Tracy described to the Board the possibilities that could exist in nearby Singapore, which he described as one of the "many thousands of beautiful and populous islands" in the immediate region. As Tracy looked around the Malay Archipelago and the surrounding region in the early 1830s, Singapore stood out for its diverse population that was drawn to its commercial center. This was a recent development. In 1819, when the East India Company established its first trading post on the island, Singapore had a population of approximately one thousand residents and little importance in regional commerce. The British had initially seen it as a possible means of halting Dutch expansion in Southeast Asia by opening a new center of trade. Although this project began with some uncertainty, it was enormously successful. By the mid-1820s, the EIC negotiated stronger treaties that recognized its sovereignty over the island, and Singapore emerged as a major center of commerce in Southeast Asia.[10]

American merchants and diplomats were certainly aware of these developments. In the 1820s and early 1830s, these groups attempted to strengthen America's position in East Asia and focused on Singapore. For American merchants, Singapore introduced a way to bolster their income from the lucrative China trade. Stopping in Singapore would allow them to bring valuable goods from the Malay provinces to the Canton market, making it easier for them to obtain the Chinese goods they wanted for their American consumers. The legality of American trading in Singapore, however, was not clear in the 1820s and early 1830s. Nations were not automatically granted the right to trade in the holdings of the East India Company, and American trade relations were based on the treaty that ended the War of 1812. This included a list of the places where Americans were explicitly allowed to trade, including Calcutta, Madras, and Bombay. Singapore, on the other hand, was not a part of the East India Company when those lists were drawn up in 1815, and so it raised some questions. Some British officials assumed that because they did not have explicit permission, Americans had no right to be there in the 1820s and 1830s.

Difficulties

The question of the rights of Americans to trade in Singapore figured most dramatically in the "*Larne* incident" of 1825. In that year, the HMS *Larne* seized a U.S. trader, the *Governor Endicott*, which had been trading in Singapore. For this, the captain was brought to trial in Calcutta. The trial vindicated the Americans when the judge determined that Americans could, in fact, do business in Singapore. The incident caused enough concern among Americans, however, to keep them out of Singapore for nearly a decade. Instead, American ships focused on nearby Riau, a small, commercially unimportant port. In the 1820s and early 1830s, American merchants and diplomats, along with British colonists in Singapore and officials in London discussed the legality and propriety of Americans' presence in Singapore. For every one who thought that Americans ought to stay out of Singapore, there were many others who felt that Americans should be able to trade there. American merchants brought specie into the island, and many in the East India Company worried that if Americans were unable to trade with the British in Singapore, they would instead trade with the Dutch in their Malayan colonies. It took until 1836, though, for the issue to be fully resolved. Until that year, the officers of the East India Company in Singapore and Calcutta continued to ask the Board of Directors in London for advice, and the Board of Directors sought outside legal counsel. Once they did so, they reported to those in Singapore that Americans ought to be received "on the footing of the most favoured Nations." It took multiple instructions from London to see that Americans would enjoy the right to trade in Singapore.[11]

As the Board of Directors conferred with the lawyers of the East India Company and of the Crown about America's commercial rights in Singapore, the United States carefully attempted to obtain diplomatic footing there as well. Shortly before the arrival of the American missionaries, the United States sent its first consul to Southeast Asia. In 1833, Joseph Balestier arrived in Singapore as the consul to Riau, though his official commission granted that his work would not be confined to that port. The real focus of Balestier's work would be Singapore, where he resided, even as the State Department was not sure whether they would be welcome there. It was not until 1836 that his appointment to Singapore was made official by the United States. In November of that year, the directors of the East India Company consented to recognize his appointment. News of this welcome would not reach Singapore until 1837. The American position in Singapore, then, was unstable and unclear through the 1830s, though this fact did little to keep Americans away.[12]

As merchants and diplomats attempted to take advantage of the commercial benefits of Singapore, missionaries, too, became interested in the possibilities there. Its commercial power made Singapore attractive to missionaries, for it meant that Singapore had a large and diverse population of

Asian settlers. Throughout the 1820s and 1830s, the population expanded dramatically. By 1821, five thousand Malays, Chinese, Bugis, and others were living in Singapore; the 1824 census counted eleven thousand residents. Around the time of the arrival of the American missionaries in the mid-1830s, that population had more than doubled again to thirty thousand, and missionaries reported that about fifteen hundred vessels traded in Singapore annually from the region.[13] While these numbers included a steady trickle of European immigration, mostly British, Europeans were a tiny minority in Singapore. By and large, this population growth was the result of Asian immigration, particularly from Malaysia and China. These immigrants were attracted by the commercial opportunities of Singapore. In order to attract trade, the early governors of the colony had instituted a policy of free trade. Goods were not taxed, and there were initially no port fees. While this could be problematic for the maintenance of the government and of social services, it was incredibly attractive to immigrants who hoped to make their fortunes in Singapore and, in many cases, return home with their newfound wealth.[14] In Singapore, Tracy came to believe, missionaries could reach Malay, Indian, and Chinese individuals, who would not only have the chance to hear the Gospel themselves, but who might also travel home and spread the word about God and, perhaps, the benevolence of the missionaries. A mission in Singapore might hasten the day of a thriving mission to China.

Singapore seemed to offer so much potential to the American mission, in fact, that Tracy left China in order to lead the mission at Singapore. In 1833, he had been busy learning Mandarin in Canton and helping Morrison and Bridgman with the publication of the *Chinese Repository*. Yet by the end of that year, he began listing the reasons why he might be required instead to go and work in Singapore. In the first place, the Canton missionaries were concerned that they needed a place to both produce and safely keep books in Chinese and other languages. Canton would not serve that purpose. It was illegal to distribute missionary texts in China, and the missionaries worried about this. For Tracy, it was endlessly frustrating to be surrounded by those he considered "eager for books, books containing the bread of life" when he was "able to give them this bread, but forbidden by the laws; and if we do it, we are culprits in the view of those laws, and the punishment may come upon some innocent Chinese, and cost him his life." In contrast to the legal constraints that missionaries faced from the Chinese in Canton, the missionaries expected safety and perhaps even encouragement from the British in Singapore. There, Tracy insisted, not only would their books be kept safe, but the missionaries, too, could be safe "from the persecution of pagan or Christian governments, from sickness caused by excess of labors, or any other cause, and perhaps, I should add, where their families may live in safety and have a *home*." It was further believed to be a healthful location, and one that could operate as a central location for the distribution of tracts and books in the region. It had a sizeable population and as yet, only one LMS missionary, Claus Hinrich Thomsen, who worked exclusively with the Malay. The logic of the hierarchy of heathenism continued to guide American missionaries as they tried to follow where Providence led them. Tracy hoped to work among the Chinese there, and the brethren who might arrive to aid him could be expected to work in additional languages.[15]

The first description of Singapore in the Board's published writing explained that it was "a flourishing commercial entreport [*sic*] south of the Malayan peninsula."[16] Singapore was attractive because it brought together the people of the Malay Peninsula, surrounding islands, and China in a center of trade. In their unpublished letters, the missionaries expanded on this description to make Singapore stand out as an ideal location for the Board's work. Here, missionaries could easily reach people from many different places at once. Many of these people, further, were mobile. The Board missionaries estimated that over a hundred ships came to Singapore monthly, from forty different ports. This "frequent intercourse with all the ports of the neighboring countries and islands" gave Singapore "peculiar advantages" for missionary exertion. Once the missionaries had preached to them, educated them, or given them tracts, they could be expected to return home and spread the word even further. Providence seemed to direct the Board there. Shortly after the missionaries had determined to work in Singapore, they were offered the sale of an extensive printing establishment from a former LMS missionary. This station seemed promising enough that the Board removed one of its Canton missionaries to take the lead there. Singapore, the Board decided, would be "the central point in respect to all our operations in that part of the world."[17]

It became the hub

An American Colony

Ira Tracy arrived during the summer of 1834 along with Daniel Bradley as the Board missionaries to Singapore. As he looked over his new field of labor, Tracy found much work to do. He was saddened by his reflections on all the missionary labor that had preceded his arrival. The London Missionary Society had been active in Singapore for almost twenty years, he reminded the Board, and yet he looked "in vain to discover any good effects" of their work. The London missionaries had so far focused their energies on the distribution of tracts and sacred writing to little avail. The American missionaries, he wrote, ought to "concentrate" their efforts. They needed "to bring the truth more frequently and forcibly before the minds of some individuals" through the establishment of an extensive educational system. Tracy had a few ideas shortly after his arrival: he would begin an English school, where Chinese students eager to learn that language for its value in commerce and government might come for instruction in religious subjects as well. In addition, the Singapore missionaries could begin a boarding school on the model of the domestic education program in the Cherokee and Ceylon missions. They could thus separate male and female students from the bad examples "of the adult Chinese generally" and bring them under American Protestant influence. The mission might even take over the government's Singapore Institution, the planned college for youth from Singapore and the region. The missionaries thought about turning it into a missionary school that would teach the arts and sciences "only as auxiliaries" to the important subject of the "spirit of the gospel."

These, though, were not the only plans for what missionaries might do in Singapore. Daniel Bradley, for his part, had long been thinking about the benefits of creating a Christian colony in Asia. The year before he came to Singapore, he spent some time in Burma visiting with American missionaries there and began to think seriously about putting this idea into action. This type of colony, Bradley wrote, would involve sending "more laymen of various occupations to engage in the work of Christian missions." They would not be missionaries in the sense of being preachers, but they would be teachers and evangelists of a sort. They would demonstrate Christian living to those around them and teach in mission schools. The colonists would "support themselves while they reap an abundant harvest of souls," Bradley predicted. Able to work in whatever field they were trained in, they would be able to sustain themselves financially while still contributing to the mission's goal of converting the world. In a letter from Moulmein, Bradley described this plan as a "favorite theme of mine." So long as governments would support the work, Bradley believed that this would be an ideal way of bringing about the conversion of the world.[18] Tracy clearly agreed, and the two expected that the British Empire would be able to support this kind of endeavor. To this end, they began to reach out to American and British officials to learn more about "what can be done by [American] farmers and mechanics for the heathen in these regions." Within a year, the missionaries had their answers and had formed their proposal for a Christian colony at Singapore.[19]

To name a missionary enterprise a "colony" was certainly new, but when American missionaries proposed their colony, they were in fact acting in the tradition of what American missionaries had been doing for the past several decades. In all of its missions, the "conversion of the world" that the Board hoped to accomplish could not, its members believed, be accomplished by preaching alone. Missionaries worked in several branches—teaching and translation being the most important—as they tried to spread the word of the Gospel. Through these aspects of mission work, nonordained Americans could become part of the mission family, and indeed every mission included assistants who were not ordained ministers. Some of the missions employed printers, for example, to work at mission presses. All of the missions established schools. In some locations these were extensive boarding establishments that taught not only academic subjects, but also the so-called "arts of civilization," including husbandry and needlework. This was part of what Bradley and Tracy meant by a Christian colony. In Singapore, they were in many ways hoping to re-create the settlement-style mission of the Cherokee Nation and Sandwich Islands in the British Empire.

On the one hand, this plan was focused on the needs of Singaporeans. At the same time, though, the missionaries hoped to inaugurate a change in American religious culture by providing a means for more people to become engaged in mission work. When the Singapore missionaries reflected on the Americans they met before their departure, "whose hearts burned with love to Christ and the souls of the poor heathen, and who expressed to us a wish to become our fellow laborers in the missionary work," it seems only natural that they would resolve, as they did, to find out whether such individuals could be "useful" to the mission. Indeed, such individuals had found important roles in other missions of the Board. The missionaries and their leaders in the Board all agreed that there were not enough men and women currently working as missionaries. The Singapore missionaries were sure that if a colony could be established that followed their plan, these "uneducated Christians" could be "very useful," as well as able to "obtain a livelihood and promote the temporal and eternal good of the heathen."[20]

Once Tracy and Bradley began to think about a colony in Singapore, they began to research what it would take to put this plan into action. They wrote to the governors of Singapore, Malacca, and Penang, sending a

list of questions to each. They also discussed the matter with other prominent British members of society in Singapore. Their questions were quite
detailed. They asked about obtaining land and paying rent, about soil cultivation, and about what types of occupations American colonists should
have. They asked where the colony should be located, in the town or the
country, and whether the correspondent agreed with them that such a
project was a good idea. While they "explicitly promise[d]" these leaders
that no such colony had yet been established, their questions were detailed
enough to attract attention. They asserted that while such a colony would
be independent of the mission, its goals would be "in harmony" with the
Board's plans in Asia.

Their responses were, as Bradley described them, "very encouraging."[21] Perhaps the most important question that the missionaries asked was
whether the English government would "countenance a Christian Colony
in Singapore? Would the government afford the necessary protections?" To
this, they received the answer that the Singapore government "doubtlessly
would—whether from benevolent or political motives. The authorities
cannot but see that any attempt to ameliorate the moral and civil condition
of the people must ultimately tend to the advantage of the rulers."[22] Most
of these correspondents agreed that the Singaporeans would anxiously welcome those willing to teach them. Other responses were similarly positive
toward the project and suggested that the British would allow an American colony of this sort to exist within Singapore. The Americans expected
to be able to obtain land rent-free for the purposes of their colony, and
their research led them to believe that the colony would quickly become
self-supporting. The director of the police promised "all the protection in
his power" to the American colony.[23]

When they proposed the colony to the Board, these missionaries had to
explain what a colony could do that a mission on its own could not. Bradley
and Tracy set out the ultimate goal of the colony as to improve "the temporal, and most especially the eternal good of the heathen or Mohammed-
ans, among whom it should be located." The missionaries spent the largest
portion of this communication answering whether a colony was the best
means of accomplishing that object. Unsurprisingly, they insisted that it was.
The Malay language could be learned, they insisted, in a matter of months,
from which point colonists could speak to natives about the simple truths of
the Gospel. They went into great detail explaining their plans to the Board,
writing a thirty-five-page joint letter, accompanied by documents from
other supporters of their ideas within Singapore and the surrounding area.

By the time that they approached the Board about the idea, they had a pretty clear idea of what this colony would look like. It would be a settlement of about twenty families of pious Americans, including a clergyman, a physician and surgeon, male and female schoolteachers, several farmers, a blacksmith, a carpenter and cabinetmaker, tool and machine makers, a millwright, a goldsmith, a clock maker, and a cobbler. The first several of these were common, or becoming so, at missions around the world, but the latter categories were more specialized than missions employed. The colony would also require women, of course, and on this matter the Singapore missionaries also showed their similarities to the settler-style missions. They encouraged the employment of single women as teachers in Southeast Asia in the mid-1830s, when the practice was very rare indeed at the Board's overseas missions. These women, missionaries hoped, would be better able to reach the "countless" children and women to whom the missionaries had little access. Women were needed to "go into their dwellings" armed with Christian texts, to "win the confidence of their mothers, enlist the affections of the children . . . and gather them into day schools and Sabbath schools."[24] To find such women and men, and to supervise the colony, the missionaries suggested that Americans form a "'Christian' or 'Missionary Colonization Society.'"[25] That this society would in fact govern the colony suggests that the missionaries had something more in mind than simply encouraging American settlement. They did not adopt the language of colonies lightly.

This colony would serve as a "Christian example" to Singaporeans, revealing all the benefits of both the Protestant religion and civilization. In particular, the mission hoped the colonists would teach the virtues of industry, as the missionaries felt idleness to be a particular problem for the Malay, leading to poverty and preventing them from advancing in civilization. Missionaries expected that a colonial example would be effective because they believed that all those they met in Singapore were "in the habit of looking up to Europeans and Americans as their superiors and hovering around them for employment." The colonists, then, could expect both access to the people and a willing audience for conversations. "Example is better than precept," the missionaries insisted, and the Board would have agreed with this. Indeed, missionaries had long been understood to serve this important role of exemplifying the Christian and civilized lifestyle. What was different here was only that the examples would not only be provided by missionaries, but by laypeople as well.

The colonists would be men and women with something like a missionary spirit: marked by "fervent" love of God and men, with a "humble but firm dependence on God," with "economy and self-denial," "prudence and aptness to teach the natives simple truths and how to do common things." The missionaries expected this to be a great help to their evangelization, allowing them to "point the heathen to an example of that purity and holiness of life, which he enjoins upon them; but of which, without such example, they can form no definite conception."[26] Much of these descriptions of who the colonists would be sounded a lot like descriptions of who the missionaries would be, though there were key differences. What set colonists apart from missionaries was that, while missionaries pooled their resources and depended on the donations of American supporters to keep their work going, the colonists could expect to make a living in Singapore. They would still make their property a common stock, but there was less of an expectation that they should necessarily be living frugally. Missionaries were attentive to this issue and researched how much Americans would be able to charge for their labor relative to Singaporeans and whether they would be able to support themselves, given that they would in all likelihood charge more than their native competitors. The colony would only work if the colonists could expect to be rewarded for their services.

Reflecting their assumption of the superiority of American workers, missionaries never suggested that colonists consider charging less for their labors. The missionaries and their supporters in Singapore believed that the American colonists would be able to survive even with higher prices, because they would necessarily be more skilled in their work and could therefore justify the cost to discriminating customers. This dynamic of competition was wholly different from anything that could have been proposed as part of a mission itself. Indeed, when British residents in Singapore suggested that the colony could benefit from a watchmaker, they did so because there currently were none in Singapore, and the European community would appreciate having such skilled labor. The colony, then, would not be wholly focused on the non-Christian and non-European population. It would in a very real way be an extension of a Euro-American colonial presence in Singapore.[27]

The colonists would serve as teachers—some in the informal sense of teaching by example, and others in the formal sense of instructing children in schools. As the missionaries described the importance of schools within their colony, they did not say anything particularly different from what missionaries had long been saying about schools within missions. They described Singapore as "swarm[ing] with children" who were currently without any educational opportunities. The result of such an upbringing was obvious to missionary observers. Education was important because it was those who "educate the children of the present generation" who would "form the character of the next." Without the right kind of educators, children would grow up into the habits of "idleness and vice" that missionaries insisted plagued Singapore. Missionaries in the region had little difficulty finding students, even more than they could possibly handle. Illiterate parents, they reported, "despise their own language, have not literature, and feel their inferiority to Europeans." They came to missions begging for their children to be educated and saddened to learn that the missionaries could not educate them. With a colony, the missionaries urged, Christian schools could be easily established in which children could come and break the cycle of "wretchedness in this life and misery in the future." They would not only learn academic subjects, but also the "cultivation of the earth," which missionaries felt was "absolutely necessary for the improvement of the state of the natives generally." For less than two dollars a month, the missionaries insisted, these children could be fed, clothed, and boarded in the schools away from the bad examples of their families. In twenty years, the missionaries imagined, Singapore would be transformed.[28]

The schools that they proposed here sound a good deal like the boarding schools that were, in fact, present at most of the mission stations of the Board. In light of these similarities to other Board missions, it is somewhat surprising that the Board reacted as negatively as it did. The Prudential Committee called the colony "both inexpedient and impracticable." One of the missionary assistants at Singapore referred to the plan as a "crazy project." The Prudential Committee held a special meeting after receiving the proposal from the Singapore missionaries and passed three unanimous resolutions condemning the idea. They declared that no such colonies would be formed in Singapore or anywhere else, criticized the missionaries for discussing this plan with officials from the East India Company, and authorized a leader of the London Missionary Society to deny Americans had any plans to colonize EIC territories to the directors of the East India Company in London. Though individual members of the committee admitted that they would "rejoice" to see American laymen move to "different parts of the heathen world" where they might "while pursuing their respective secular vocations . . . exert a direct and efficient influence in propagating the gospel of Jesus," such a colony would be impossible.[29]

This conclusion had a great deal to do with location. Singapore, of course, was under the control of the East India Company, and that made at least some of the difference. To colonize any part of the world from the

United States would be, as the Board explained, a "subject of so much delicacy," but because of the Board's dependence on the East India Company for its many missions in South Asia, this was even more delicate. The Board was horrified to hear that the missionaries had already approached East India Company governors with this proposal. They were most alarmed, perhaps, by the discussion of how this colony would relate to the East India Company itself. "The colony will of course become subject to the laws of the Government whose protection and favor it enjoys," Tracy and Bradley wrote to the governor of Singapore and Malacca, although they expected also "to participate all the rights of conscience and religion which they possess in the land of the Pilgrims." That is to say, they recognized that their colony would be dependent on the East India Company's government, but expected to be treated as Americans and to enjoy certain freedoms of religion as such. The basis for such expectations was unclear. The "land of the Pilgrims" had no authority in Singapore. At this point, the United States did not even have a recognized consul there. Still the missionaries expected the privileges of citizenship to follow Americans as they settled overseas. Politically, this could be awkward. It certainly suggests that the missionaries were not using the term *colony* lightly—they did expect some sort of sovereignty to exist within the colony separate from the British government.[30]

The Prudential Committee was worried because of its prior dealings with the East India Company. As part of the EIC's holdings, Singapore could not be considered in isolation. Although some of the missionaries' supporters believed that the English government would support such a colony from both benevolent and political motives (recognizing that the improvement of the "moral and civil condition of the people must ultimately tend to the advantage of the rulers," as one of these supporters explained), the Board was not so sure.[31] If the British East India Company became angered by this attempt to establish an American colony, then many of the Board's missions could be put at risk. The governor of Singapore, they pointed out, would be duty-bound to forward the missionaries' correspondence to the Governor General in Bengal, and from there, it could be sent to London.

Only a year before, the Board had been unsure whether the East India Company would allow missionaries to operate within its territories on the grounds that they were American. Now, the missionaries were canceling out all earlier attempts to make the American missions appear apolitical and disinterested in imperial politics. All of their missions in Asia, they worried, were at risk. The Board was hardly being paranoid here. Within the next year, the Board was receiving reports from South Africa that some British

officials there were being accused of traitorous behavior for supporting
the American mission at Port Natal. There, newspapers included "tirades"
against the American mission, with the "grand objection . . . that our *mission
will only be a forerunner of a colony*—an *American colony*."[32] The Board was
concerned enough that Rufus Anderson quickly wrote to William Ellis of
the LMS, authorizing him to speak to the Board of Directors of the East
India Company on their behalf. The Board found the idea "inexpedient and
impracticable," Anderson told Ellis, and they were upset that the missionaries had opened correspondence with the East India Company on such a
delicate subject.[33]

The Board's concerns about the implications of this colony went
beyond worrying about the status of missionaries. Americans in general
had a somewhat precarious position within Singapore. The missionaries
ought to have been well aware of this situation. Balestier was well known
to the missionaries. Within the first month of Tracy's time in Singapore,
he had spent a considerable amount of time with him, during which they
discussed the extent of trade in Singapore, the possibility of the Americans
taking over the Singapore Institution (Balestier was in favor of this), and
the possible opportunities for American laymen to live and help the people
of Singapore.[34] It was not only Tracy that had this sort of relationship with
the consul. The most enthusiastic supporter of the Christian colony, Daniel
Bradley, had lived with Balestier upon first arriving in Singapore in 1834.
The two seem to have stayed in touch; when Bradley asked for advice about
his proposed colony, Balestier's reply assumed that the missionary had been
aware of some health problems the consul had been enduring.

Surprisingly, Balestier was considerably less concerned than the Board
proved to be about the proposed American colony. His answers were mostly
matter-of-fact descriptions of soil and produce, though he did remind the
missionaries that "the East India Company are the Lords of all the territory" and they should not expect any particular deal on obtaining land and
rents. His most negative comment concerned the difficulty that American
farmers would have in surviving the climate: "You are aware," he wrote,
"that no American constitution could endure working in the field" in
that region of the world. He was enthusiastic, though, about the importance of teachers and the medical dispensary that the mission had already
established, both aspects of the mission that would not require such a large
scale and had been successful elsewhere within the East India Company's
holdings. He suggested that the mission begin holding a series of public
lectures in the Malay language.[35]

As they had done earlier in India, the Board missionaries leapt into the planning of their mission without sufficient consideration of their position as Americans in the British Empire. If the officers of the East India Company in Asia and London had to correspond repeatedly about whether or not American ships might be welcome in their ports, American farmers calling themselves colonists certainly would not be welcome.

The Board's scolding letter to Tracy and Bradley highlight the ways in which the Board had, by the late 1830s, shifted away from political engagement. Even as the Prudential Committee suggested its approval of the colonial project in the abstract, the cumulative experience of the Board's experience around the world had by this time soured its leadership against schemes like this. In writing to the Canton missionaries about this proposal, Anderson compared the Singapore colony to Liberia when he explained, "This is not the time for proposing in this country another Colonization Soc't." His reasons for this referenced the difficulties of finding the "right organization" for such a society, as well as the "immense and insufferable difficulties in selecting the colonists, and in importing the necessary restraints upon them when upon the ground they are to occupy." At the same time that Anderson was discussing colonization in Singapore he was also, of course, discussing colonization in Liberia with John Leighton Wilson and others. That context was clearly at the back of his mind as Anderson and others on the Prudential Committee received these proposals from Singapore. The controversies of Cherokee removal and American colonization in Liberia represented major challenges to the implementation of the Christian imperialism that Bradley and Tracy exhibited and that had defined much of the early mission movement.[36]

The Singapore Mission and Seminary Education

No colony was established at Singapore, but it did become the center of the Board's work in the region. Singapore was the location of a major missionary press, as well as the Board's seminary for "native helpers." All of the reasons that the earlier missionaries had felt it to be an ideal location for a colony made it seem perfect for these other purposes. It was centrally located, and easy to reach from many different places. Accordingly, it became the "central station," as the Board explained to a group of new missionaries. It was quite well staffed, with around a dozen missionaries, wives, and assistants throughout the 1830s. Additionally, missionaries destined for

other locations frequently stopped in Singapore, staying with the missionaries there before proceeding to their final stations.[37]

Once the colonial plan was quashed, much of the business of the Singapore mission proceeded in the same manner as the Board's other Asian missions. Ira Tracy, James Dickinson, William Arms, and Alfred North divided
their labor among themselves and turned their attention to education. They
established schools for boys and girls. Gradually, they began taking control of a number of local schools, as when they took over a Malay school
that they reported the parents had established "for the purpose of instructing their children in chanting the Koran in Arabic." The Arabic studies
were exchanged for classes in Malay.[38] They took some of these students
in as boarders, building them a separate building for eating and sleeping in
August 1836, and arranging for someone to care for their laundry. Previously, the boys had been in charge of their own cleaning, which apparently
was not satisfactory. In September, they discussed whether it would be a
good idea to "secure native boys by indenture, in order to [have] a more
efficient government of the schools." This educational system was certainly
not on the scale of the Sandwich Islands or the Cherokee missions, but
it was by no means a small one. They were following the general mission
protocol of establishing as large scale a mission as they could, given the
constraints of the political context in which they worked.[39]

These schools, though, were not the primary focus of the mission. The
Board emphasized to its missionaries that there were two main priorities for
Singapore: the press and the seminary. The Board had purchased a printing
press complete with typesets from a retiring British missionary in 1834, and
so found itself immediately stocked to begin printing on a large scale in a
number of languages. Despite some legal confusion about the transfer of
the press from the British to the Americans, this meant that the Singapore
mission could emphasize translation and distribution of scripture and tracts.
This seemed to be a wonderful prospect. Here they could print the materials missionaries would need not only in Singapore, but in Southeast Asia
more generally because of its position in regional trade. The Dutch colonial
government on many of the nearby islands would not allow missionaries
to reside and create tracts within their territories, and the Siamese government similarly was not receptive to work on the scale that the missionaries
envisioned. Charles Robinson, one of the missionaries planning to work in
Siam, expressed this concern when he wrote that he did not know "*what we
can do at Siam* if the *press here should be abandoned.*" In Singapore, "a free port,
and under British rule," as the Board reminded its supporters, missionaries

would be able to create the texts that would have important effects on the people of the region. American supporters were similarly excited about these prospects. In 1834, the American Tract Society and American Bible Society both granted over twenty thousand dollars to the Board's press in Singapore. The missionaries were pleased with this news, and by the implications that through it, their country would "act a conspicuous part in the evangelization of the world."[40]

By the end of 1835, the Singapore mission was printing more than 2 million pages annually, in more than forty-four thousand tracts in Chinese, Malay, and Bugis; the following year, the Board issued a partial report claiming some hundred thousand tracts printed in 1836. Only some of those were distributed in Singapore, the rest were sent on to other distributors in Siam and China. As the missionaries described this situation to their supporters in America, they explained that the Chinese were a "reading people," and so when missionaries attempted to distribute texts, they were "eagerly" received. The missionaries would spend several hours a week visiting ships in the harbor and distributing the tracts among those they met. In this way, the missionaries were able to imagine their reach extending from Singapore into China, Cochin China, Siam, Borneo, and Celebes.[41]

Within a few years, though, the Singapore missionaries' enthusiasm for the press had waned. The number of readers, they reported, was "smaller than has been supposed." While the Board's printed reports did not go into much detail about this, the mission's printer, Alfred North, wrote extensively about the problem of distributing texts in Singapore. He had visited a number of ships at harbor in Singapore in order to conduct an unofficial survey of the men they hoped to reach through their printed materials. Of the Malay and Bugis men he spoke to, only a small proportion, "less than one in eleven," he found "even pretended to read," and of these, few could read intelligibly. Because there were so few readers, he explained, there was not much point in printing extensively. As the Board in Boston considered sending more printers and bookbinders to Singapore, and wondered about shipping a power press, North insisted that there was "scarcely anything to print." Translation efforts had not been as quick as he had hoped, and there were only a few tracts ready for distribution. When this was combined with the low level of readership, the effect was clear. In just a few weeks, he wrote, they could print enough of those tracts "to supply all the Bugis and Javan readers in the world, if access could be had to them."[42] As expected, there were more Chinese readers, but he informed the Board that the differences between the groups was not so great "as seems to be supposed in America."

Printing gradually slowed as a result. By 1839, the mission was printing fewer books than before, but still "enough to meet the demand." This was not cause to abandon the mission, however. For the Board, this served as a call to expand their efforts with education.

It was not lost on any of the missionaries that by the time they reached the island, there had been efforts at evangelization there for two decades. British missionaries had emphasized the distribution of tracts and books. By 1836, North had declared them improvident: their time in Singapore had "left scarcely a trace of their long labors. . . . They seem not to have been aware that the surest and quickest way of spreading Christianity is to aim at making *deep impressions on particular minds*, and not a general, indistinct impression on the mind of multitudes."[43] The way to do this, the American missionaries were sure, was through education. The Board reminded its supporters that "it is no less scriptural to teach people to read the word of God, than it is to circulate that word." The mission needed to teach, not only to allow their students to access the texts that they were printing, but to enable them to teach even more of their countrymen so that they, too, might be able to read tracts and Scripture.[44]

The Singapore Seminary was only one of several proposed seminaries across the Board's many missions. They hoped to have as many as fifteen such institutions opened throughout the world. Everywhere, the missions needed teachers and evangelists whom they could trust. While they frequently hired indigenous teachers, these rarely shared a religion with the missionaries themselves. Accordingly, the schools could only do so much to advance their religious goals. The seminaries were supposed to help fix this problem. Further, the Board insisted that it was "utter[ly] hopeless" to think that the United States and Europe could send "an adequate supply of preachers" for the "heathen," and so the only solution was to "thoroughly educat[e] a select number of native inhabitants." These "native helpers" would be at a major advantage over foreign missionaries: "The climate will be natural, the language vernacular, the manners, habits, and customs of the people familiar; and who, to use the expressive language of a convert from heathenism, 'having been heathen, know how heathen think.'"[45]

By providing advanced education to the best of the missions' students, the seminaries would train future teachers who would be allied with the goals of the mission. They would be, in the Board's phrasing, the "native helpers" of the missions. They would be able to touch people beyond the reach of the missionaries. They would teach and itinerate, and eventually would help transition the missions into native churches. This would be a long process, but the Board was committed to it and was to become more so over the course of the nineteenth century. Accordingly, the plans for the Board's seminaries reveal what they had come to believe the "heathen world" needed in order to become fully Christian. In training seminary students, the missionaries were training the future leaders of the native church. This was important work, and they had very clear goals for what they wanted to see these students learn over the course of their education.

The seminary would educate young men who had previously distinguished themselves in the lower mission schools. They would board at the mission for several years. Their education itself would be directed toward making them mission workers. While the Board recognized that not all of the students would go on to work in the mission, they were explicitly not training young men to become lawyers, doctors, merchants, or civil servants. That was the work of government-sponsored schools. The seminaries were to combine the projects of colleges and theological schools, remembering that it was their duty to do "all in our power to fit [their students] for usefulness on earth, and prepare [them] for heaven." Accordingly, they would use "THE GOSPEL OF JESUS and the BIBLE" as their "text-book."

The missionaries would teach in English, deemed the best way to "open the world of truth to the contemplation of our select pupils." English-language training would, they believed, "place them almost a century in advance of the great body of their countrymen." Language, the Board believed, was connected to "the opinions, prejudices, and intellectual and moral habits" of a nation; teaching in English, rather than Asian languages, would thus remove the students from some of the problems missionaries saw among those non-Christian cultures. "Native literature" would also be studied, but for specific purposes. Mainly, this would teach both the students and the missionaries themselves what the "actual state of the native mind" was like, for only through such study could they expect to "remove its errors" or "guard their message from being fatally misapprehended." The students, too, would need such study in order to gain the respect of their countrymen.

Because graduates of the seminary were to become teachers in one way or another, much of their education was designed with this in mind. They were to "feel for the ignorance of other minds," and learn how to teach others. The missionaries recognized their own limitations here. They knew that they were not always the best vessels of the Gospel for the "heathen world." They were outsiders, but these students would be insiders. The difficult part of training them, then, would be to find the balance between being sufficiently allied with the missionaries without losing the thing that would make them so valuable to the mission: their "native" status. Lest they be accused of abandoning their native cultures and assimilating too fully to missionary norms, the Board wanted them to be able to be learned in their own literature as well. Then they might be better able to gain trust and convert their hearers. Such study would also help them to be able to prepare books in native languages for the press. The whole program of the seminary, then, was designed to expand the missions.

The Board, characteristically, had grand visions for the effects of these schools. If they were able to open the fifteen seminaries they hoped for, and if each of these could have sixty pupils, they would, in twenty years, see some three thousand graduates. Even if only a third of these worked for the missions, they estimated, that would still leave one thousand "educated native helpers." Within a few years of the planned American colony, the Board was planning a different sort of expansion. If *The Conversion of the World* had thrilled evangelical supporters in America with estimates of how easily huge numbers of missionaries might be found to embark on the work of foreign missions two decades earlier, now American readers could envision the training up of a native army of evangelists, educated by the American mission but not financially supported by American Christians (an important consideration after the Panic of 1837). American farmers would not serve as the examples of Christian living for the "heathen world." That job would be undertaken by native seminary graduates.

In earlier years, the Board had attempted to create these helpers at the Foreign Mission School in Cornwall, Connecticut. That school had closed in 1827, however, and the seminaries emerged as a new possibility. The Cornwall school was designed to train "heathen" youth within the United States. By bringing them into the heart of civilization, it was hoped, they would come to adopt the lifestyle of Americans and might even convert to Christianity. They could then return home as civilized Christians, ready to teach others what they had learned. However, this idea of training foreign students in New England seemed doomed from the start. Graduates did not go on to help the missions to the extent that the Board expected. In spite of the seeming promise of Oobookiah and his fellow Hawaiian students, as a whole, the school did not produce missionary assistants. When two Cherokee students married white women from Connecticut, further, the resulting scandal led to some bad press for the Board. Educating "heathen" students among civilized families seemed dangerous, inappropriate, and what was worst of all to evangelical viewers, not likely to result in the conversion of students or their nations. Accordingly, the school was quietly closed, but the issue of training native assistants did not disappear. The seminaries emerged as a new plan that might serve the same goals without the problems inherent in bringing students from overseas into America.[46]

The Singapore Seminary was slow in getting started. The mission was not able to enlist its sixty pupils. Only twenty-two boys were enrolled in 1838, even as the Board insisted to its supporters that "no better place can be found, at present, in that part of the world" for such an institution. Attracted by the cosmopolitanism of the island, missionaries were troubled when parents were reluctant to enlist their children in a multiyear boarding school with the explicit goal of changing their children's religion. Malay and Bugis parents were, the Board reported "bigoted Mohamedans, indifferent to the education of their children, and fearful to trust them a long time with the missionaries as boarding scholars, lest they should become Christians." Chinese parents, as well, were "indifferent and deceptive." Children from Siam could not be educated at the seminary either, as native-born subjects were legally prohibited from leaving the kingdom. Nothing, they decided, could be accomplished until parents would be willing to leave their children with the missionaries for "a certain number of years." This would take time.[47]

The American missionaries were not alone in their difficulties to establish a seminary in Singapore. British missionaries and colonists, too, were interested in education in this region, and their work with the College at Malacca and the Singapore Institution shared many of the same problems that the Board faced. LMS missionaries, including Robert Morrison, founded Malacca College in 1820. Morrison brought a combination of evangelism, linguistic interest, and commercial connections to bear on the creation of the college. Malacca College was designed to serve God, Morison insisted, but its curriculum focused heavily on the Chinese language, and it prepared students for careers in law, medicine, and business. Among LMS missionaries, the college caused a fair amount of controversy: over the prioritization of Chinese over Malay studies, over religious versus secular subjects, and about the propriety of missionaries running a school of this sort at all.

In Singapore itself, the colony's founder, Sir Stamford Raffles, had established the Singapore Institution with similar goals. He had at several points tried to bring the LMS missionaries to combine their efforts with the institute. This would, he hoped, make the Singapore Institute a valuable educational option for young men in Singapore. He, too, combined religious and secular concerns, with a general assertion that the school would serve the cause of God. Yet the LMS missionaries insisted that it was too secular, and they did not join in the school. Neither of these schools was particularly successful in attracting students or keeping them enrolled. Both attempted to engage students for several years at a time and experimented with offering stipends to students to keep them from leaving the school for employment. European observers complained that neither was able to rise up to the high levels that their programs promised; the Malacca College was called "an elementary school" by one such visitor. By the time the American missionaries had arrived in Singapore, it was these schools that stood out as their examples and, to a certain extent, their competitors.[48]

The boarding aspect of the seminary is reminiscent of the boarding schools that the Board established around the world, including those at the settler missions. Aspects of the planned Christian colony, then, did make it into the mission that was ultimately established at Singapore. The only missing component was the population of nonmissionary support staff, which was deemed impossible by the political context Americans faced in Singapore in the 1830s.

The clear resemblance of the proposed colony to other—uncontroversial, even celebrated—American missions is further telling of the difference that terminology made for American mission supporters in these years. In their denial of the proposed colony, the Board was denying an American interest in colonization. Politically, it was inexpedient to form an American colony in Asia in 1836. The logic behind such a proposal, however, was far less controversial. No one argued with the central premise of such a colony: that Singapore's culture needed to change, and that American Christians could serve as appropriate models for civilization. The plan was also based on the idea that Americans were active in the world, that even uneducated laymen and women were invested in the fate of the "heathen" from around the globe and wanted to do their part to help bring about "the conversion of the world." As other Americans looked west for the expansion of American territory and influence, supporters of world mission looked east. As missionaries and their supporters debated the creation of colonies in Singapore and elsewhere in Asia, they spoke about a sort of secularization of the mission project, and a larger American claim to leadership on a world stage.

In their attempt to establish a distinctly American mission station in Singapore, the missionaries again struggled with the reality of working within a British imperial field. In addition to the proposed colony, Singapore created problems for the Board by being the occasion of the first major conflicts with their peers in London over competition for mission locations. In 1812, when the Board was sending Judson, Nott, Newell, Hall, and Rice to India,

Samuel Worcester had instructed the missionaries that when it came to missionaries from Europe, "your only competition will be, who shall display most of the spirit, and do most of the honour of Christ." By the 1830s, though, missionaries from both sides of the Atlantic had begun to talk about "interference" and to feel more direct competitiveness over regional control and property. This anxiety underscored the transfer of the Singapore press from English to American hands, and it became an important topic in the correspondence of the directors of the two groups.[49]

Missionaries, too, worried that the British would feel that they were attempting to compete by entering this region. Charles Robinson, for example, wrote to the Board that the LMS missionaries in Malacca and Batavia would "remonstrate with our Board for sending missionaries here." These were not "reasonable" objections, he felt. The Singapore mission was the headquarters of the press, not a full mission in its own right. His solution was not to leave Singapore, though, but to purchase land and settle themselves more securely on the island. If they owned land, he explained, "we shall, as it were, be fellow citizens, entitled to equal rights of the land and buildings" and thus better able to go about their work.[50]

By the end of the 1830s, the American and British mission boards had resolved to cooperate with each other. The Board had discussed this in its 1838 Annual Meeting and had concluded that it was essential for the different groups to come to a mutual understanding in regard to the territorial boundaries of their work. They suggested that, going forward, whenever a missionary society hoped to establish a new mission in a region that another society occupied, the two groups should consult with each other before anything new be attempted. In that spirit, they asked if the London Society would object to American missionaries at Batavia or the Prince of Wales Island. The minutes of the LMS's board meetings in that year reveal resolutions to send letters to the ABCFM, informing them of the British society "cordially approved" of the newly proposed American missions. When the Board prepared to end its work in Singapore at the end of the decade, as it became easier to send missionaries into China, they offered to sell their land and premises to the London Society. By the 1840s, the Board had become closer than ever to actually being a partner with the British in the work of world evangelization. Such a partnership, however, was constrained by the realities of the British and American overseas imperial presence. For while the British missionaries could be more sure of their standing in Asia because of the British Empire, Americans had no such clarity. For there were no American colonies in Asia, at least not in the 1830s.

Missions and colonies often went hand in hand, of course. This was evidently the case for the European experience in the nineteenth century. It stood to reason that it could be the case for Americans, too. But Americans did not generally identify as a colony-forming people at this time, and so the history of the American colony at Singapore seems an odd one. If nothing else, it reminds us that some Americans at the time were, in fact, thinking about colonies. After all, at the same time as the Board was dealing with the proposed colony at Singapore, they were beginning to feel the strain of operating a mission within another American colony—that of the American Colonization Society in Liberia. By the late-1830s, too, the Board had seen its celebrated missions to the Cherokee, which resembled the proposed colony to a remarkable degree, torn apart by Indian removal. After a decade of cooperation between the American government and the Board, the missionaries' faith in cultural transformation through secular means was challenged.

American missions brought Americans into contact with the rest of the world long before the beginning of what is generally understood to be the imperial age of the United States. As the Singapore mission reminds us, there were some Americans who were thinking in imperial terms even before the American entry into the Philippines in 1898, and there were alternate visions of what an American colony in Asia would look like. The Christian imperialism of the missionaries of the early republic consistently came up against the empires of governments, but it represented a significant vision for a global America.[51]

Conclusion

Missionaries and American Imperialism

In 1846, the ABCFM reflected on the first third of a century of their work. Thirty-four years after the Bombay missionaries first left America, the Board could claim mission stations across the globe. Now, with all of their past experiences to guide them, they wondered how successful they had been. They wondered, too, how a missionary ought to measure success. Was it just a matter of conversions and baptisms, or were they also looking for a larger kind of transformation? The members of the Board knew that their work was not done in 1846. Even though they understood that to many of their supporters, "it would almost seem as if a single missionary in a city, or a dozen in a kingdom, might speedily transform an ignorant, sensual, idolatrous, and selfish community into a nation of intelligent, moral, Christian freemen," such was not the case. Perhaps part of the reason for this lay in their understanding of what success would look like at this point. As they continued their reflection, they suggested that their work would be done only when the missionaries could "put a British or American face on the whole Chinese empire."[1]

By the mid-1840s, the Board and its missionaries were not the only Americans thinking about the role their country would play on the world stage. The merchants and missionaries who envisioned a global reach of

American influence in the early years of the century were now joined by the expansionists who claimed it was the manifest destiny of the United States to spread its reach across the continent and into Latin America. The year 1846 not only marked the end of the first third of a century of the Board, it also marked the beginning of the war between the United States and Mexico. In that conflict, American soldiers fought Mexicans whom they described as mongrels in order to gain new territory for the expansion of U.S. sovereignty and white plantation agriculture. Like the missionaries, they saw a divine hand guiding their actions on behalf of their country, although their ideas about where Providence was leading them was very different. The Board and its supporters, indeed, were not among the supporters of that war. Its aggressive version of American imperialism did not gain their sympathy. Though the Board well understood that war could be helpful to their work, opening up new lands for missionary efforts (as it had in China), they did not see Texas and Mexico as a new location for their evangelization. Perhaps this was because Catholicism seemed too entrenched there. Missionary excursions to South America had reported difficulties with this earlier in the century. Catholicism was not enough to keep them out, though. The missionary vision for the role of the United States in the world, and for its adoption of a kind of Christian imperialism, was thoroughly distinct from the version of American empire put forth by the War Hawks. This was the battle over Cherokee removal all over again, and this time, the Board did not engage but continued to focus its attention on the rest of the world and on a transnational identification with British missionaries and their empire.

In their North American missions, though, the Board did contend with this new form of American imperialism. This occurred most notably at the Oregon mission, where Marcus and Narcissa Whitman had been sent to work among the Cayuse. They are as remembered for their role in American westward migration and Narcissa's position as the first white woman who traveled across the Rockies as they were for their mission work, which suggests that the 1840s were a transition period in the ways that Americans thought about themselves relative to the other peoples of the world. This was not a very successful mission, and the Whitmans soon came to focus most of their efforts on the pioneers who made their mission a common stopping point along the Oregon Trail. It became, then, a home mission, focused on keeping the West a place of religion and morality, rather than a foreign mission, focused on converting the world. In many ways, the Whitmans were doing what the Wilsons had been told not to do: focusing their attention on colonists over natives. The mission was abandoned in 1847, when the Whitmans were murdered by the people they had ostensibly come to serve. Angered by the influx of white American settlers and the illnesses that had come among them, the Cayuse struck against the symbol of the American presence there: the mission. In this mission, the missionaries had embraced the American settlement of the land and paid for it. The Whitmans' acceptance of Manifest Destiny's version of imperialism broke with a central premise of the foreign mission movement up to this point: that an important goal of empire ought to be the betterment of the lives and conditions of the "heathen" in colonized lands.

The Board's Christian imperialism was never realized, and indeed probably never could have been. When they described the wide extent of a missionary's labor in 1846, the Board hoped to explain the difficulties that a missionary faced. He alone was responsible for preaching, translating, printing, and distributing religious texts. "If any thing is to be done in the way of education," they continued, he must create the schools and the books to be used within them. The missionary was also responsible for "the social welfare of the people" and anything done "to improve their character and habits." This wide list of duties begins to sound more and more like the work of a government as the list goes on. The Board's missionaries did not trust most governments to do this, for they thought it was not sufficient to simply trade with or settle a new land. These places had to be improved. The missionary, they explained, "stands alone on an elevated platform, and his work is, God strengthening and blessing him, to raise the depressed community around him up to his level." Bringing the whole of the world up to their own level in terms of religion and civilization was the goal of the Board's Christian imperialism. It was this cause that brought them into engagement with the world around them in the early republic.[2]

The early American foreign mission movement reminds us that Americans of the early republic were attuned to the events and peoples of the world around them. Missionaries and their supporters were committed to a kind of Christian imperialism that they thought would make the world a better place by spreading the Kingdom of God. This idea emerged from the politics of their day. Missionaries of the early republic lived in a world defined by the British Empire. Even as they were creating a new republic, these Anglophilic evangelicals kept one eye across the Atlantic, measuring themselves against England's model. Unsurprisingly, when missionaries imagined what sorts of forces could bring about the ends they desired, they did so in the terminology of their time: empires and colonies. Even when they criticized the real applications of these types of imperialism in Asia, America, and Africa, they held out hope that somehow, in the right hands, a truly Christian empire could be created on this earth.

This is not a picture of the early republic we are used to considering. The missionary public was Anglophilic and conservative, but possessed a hopefulness and industriousness that marked them as products of the early American republic. Their continued focus on England and the world touched by the British Empire reveals how much continuity existed in the postrevolutionary era in the Atlantic world. Indeed, the major change that occurred after the Revolution for these Americans was that the Atlantic became a gateway to the larger world.

Not all Americans in the early republic were interested in world missions, of course. For American Protestants, the mission movement would have been something they were at least aware of, if not deeply committed to. Many Americans, though, were committed. As they learned about the rest of the world, they were proud and glad to be from the United States, where they lived in a Christian civilization. Missionary literature reminded Americans of the blessings that they enjoyed, as well as the duties that they had to bear. For when Americans thought about the "heathen world," they did not simply sigh with relief that they were not part of that world, they wept for the fate of those who did not know Jesus, and who would accordingly be damned in the next life, even as they were miserable in this one.

Missionary supporters believed that everyone could and should be saved. Their sense of their own superiority in terms of religion, culture, and race combined with this conviction that ultimately, all people stood equally before God. As the people who already possessed knowledge of the Gospel and the means to teach others, they needed to engage in mission work. Religiously, this makes sense in light of the increase of religious reform movements through the Second Great Awakening. Politically, however, the mission movement does not quite fit with our understanding of this period. In order to act on their convictions, missionaries and their supporters needed to take advantage of the imperial and commercial networks that could connect them to the wider world. They needed to rely on their shared religious and cultural identities with British evangelicals for access to lands under the domain of British powers.

American evangelicals entered the foreign mission movement with a conviction that they should, and could, transform the world. Alongside the expansion of British and American imperial power, they sought to bring the "blessings of the gospel," which included not only faith in Jesus Christ, but also the "arts of civilization." As board secretary Rufus Anderson would explain, American evangelicals in the early republic thought that they would have succeeded when they could see the "heathen world" transformed into "a state of society such as we enjoy," complete with public education, settled agriculture, a particular organization of gender roles, and other markers of civilization. In India, the Cherokee Nation, Hawaii, Liberia, and Singapore, it was this sort of transformation that missionaries sought between the 1810s and 1840s. Only as a result of the political encounters that missionaries faced in these places and at home did the Board come to shift its theological understanding of the definition of its work, and of the relationship between Christianity and civilization.[3]

In the first decades of the foreign mission movement, American missions were dependent on the expansion of British and American power overseas. Foreign missions were only possible when the missionaries could physically reach non-Christians and find support. The imperial expansions of the early nineteenth century provided those opportunities for both British and American evangelicals to begin the work of world mission. Anglo-American missionaries hoped that these opportunities would mean not only that they could physically reach new places, but that they could expect cooperation and some unity of purpose between their work and that of the imperial powers, whether that meant the British East India Company, the U.S. government, or the American Colonization Society. From the missionary perspective, the access to new lands that these expansive political groups provided was providential. This too often led them to assume that the two groups had shared goals, and that the imperial vision of these governments would evenly map onto their own vision of the creation of God's kingdom throughout the world.

The missionaries saw the connection between their work and that of these governing bodies in the shared emphasis on civilization. Though they clearly saw a distinction between their work and the secular aims of empire, they saw the real value of the expansion of Anglo-American influence to be the spread of Anglo-American culture across the globe. This culture, they felt, was deeply entwined with the expression of "true Christianity," and thus their work was connected to that of imperialism. They had high hopes for the creation of a Christian imperialism that would unite these projects and bring about the conversion of the world. It was this link that led Samuel Newell and Gordon Hall to remind American evangelicals that concerns about mortality and risks in the "heathen world" were not so strong "as to deter the devotees of Mammon, from penetrating them for the sake of earthly treasures."[4]

The connection between civilization and Christianity was hard for the missionaries to disentangle, and this had to do both with the ways that they defined the two and their attempts to measure the genuineness of conversions. If evangelical Protestants of the early republic believed that one had only become a Christian when one's heart was changed, this was a difficult transformation to quantify or measure. While they reported huge crowds during itinerant preaching tours and significant numbers of hearers at regularly appointed services, very few "heathen" actually converted to Christianity under the watch of the Board's missionaries in these years. To be baptized and then received into church membership, the missionaries required "heathen" inquirers to display profound changes in their cultural behavior. To be Christian, they insisted, one had to be civilized.

In India, this meant that potential converts had to renounce caste. They had to enter monogamous marriages recognized by the mission. In the Cherokee Nation, missionaries emphasized dress and farming practices. Abandonment of her jewelry was a major sign of Catherine Brown's conversion. In Africa, dress was again emphasized, though less emphatically, and monogamy again became a major signal of religious transformation. In all of these places, missionaries emphasized education in their work, linking education and Christianity in both their own minds and those of potential converts. Gender norms, too, were central to this missionary construction of civilized Christianity. Missionaries themselves did their best to retain their Anglo-American culture, not adopting native practices themselves beyond the architecture of their buildings. Missionaries, the Board, and potential converts associated the form of Christian practice with its content.

The connection of mission work and civilization was evident not only in how the missionaries performed their work but in where they chose to go. In its discussions of potential mission sites, the Board relied on a "hierarchy of heathenism" that weighed both the current culture and the potential for civilization in deciding whether a given population would be likely candidates for conversion. Populations such as those in India, the Cherokee Nation, and West Africa, which were ultimately seen as being likely to obtain civilization, were chosen for mission sites. The slowness with which the Board entered Africa, however, is indicative of the ways that racial considerations were always present in these judgments of civilization.

Proximity to Anglo-American power was also important in the ways that the Board chose its mission locations. The British Empire, the imperial expansion of the United States into Indian Country, and the American colonization movement's colony in Liberia all provided missionaries with the physical support and cultural base that they thought they needed to pursue their work. As was particularly evident in the experience of the missionaries in India during the War of 1812, the ability to connect with the Board in Boston was extremely important, and when that was impossible, having another source of support made all the difference in the world. The ability for missionaries and then new converts to disseminate the Gospel was extremely important, missionaries thought, for the success of their work, and they believe that proximity to British and American governments would provide this.

While missionaries linked civilization with Christianity and saw the work of world mission and that of imperialism to be linked, governing powers often did not. In India, the Cherokee Nation, and Liberia, American missionaries came into conflict with the governments and found their project becoming too closely blended with politics. In Bombay, American missionaries were allowed to remain only with permission of the East India Company, and this permission could be difficult to obtain when the company was concerned with avoiding offending native non-Christians. During the War of 1812, the relationship between the missionaries and government was particularly tense. The missionaries to the Cherokee, too, confronted similar issues when the federal government shifted its Indian policy with the rise of Andrew Jackson. Under the new policy of forced removal, the goals of the mission and the government were no longer united. Similarly, in Liberia, missionaries came into conflict with the government of the Maryland Colonization Society when it became clear that the governor and colonists did not share the missionaries' goals of bringing civilization to Africa.

These conflicts all brought the missionaries into the realm of politics, most directly in the late-1820s and 1830s. In the Cherokee Nation and in Liberia, missionaries were particularly emphatic about the failure of governments to do their part to help the "heathen," perhaps because in both of these cases the governments in question were American. In both cases, missionaries felt betrayed when they found that their understanding of the governments' goals was not shared. The Board had hoped that the Civilization Fund of the federal government and the Colonization Society's commitment to "redeeming" Africa meant that the missions would be supported in their work of bringing civilization to non-Christians. Yet this was not the case. The arguments—and in the case of the Cherokee missionaries, the lawsuits—that emerged out of these misunderstandings about the goals of each group occurred because the missionaries felt it was their duty to become involved in politics when morality was in question. This had guided their work in India as well, and it shaped the course of their inter-actions with the federal government and the Colonization Society.

The missionary understanding of moral politics was based in a broad understanding of their work. They saw that their calling to convert the world was not only a theological matter, but a cultural one as well. In fact, these two were so closely aligned that they did not seem to need to disentangle them until their political involvement came under scrutiny by less sympathetic Christians. In the Cherokee Nation, this happened when observers critiqued the extent to which missionaries took their opposi-tion to Indian removal by challenging the laws of Georgia in the Supreme Court. The timing of this stand forced the missionaries to confront the Nullification Crisis, a political context that the Board could not justify as an issue that concerned their missionaries. In Liberia, the conflicts between missionary John Leighton Wilson and Governor John Russwurm became so heated that the missionaries left Liberia for Gabon to be outside of the reach of the colony. These experiences left the Board wary of the close association of its work with the issues of politics. The new mission to Sing-apore, established as these other crises were at their peak, reveals the ways that Christian imperialism guided and challenged missionaries by the end of this period.

It was in this context that the Board separated itself from antislavery politics in the 1840s, when abolitionists demanded that the Board take a firm stance on that issue. Slavery seemed to be a political question that quite clearly fit the definition of "moral politics" that had governed the Board's missionaries for decades. All that abolitionists were asking was that the Board declare itself to be an antislavery organization and require potential converts to give up slave-holding just as they had to give up other social vices such as polygamy. Yet the Board could not do this, and its reaction to the push of abolitionists led to a reformulation of its role in the world and of the duty of missions in bringing civilization. Moral politics no longer concerned the Board; only the dissemina-tion of Christianity would be its concern.

The missionary relationship to government, and of the connection between culture and Christianity, continued to plague the mission move-ment throughout the nineteenth and twentieth centuries. Even today, churches and missionaries struggle with what it means, exactly, to fulfill the call to bring the Gospel to the world. It has never been clear to those who seek to evangelize others how much of Christianity is "pure religion" and how much is culture and politics. The legacy of these struggles can be seen as the churches that were planted by Western missions now claim authority to govern themselves and to have a powerful voice in the global church, even as churches from around the world disagree about important cultural and political issues including the rights of women and homosexuality.

For the Christians at the height of the mission movement in the late nineteenth and early twentieth centuries, the role of missionaries was to introduce Christianity along with the benefits of Christian culture, including medical care. They agreed with their predecessors that Christianity was not just a theology; it was a religion that brought with it a superior culture. While there were differences between the movement at the end of the century and its form at the beginning, this conviction linked them. It was in this context at the beginning of the twentieth century that the title of the first missionaries' call to the American church was revised to become a new spur for American evangelicals. With the end of the century, missionary supporters were imagining it possible to see "the evangelization of the world in this generation." This phrase was the "watchword" of a new generation of young evangelicals who saw themselves as called to join the work of world mission. By this time, it was understood that the missionaries' work was only to provide the tools for conversion: preaching, teaching, and the Gospel. The effects of these means were left to God's grace and the actions of those to whom they preached.[5]

For American evangelicals of the early republic, however, their goal really was the conversion of the world—both in its religion and in its culture. The early foreign mission movement was shaped by the vision of young evangelicals like Newell and Hall who saw the movement as having the potential to change everything. The movement was their attempt to step in as the partners of Britain in bringing Anglo-American civilization along with evangelical Christianity to the world. Throughout their work, they struggled with the relationship of religion to culture, and of the missions to government. In the first decades of their work, though, they saw religious change to require a shift in cultural values as well, and this requirement brought them into political action. In Asia, Africa, and North America, and indeed, everywhere they went, the Board's missionaries attempted to bring about the conversion of the world in the early republic.

Notes

Prologue

1. Francis Wayland, *Memoir of the Life and Labors of the Rev. Adoniram Judson, D.D.*, vol. 1 (Boston: Phillips, Sampson, and Company, 1853), 30.

2. Ibid., 28–29.

3. Clifton Jackson Phillips, *Protestant America and the Pagan World: The First Half Century of the American Board of Commissioners for Foreign Missions, 1810–1860* (Cambridge, MA: East Asian Research Center, Harvard University, 1969), ch. 1; ABCFM, *Annual Report* (1810), in ABCFM, *First Ten Annual Reports, with Other Documents of the Board* (Boston: Crocker and Brewster, 1834), 9–14.

4. Samuel Worcester to Adoniram Judson, Salem, Dec. 25, 1810, Papers of the American Board of Commissioners for Foreign Missions, Houghton Library, Harvard University (ABC) 1.5, vol. 2.

5. Wayland, *Memoir*, 70–73.

Introduction

1. Rosemarie Zagarri, "The Significance of the 'Global Turn' for the Early American Republic: Globalization in the Age of Nation-Building," *Journal of the Early Republic* 31, no. 1 (spring 2011): 1–37; Michael A. Verney, "An Eye for Prices, an Eye for Souls: Americans in the Indian Subcontinent, 1784–1838," *Journal of the Early Republic* 33, no. 3 (fall 2013): 397–432; Emily Conroy-Krutz, "Engaged in the Same Glorious Cause: Anglo-American Connections in

the American Missionary Entrance into India, 1790–1815," *Journal of the Early Republic* 34, no. 1 (spring 2014): 21–44.

2. Charles Foster, *An Errand of Mercy: The Evangelical United Front, 1790–1837* (Chapel Hill: University of North Carolina Press, 1960); Mark A. Noll, *The Rise of Evangelicalism: The Age of Edwards, Whitefield, and the Wesleys* (Downers Grove, IL: InterVarsity Press: 2003); Thomas Kidd, *The Great Awakening: The Roots of Evangelical Christianity in Colonial America* (New Haven: Yale University Press, 2007), ch. 4.

3. On the role of missionaries in nineteenth-century foreign policy, see Mark R. Amstutz, *Evangelicals and American Foreign Policy* (New York: Oxford, 2013), ch. 3.

4. Of the total, 709 were female, most married to missionaries or missionary assistants, but many, especially in Native American missions, served as missionary assistants in their own right. Rufus Anderson, *Memorial Volume of the First Fifty Years of the American Board of Commissioners for Foreign Missions* (Boston: American Board of Commissioners for Foreign Missions, 1862), appendix V, 414–432.

5. "American Board of Missions," *Missionary Herald* (August 1826), 261.

6. Jeffrey Cox, *Imperial Fault Lines: Christianity and Colonial Power in India, 1818–1940* (Stanford: Stanford University Press, 2002); Elizabeth Elbourne, *Blood Ground: Colonialism, Missions, and the Contest for Christianity in the Cape Colony and Britain, 1799–1853* (Montreal: McGill-Queen's University Press, 2002); James Greenlee and Charles Johnston, *Good Citizens: British Missionaries and Imperial States 1870 to 1918* (Montreal: McGill-Queen's University Press, 1999); Anna Johnston, *Missionary Writing and Empire, 1800–1860* (New York: Cambridge University Press, 2003); Andrew Porter, *Religion versus Empire? British Protestant Missionaries and Overseas Expansion, 1700–1914* (Manchester: Manchester University Press, 2004); Catherine Hall, *Civilising Subjects: Metropole and Colony in the English Imagination, 1830–1867* (Chicago: University of Chicago Press, 2001); Jean Comaroff and John Comaroff, *Of Revelation and Revolution*, 2 vols. (Chicago: University of Chicago Press, 1991).

7. Martin Marty, *Righteous Empire: The Protestant Experience in America* (New York: Harper Torchbooks, 1970), 11.

8. On exceptionalism, see Ian Tyrrell, "American Exceptionalism in an Age of International History," *American Historical Review* 96, no. 4 (Oct. 1991): 1031–1032. For a recent argument against the use of "empire" for American history, see Elizabeth Cobbs Hoffman, *American Umpire* (Cambridge: Harvard University Press, 2013). For an argument in favor of applying imperial study to American history, see Ann Laura Stoler, "Tense and Tender Ties: The Politics of Comparison in North American History and (Post) Colonial Studies," in *Haunted By Empire: Geographies of Intimacy in North American History*, ed. Ann Laura Stoler (Durham, NC: Duke University Press, 2006), 23–67.

9. Ian Tyrrell and Jay Sexton, eds., *Empire's Twin: U.S. Anti-Imperialism from the Founding Era to the Age of Terrorism* (Ithaca: Cornell University Press, 2015); Amy S. Greenberg, *Manifest Manhood and the Antebellum American Empire* (New York: Cambridge University Press, 2005); Edward G. Gray, "Visions of Another Empire: John Ledyard, an American Traveler across the Russian Empire, 1787–1788," *Journal of the Early Republic* 24 (fall 2004): 347–380; Eugene S. Van Sickle, "Reluctant Imperialists: The U.S. Navy and Liberia, 1819–1845," *Journal of the Early Republic* 31, no. 1 (spring 2011): 107–134; Julian Go, *Patterns of Empire: The British and American Empires, 1688 to the Present* (New York: Cambridge University Press, 2011).

10. Andrew Porter, *Religion versus Empire? British Protestant Missionaries and Overseas Expansion, 1700–1914* (Manchester: Manchester University Press, 2004).

11. Peter Onuf, *Jefferson's Empire: The Language of American Nationhood* (Charlottesville: University of Virginia Press, 2001).

12. Adam Rothman, *Slave Country: American Expansion and the Origins of the Deep South* (Cambridge: Harvard University Press, 2005).

13. Greenberg, *Manifest Manhood.*

14. Kariann Akemi Yokota, *Unbecoming British: How Revolutionary America Became a Postcolonial Nation* (New York: Oxford University Press, 2011).

15. Jack P. Greene, *Evaluating Empire and Confronting Colonialism in Eighteenth-Century Britain* (New York: Cambridge University Press, 2013).

16. Bruce Dorsey, *Reforming Men and Women: Gender in the Antebellum City* (Ithaca: Cornell University Press, 2002), ch. 4.

17. Paul Kramer, "Power and Connection: Imperial Histories of the United States in the World," *American Historical Review* 116, no. 5 (Dec. 2011): 1349.

18. Amy Kaplan, *The Anarchy of Empire in the Making of U.S. Culture* (Cambridge: Harvard University Press, 2002).

19. John Keay, *The Honourable Company: A History of the English East India Company* (New York: Scribner Press, 1994).

20. Peter S. Onuf, *Jefferson's Empire: The Language of American Nationhood* (Charlottesville: University Press of Virginia, 2001).

21. Van Sickle, "Reluctant Imperialists."

22. Here I am defining a settler colony as one in which a group of colonizers settle in a foreign space, removing the indigenous population and implanting their own system of governance.

23. Amos J. Beyan, *The American Colonization Society and the Creation of the Liberian State: A Historical Perspective 1822–1900* (Lanham, MD: University Press of America, 1991); John Leighton Wilson, "On Colonization, No. 3," ABC 15.1, vol. 2. The Maryland Colonization Society, for example, received ten thousand dollars annually from the Maryland state government for the creation and maintenance of their colony at Cape Palmas in Liberia. Winston James, *The Struggles of John Brown Russwurm: The Life and Writings of a Pan-Africanist Pioneer, 1799–1851* (New York: NYU Press, 2000).

24. Sylvana Tomaselli, "The Enlightenment Debate on Women," *History Workshop* 20 (autumn 1985): 101–124.

1. Hierarchies of Heathenism

1. John 4:35 (KJV).

2. John Treadwell and Abel Flint, on behalf of the Connecticut Missionary Society, to the Directors of the London Missionary Society, Hartford, April 20, 1803, London Missionary Society Archives, School of Oriental and African Studies Library, University of London (LMS) 8, Box 1, Folder 1, Jacket A

3. Samuel Miller to Joseph Hardcastle, New York, Aug. 23, 1802, LMS 8, Box 1, Folder 1, Jacket A.

4. Abel Flint to Joseph Hardcastle, Hartford, March 20, 1805, LMS 8, Box 1, Folder 1, Jacket B.

5. John Treadwell and Abel Flint, on behalf of the Connecticut Missionary Society, to the Directors of the London Missionary Society, Hartford, April 20, 1803, LMS 8, Box 1, Folder 1, Jacket A.

6. "Religious Intelligence: London Missionary Society," *Christian Observer* (Nov. 1805), 700.

7. Claudius Buchanan, "The Star in the East," in *The Works of the Rev. Claudius Buchanan, L.L.D. Comprising His Christian Researches in Asia, His Memoir on the Expediency of an Ecclesiastical Establishment for British India, and His Star in the East, with Two New Sermons. To Which Is Added Dr. Kerk's Curious and Interesting Report, Concerning the State of the Christians in Cochin and Travencore* (Baltimore: Neal and Wills, 1812), 293–295.

8. ABCFM, *Annual Report* (1810).

9. The relationship between "civilization" and mission work was contested in the nineteenth century and continues to be debated by historians today. Hutchison argued in his classic study of American missions, *Errand to the World*, that by the mid-nineteenth century, there was a concerted effort (although not an entirely successful one) to deemphasize the civilizing thrust of conversion efforts and focus on Christ over culture. Current research by Barbara Reeves-Ellington challenges this notion, looking at how even after this policy was pushed by mission boards, missionaries continued to be active in politics abroad, seeing "culture" and "civilization" as central to their evangelical work. In the British context, the relationship between "Christ and civilization" is similarly debated. In his article "Commerce and Christianity," Andrew Porter argues that these were separate, if related, categories and missionaries debated which needed to come first in the late eighteenth and early nineteenth centuries. Nonevangelicals in particular felt that "civilization" under a British government should come first (along with commerce) and bring Christianity in its train. British evangelicals found this to be a problematic prioritizing of commerce over religion and consistently pushed to have religious interests more fully represented in the empire. See William R. Hutchison, *Errand to the World: American Protestant Thought and Foreign Missions* (Chicago: University of Chicago Press, 1987), ch. 2; Barbara Reeves-Ellington, "Religion, Diplomacy, and Anglo-American Relations in Nineteenth-century Istanbul," Annual Conference of the SHAFR, Lexington, KY, June 19, 2014; Andrew Porter, "'Commerce and Christianity': The Rise and Fall of a Nineteenth-Century Missionary Slogan," *Historical Journal* 28, no. 3 (Sept. 1985): 597–621; Penelope Carson, *The East India Company and Religion, 1698–1858* (Rochester, NY: Boydell Press, 2012).

10. This phrase (and variations of it) were used frequently by the ABCFM. See for example: Rufus Anderson, "'Instructions of the Prudential Committee to the Rev. John Leighton Wilson, missionary to West Africa; read at a public meeting, held at Philadelphia, Sept. 22, 1833,"ABC 8.1, v. 2.

11. Buchanan, *Works of the Rev. Claudius Buchanan*, 282.

12. Quotation is from ABCFM, *Annual Report* (1828), 55. George W. Stocking Jr., *Victorian Anthropology* (New York: Free Press, 1991), ch. 1.

13. For example, Samuel Worcester to Rev. Ard Hoyt, Salem, Jan. 15, 1817, ABC 1.01, vol. 1.

14. Joseph Hardcastle, "Observations on the Instructions to the Missionaries," London, March 29 [no year], LMS 3, Box 1B, Folder 5, Jacket B; The Directors of the Missionary Society to the Officers, Directors, and Members of the New York Missionary Society, London, July 1799, LMS 8, Box 1, Folder 1, Jacket A.

15. Hutchinson, *Errand to the World*, ch. 1; Thomas S. Kidd, *The Great Awakening: The Roots of Evangelical Christianity in Colonial America* (New Haven: Yale University Press, 2007), ch. 13.

16. Gordon Hall and Samuel Newell, *The Conversion of the World or the Claims of Six Hundred Million and the Ability and Duty of the Churches Respecting Them*, 2nd ed. (Andover, MA: The American Board of Commissioners for Foreign Missions, 1818), 32–33.

17. Ann Judson, at sea, to her sister June 17, 1812, as excerpted in James D. Knowles, *Memoir of Ann H. Judson, Missionary to Burmah* (Boston: Gould, Hendall, and Lincoln, 1846), 65.

18. Susan Bean, *Yankee India: American Commercial and Cultural Encounters with India in the Age of Sail, 1784–1860* (Salem, MA: Peabody Essex Museum, 2001), 40.

19. In 1793, Captain John Gibaut's *Astrea* was commandeered up the Irrawaddy River by the Burmese emperor. According to Morison, Gibaut collected curiosities on his way and deposited them in the East India Museum. There is no record of this donation, however, and so the story remains a possibility if not a certain fact. Samuel Eliot Morison, *The Maritime History of Massachusetts, 1783–1860* (Boston, 1921), 92; Courtney Anderson, *To the Golden Shore: The Life of Adoniram Judson* (Boston: Little, Brown, 1956), 132; and John L. Christian, "American Diplomatic Interest in Burma," *Pacific Historical Review* 8, no. 2 (1939): 139. On the society generally, see Bean, *Yankee India*, 78–79.

20. Carey, "Religious Intelligence," *The New-York Missionary Magazine, and Repository of Religious Intelligence* (1801), 307.

21. "East Indies," *Panoplist* (March 1806), 559.

22. Morison, *Maritime History of Massachusetts*, 92.

23. "Extract of a Letter from Rev. Carey Dated Calcutta, July 30, 1807," *Panoplist* (February 1808), 421; "Later Intelligence from India," *Massachusetts Baptist Missionary Magazine* (March 1810), 270.

24. *Embassy to Ava* was published in London ten years earlier (1800), perhaps explaining why it was published in the United States so long after the information it contained was regarded as inaccurate by those in British India. Frank N. Trager, *Burma from Kingdom to Republic: A Historical and Political Analysis* (New York: Frederick A. Praeger, 1966), 24.

25. Quotes are from Michael Symes, *An Account of an Embassy to the Kingdom of Ava, in the Year 1795. By Lieut-Colonel Michael Symes, to Which Is Now Added, a Narrative of the Late Military and Political Operations in the Birmese Empire. With Some Account of the Present Condition of the Country, Its Manners, Customs, and Inhabitants*, 2 vols. (Edinburgh: Constable and Co., 1827), 40 and 251. On the influence of Symes on Judson, see Francis Wayland, *A Memoir of the Life and Labors of the Rev. Adoniram Judson, D.D.* 2 vols. (Boston: Sampson and Company, 1853), 37–38.

26. Judith L. Richell, *Disease and Demography in Colonial Burma* (Singapore: National University of Singapore Press, 2006), 15–16; Wayland, *Memoir of Adoniram Judson*, 131.

27. Prudential Committee Report (September, 1811), in ABCFM, *First Ten Annual Reports*, 23–24.

28. ABCFM, Minutes of the Second Annual Meeting in *First Ten Annual Reports* (1811), 22.

29. William Carey, "Extract of a Letter from the Rev. Dr. William Carey, dated at Calcutta, Jan. 20, 1807," *The Panoplist* (July 1807), 86; William Carey, "Extracts from letters just received by the Susquehannah, from the Rev. Dr. Carey, Serampore," (December 1807), 301.

30. Samuel Worcester to Jeremiah Evarts, Salem, July 1, 1815, ABC 1.5, vol. 2. Worcester is quoting from John 4:35–36. Samuel Worcester to Elisha Swift, Salem, October 22, 1817, ABC 1.01, vol. 1.

31. Gideon Blackburn, "Letter 1," *The Panoplist* (June 1807), 39; Blackburn, "Letter II," *The Panoplist* (July 1807), 84; Blackburn, "Letter III," *The Panoplist* (Dec. 1807), 322.

32. Gideon Blackburn, "Letter 1," *The Panoplist* (June, 1807), 39; Blackburn, "Letter IV," *The Panoplist* (March 1808), 416, 475; Blackburn, "Letter II," *The Panoplist* (July 1807), 84; Blackburn, "Letter III," *The Panoplist* (Dec. 1807), 322; "Religious Intelligence," *The Panoplist and Missionary Magazine* (July 1808), 83; KC [Cyrus Kingsbury], "Sketch of a Plan for Instructing the Indians," *The Panoplist and Missionary Magazine* (April 1816), 150; Gideon Blackburn, "Letter from Rev. Mr. Blackburn to Dr. Morse," *The Panoplist and Missionary Magazine* (March 1810), 474; ABCFM, *Annual Report* (1815), in *First Ten Annual Reports*, 125–126.

33. Rufus Anderson to Samuel Worcester, Rio de Janeiro, Feb. 1, 1819, ABC 85.11.

34. ABCFM, *Annual Report* (1820), in *First Ten Annual Reports*, 304.

35. ABCFM, *A Narrative of Five Youth from the Sandwich Islands, Now Receiving an Education in this Country* (New York: J. Seymour, 1816).

36. John Demos, *The Heathen School: A Story of Hope and Betrayal in the Age of the Early Republic* (New York: Knopf, 2014), ch. 2; Bradford Smith, *Yankees in Paradise: The New England Impact on Hawaii* (Philadelphia: J. B. Lippincott, 1956), 21–28; ABCFM, *Narrative of Five Youth*; Edwin Dwight, *Memoirs of Henry Obookiah, a Native of Owhyhee, and a Member of the Foreign Mission School* (Philadelphia: American Sunday School Union, 1830).

37. ABCFM, *Annual Report* (1820), in *First Ten Annual Reports*, 306.

38. Anderson, *Memorial Volume of the First Fifty Years*, 230.

39. ABCFM, *Annual Report* (1819) in *First Ten Annual Reports*, 229–231.

40. ABCFM, *Annual Report* (1820) in *First Ten Annual Reports*, 277–281.

41. Samuel Nott to Leonard Woods, Calcutta, Sept. 8, 1812, ABC 38.

42. "Foreign Establishments," *Missionary Herald* (January 1827), 6.

43. Rufus Anderson, "Instructions of the Prudential Committee to the Rev. John Leighton Wilson, missionary to West Africa; read at a public meeting, held at Philadelphia, Sept. 22, 1833," ABC 8.1, vol. 2. Emphasis in original. Archibald Alexander, *A History of Colonization on the Western Coast of Africa* (1846; reprint New York: Negro University Press, 1969), 40.

44. Christopher Leslie Brown, *Moral Capital: Foundations of British Abolitionism* (Chapel Hill: University of North Carolina Press, 2006), 261.

45. Cassandra Pybus, *Epic Journeys of Freedom: Runaway Slaves of the American Revolution and their Quest for Global Liberty* (Boston: Beacon Press, 2006), chs. 7 and 9; Alexander, *A History of Colonization*, 45; Maya Jasanoff, *Liberty's Exiles: American Loyalists in the Revolutionary World* (New York: Alfred A. Knopf, 2011).

46. Alexander, *A History of Colonization*, 48–49.

47. "Mission of the Church Missionary Society in West Africa," *Missionary Herald* (July 1830), 220; on the German missionaries, see J. Kofi Agbetti, *West African Church History: Christian Missions and Church Foundations: 1482–1919* (Leiden: E.J. Brill, 1986), 23. For further examples of the American coverage of Sierra Leone, see *Missionary Herald* (November 1823), 355; *Missionary Herald* (December 1825), 389.

48. "Western Africa. Sierra Leone," *Missionary Herald* (May 1821), 163. Later issues corroborated this account with the reports from Mr. Thomas Morgan, who replaced Mr. Johnson. "Western Africa. Sierra Leone," *Missionary Herald* (November 1821), 366; "Western Africa. Sierra Leone," *Missionary Herald* (December 1821), 398 "Mission of the Church Missionary Society in West Africa," *Missionary Herald* (May 1834), 184; John Leighton Wilson, *Western Africa: Its History and Prospects* (New York: Harper and Brothers, 1852), 420–421.

49. "Instructions of the Prudential Committee to the Rev. John Leighton Wilson, missionary to West Africa; read at a public meeting, held at Philadelphia, Sept. 22, 1833," by Rufus Anderson, ABC 8.1, vol. 2.

50. See for example, "American Colony at Liberia," *Missionary Herald* (August 1826), 245; "Western Africa. Liberia," *Missionary Herald* (Dec. 1827), 389; "Western Africa. Colony at Liberia," *Missionary Herald* (June 1828), 186; "Liberia," *Missionary Herald* (March, 1830), 86; "American Colonization Society. Results of the Society's Labors in Liberia," *Missionary Herald* (June 1830), 187; "American Colonization Society. State of the Colony at Liberia," *Missionary Herald* (Sept. 1830), 292; "American Colonization Society. Contemplated Enlargement of the Colony," *Missionary Herald* (May 1831), 160; "American Colonization Society. Colony at Liberia," *Missionary Herald* (Sept. 1831), 290.

51. Samuel Worchester to Mr. Jehudi Ashmun, Salem, August 25, 1817, ABC 1.01, vol. 1; Allan Yarema, *The American Colonization Society: An Avenue to Freedom?* (Lanham, MD: University Press of America, 2006), 41–43.

52. Rev. Mr. Ashmun to Dr. Bumhardt, Monrovia, April 23, 1826, ABC 85.11.

53. Rufus Anderson, "Instructions of the Prudential Committee to the Rev. John Leighton Wilson, missionary to West Africa; read at a public meeting, held at Philadelphia, Sept. 22, 1833," ABC 8.1, vol. 2.

54. Rev. Mr. Ashman to Dr. Bumhardt, Monrovia, April 23, 1826, ABC 85.11.

55. For a history of racial theory in this period, see Reginald Horsman, *Race and Manifest Destiny: The Origins of American Racial Anglo-Saxonism* (Cambridge: Harvard University Press, 1981), chs. 3, 5–8; William Stanton, *The Leopard's Spots: Scientific Attitudes toward Race in America, 1815–1859* (Chicago: University of Chicago Press, 1960); George Stocking, *Victorian Anthropology* (New York: The Free Press, 1991), ch. 1; Bruce Dain, *A Hideous Monster of the Mind: American Race Theory in the Early Republic* (Cambridge, MA: Harvard University Press, 2002), esp. viii–ix; David Kazanjian, *The Colonizing Trick: National Culture and Imperial Citizenship in Early America* (Minneapolis: University of Minnesota Press, 2003), ch. 2. For a discussion of the relationship of religious and racial theorists in the Enlightenment and nineteenth century, see Colin Kidd, *The Forging of Races: Race and Scripture in the Protestant Atlantic World, 1600–2000* (New York: Cambridge University Press, 2006) chs. 4–5.

56. ABCFM, *Annual Report* (Boston: Printed for the Board by Crocker and Brewster, 1826), 102.

57. Trevor Burnard, "European Migration to Jamaica, 1655–1780," *William and Mary Quarterly*, 3rd Ser. 53, no. 4 (Oct. 1996), 7775–7777. For a discussion of this sort of language in British depictions of West Africa, see Richard Phillips, "Dystopian Space in Colonial Representations and Interventions: Sierra Leone as 'The White Man's Grave,'" *Geografiska Annaler.* Series B, Human Geography 84, no. ¾ (2002): 189–200.

58. Rufus Anderson to John Leighton Wilson, Boston, Oct. 25, 1837, ABC 2.1, vol. 2; Massachusetts Sabbath School Union, *Claims of the Africans: or the History of the American Colonization Society* (1832), quoted in Kazanjian, *The Colonizing Trick*, 100.

59. Jehudi Ashmun to Dr. Bumhardt, Monrovia, April 23, 1826, ABC 85.11.

60. Rufus Anderson, "Instructions of the Prudential Committee to the Rev. John Leighton Wilson, missionary to West Africa; read at a public meeting, held at Philadelphia, Sept. 22, 1833," ABC 8.1, vol. 2.

61. Instructions to Revs. Lindley, Grant, Bernable Champion, Wilson, and Adams, ABC 8.1, vol. 2.

62. "The Committee will now address the Missionaries destined to Southeastern Africa—the Rev. David Lindley, Rev. Alden Grant, Rev. Henry J. Brenable, Rev. George Champion, Doct. Alexander E. Wilson, and Dr. Newton Adams and their Wives," ABC 8.1; "Messrs. Hope, Travelli, Robbins," June 26, 1836, ABC 8.1.

2. Missions on the British Model

1. Emphasis in original. Adoniram Judson to Rev. Dr. Bogue, Andover, April 23, 1810, LMS 8, Box 1, Folder 1, Jacket C.

2. Penelope Carson, *The East India Company and Religion, 1698–1858* (Rochester, NY: Boydell Press, 2012), ch. 8.

3. E. Daniel Potts, *British Baptist Missionaries in India, 1793–1837: The History of Serampore and Its Missions* (Cambridge: Cambridge University Press, 1967), 27.

4. William Lee and John Gordon to Rev. G. Burder, New York, June 19, 1807, LMS 9.3, Box 1, Folder 1, Jacket C; No Name to Revs. Gordon and Lee, Oct. 7, 1807, LMS 9.3, Box 1, Folder 1, Jacket C.

5. "Letter from Marshman, Carey, Ward, and Rowe dated Serampore," Nov. 21, 1809, *Panoplist* (June 1810), 44; Potts, *British Baptist Missionaries*, 51; John Gordon to Rev. G. Burder, New York, March 22, 1808, LMS 9.3, Box 1, Folder 1, Jacket C; William Lee to Fathers and Brethren, Philadelphia, Sept. 13, 1808 and John Gordon to Rev. G. Burder, New York, March 13, 1809, LMS 9.3, Box 1, Folder 1, Jacket D; William Lee to Rev. G. Burder, Philadelphia, May 1, 1809, LMS 9.3, Box 1, Folder 2, Jacket A.

6. John Gordon to Rev. G. Burder, New York, March 22, 1808, LMS 9.3, Box 1, Folder 1, Jacket C; William Lee to Rev. G. Burder, Philadelphia, May 1, 1809. LMS 9.3, Box I, Folder 2, Jacket A.

7. Abel Flint to Joseph Hardcastle, Hartford, March 20, 1805, LMS 8, Box 1, Folder 1, Jacket B.

8. ABCFM, Minutes of the Second Annual Meeting, Sept. 11, 1811, 25, ABC 91.1.

9. Samuel Miller to Joseph Hardcastle, New York, Aug. 23, 1802 and John Treadwell and Abel Flint to the Directors of the London Missionary Society, Hartford, April 20, 1803, LMS 8, Box 1, Folder 1, Jacket A; ABCFM, *First Ten Annual Reports*, 29. This theme of the particular duty of America and Britain to convert the world was also taken up in Rev. Jonathan Allen's "Farewell Sermon" to the missionary women. R. Pierce Beaver, ed. *Pioneers in Mission: The Early Missionary Ordination Sermons, Charges, and Instructions. A Source Book on the Rise of American Missions to the Heathen* (Grand Rapids, MI: William B. Eerdmans, 1966), 268–278.

10. See, for example, Fort St. George Public Department Circular 31 August 1796, IOR/E/4/882, British Library; Fort St. George Political Department, IOR/E/4/915; Public Department, 2 Feb. 1836, IOR/E/4/947; America, Missionaries, Liberty to reside in India, IOR/E/4/747.

11. Rufus Anderson to William Ellis, Boston, Oct, 24, 1837, LMS 8, Box 1, Folder 4, Jacket A.

12. Samuel Mills, quoted in Alan Frederick Perry, "The American Board of Commissioners for Foreign Missions and the London Missionary Society in the Nineteenth Century: A Study of Ideas" (Ph.D. diss., Washington University, 1974), 87.

13. Beaver, ed., *Pioneers in Mission*, 249–278.

14. George Burder to Robert Morrison, London, March 1812, LMS 3, Box 2, Folder 6, Jacket A.

15. Oliver Smith to W. May, Philadelphia, March 27, 1815 LMS 8, Box 1, Folder 3, Jacket B; Dr. Romeyn to Rev. George Burder, New York, Oct. 13, 1813, LMS 8.1, Box 1, Folder 3, Jacket A.

16. Bombay Mission Journal (BMJ), Aug. 11, 1812, ABC 16.1.1, vol. 1.

17. C. M. Ricketts to Marshman, January 4, 1813; Rickets to Marshmann, Jan. 7, 1813; Ricketts to Marshmann, Council Chamber, January 15, 1813, BMS IN/18.

18. William Carey to Fuller, Calcutta, March 25, 1813, BMS IN/13.

19. Charles Grant, Esq. "Papers Regarding Four American Missionaries," IOR/F/4/427/10461.

20. BMJ, August 10, 1812–March 8, 1813, ABC 16.1.1, vol. 1.

21. BMJ, Pondicherry, Dec. 27, 1812, ABC 16.1.1, vol. 1.

22. BMJ, Feb. 12, 1812, ABC 16.1.1, vol. 1.

23. BMJ, Feb. 11, 1813, ABC 16.1.1, vol. 1.

24. BMJ, October 17, 1812–October 4, 1814, ABC 16.1.1, vol. 1.

25. Samuel Worcester to the Rev. Messrs. Adoniram Judson, Samuel Newell, Samuel Nott, Gordon Hall, and Luther Rice, Salem, Nov. 20, 1812, ABC 8.1, vol. 4.

26. Samuel Worcester to the Rev. Messrs. Adoniram Judson, Samuel Newell, Samuel Nott, Gordon Hall, and Luther Rice, Salem, Nov. 20, 1812, ABC 8.1, vol. 4. Hall and Nott to Rev.

S. Worcester, Bombay, August 16, 1813 ABC 16.1.1, vol. 1. 399; BMJ, October 12–30, 1813, ABC 16.1.1, vol. 1.

27. BMJ, Dec. 4, 1813; Dec. 21, 1813, ABC 16.1.1, vol. 1.

28. BMJ, March 8, 1814 ABC 16.1.1, vol. 1.

29. BMJ, May 11, 1814; October 4, 1814, ABC 16.1.1, vol. 1.

30. Gordon Hall and Samuel Nott to Rev. G. Burder, Bombay, March 8, 1813, LMS 9.3, Box 2, Folder 1, Jacket A; Samuel Nott to Rev. George Burder, Aug. 21, 1813, LMS 9.3, Box 2, Folder 1, Jacket C.

31. Samuel Nott to Rev. George Burder, Bombay, Aug. 21, 1813, LMS 9.3, Box 2, Folder 1, Jacket C.

32. Gordon Hall and Samuel Nott to Rev. G. Burder, Bombay, March 8, 1813, LMS 9.3, Box 2, Folder 1. Jacket A. For a discussion of the missionaries' arrest in November 1813, see Samuel Nott to Rev George Burder, Bombay, Dec. 22, 1813, LMS 9.3, Box 2, Folder 1, Jacket C; Samuel Nott to Rev. David Bogue, Bombay, Aug. 16, 1813, LMS 9.3, Box 2, Folder 1, Jacket B; Gordon Hall to Rev. George Burder, Bombay, June 19, 1815, LMS 9.3, Box 2, Folder 1, Jacket E. For the financial connections, see William Loveless to the Directors of the Missionary Society, Madras, Aug. [October is crossed through] 23, 1813, LMS 9.3, Box 2, Folder 1, Jacket C.

33. BMJ, Sept. 10, 1812; Nov. 1, 1812, ABC 16.1.1, vol. 1. Samuel Newell to Joseph Hardcastle, Port Louis, Isle of France, Dec. 11, 1812, LMS 8, Box 1, Folder 3, Jacket A; BMJ, Aug. 21, 1812, ABC 16.1.1, vol. 1; Samuel Worcester to the Rev. Messrs. Adoniram Judson, Samuel Newell, Samuel Nott, Gordon Hall, and Luther Rice, Salem, Nov. 20, 1812, ABC 8.1, vol. 4.

34. Samuel Worcester to Rev. Messrs. Samuel Newell, Gordon Hall and Samuel Nott, Salem, March 20, 1815, ABC 8.1, vol. 4.; Jeremiah Evarts to Rev. Messrs. Newell, Nott and Hall, American Mission at Bombay, Charlestown, March 20, 1815, ABC 8.1, vol. 4.

35. On the developments between the East India Company and British Christians after the war, see Carson, *The East India Company*, 151–177.

36. Ian Copland, "Christianity as an Arm of Empire: The Ambiguous Case of India under the Company, c. 1813–1858," *Historical Journal* 49, no. 4 (2006): 1025–1054.

37. Jesse S. Palsetia, "Parsi and Hindu Traditional and Nontraditional Responses to Christian Conversion in Bombay, 1839–45," *Journal of the American Academy of Religion* 74, no. 3 (September 2006): 615–645.

38. Rufus Anderson, *History of the Missions of the American Board of Commissioners for Foreign Mission in India* (Boston: Congregational Publishing Society, 1874), 67.

39. Samuel Worcester to Rev. Messrs. Samuel Newell, Gordon Hall and Samuel Nott, Salem, March 20, 1815, ABC 8.1, vol. 4.

40. John Nichols to Samuel Worcester, Andover Theological Seminary, August 21, 1815, ABC 6; Allen Graves to Samuel Worcester, Rupert, VT, January 9, 1816, ABC 6.

41. Newell and Hall to Worcester, Bombay, Nov. 29, 1815, ABC 16.1.1, vol. 1.

42. BMJ, April 18–April 28, 1816, ABC 16.1.1, vol. 1.

43. BMJ, May 27, 1816, ABC 16.1.1, vol. 1.

44. BMJ, June 13, 1816 ABC 16.1.1, vol. 1.

45. Missionaries to Worcester, Bombay, July 20, 1820, Appendix No. 2, ABC 16.1.1, vol. 1; Rufus Anderson also adopted this language in his history of the mission. Anderson, *History of the Missions of the ABCFM in India*, 60.

46. "Extracts from the Journal of Mr. Bardwell," *The Panoplist and Missionary Herald* (Oct. 1820), 457. Allen and Read had a similar encounter in 1831. "Extracts from the Journal of Messrs. Allen and Read While on a Tour in the Deccan," *Missionary Herald* (Dec. 1832), 385.

47. Newell and Hall to Worcester, Bombay, Nov. 29, 1815; Bombay Missionaries to Worcester, Bombay, July 20, 1820, Appendix no. 2, ABC 16.1.1, vol. 1.

48. Hall, Graves, Garrett to Jeremiah Evarts, Bombay, January 6, 1824, ABC 16.1, vol. 4.

49. Jeremiah Evarts to Rev. Gordon Hall and his brethren, missionaries at Bombay, Boston, April 25, 1823, ABC 8.1, vol. 4.

50. Hall, Nichols, Graves, Frost, Garrett to Jeremiah Evarts, Bombay, August 26, 1824, ABC 16.1, vol. 4.

51. "Copy of a Correspondence between the Honorable the Governor in Council, &c. in Bombay and the American Missionaries," ABC 16.1.1, vol. 1.

52. Ibid.

53. Anderson, *Memorial of the First Fifty Years*, appendix V.

3. Mission Schools and the Meaning of Conversion

1. Hall and Newell, *The Conversion of the World*, 16.

2. Horatio Bardwell to Samuel Worcester, [Andover] Theological Seminary, Feb. 22, 1814, ABC 6, vol. 1.

3. Ibid.

4. Linford D. Fisher, *The Indian Great Awakening: Religion and the Shaping of Native Cultures in Early America* (New York: Oxford University Press, 2012); Gale Kenny, *Contentious Liberties: American Abolitionists in Post-emancipation Jamaica, 1834–1866* (Athens: University of Georgia Press, 2010), part 2; Tracy Leavelle, *The Catholic Calumet: Colonial Conversions in French and Indian North America* (Philadelphia: University of Pennsylvania Press, 2011), ch. 1.

5. Hollis Read, *The Christian Brahmun; or, Memoirs of the Life, Writings and Character of the Converted Brahmun, Babajee* (New York: Leavitte, Lord and Co, 1836), vol. 1, 115.

6. BMJ, March 30, 1816.

7. Read, vol. 1, ch. 8.

8. "Extracts from the Journal of Mr. Stone," *Missionary Herald* (June 1831), 169. See also "Extracts from Mr. Stone's Private Journal, Continued from p. 240," *Missionary Herald* (Sept. 1829), 265; "Private Journal of Mr. Stone, Continued from p. 268," *Missionary Herald* (Oct. 1829), 305.

9. "Extracts from the Journal of Mr. Stone," *Missionary Herald* (Aug. 1831), 233; "Extracts from Mr. Stone's Private Journal, Continued from p. 240," *Missionary Herald* (Sept. 1829), 265.

10. Read, vol. 1, 147.

11. On alternate missionary responses to caste, see Copland, "Christianity as an Arm of Empire," 1034; Henriette Bugge, "Christianity and Caste in XIXth Century South India: The Different Social Policies of British and Non-British Christian Missions," *Archives de Sciences sociales des Religions*, 43e Anne, 103 (July–September 1998): 87–97; Palsetia, "Parsi and Hindu," 615–645.

12. "Extracts from the Journal of Mr. Graves, Continued from p. 179," *Missionary Herald* (July 1824), 203.

13. BMJ, Dec. 20, 1813. ABC 16.1.1, vol. 1.

14. "Extracts from the Journal of Mr. Graves at Mahim, Continued from p. 373," *The Panoplist and Missionary Herald* (Sept. 1820), 409.

15. Lata Mani, *Contentious Traditions: The Debate on Sati in Colonial India* (Berkeley: University of California Press, 1998); Jonathan Allen, quoted in Beaver, ed. *Pioneers in Mission*, 277.

16. BMJ, January 1816. Additional entries on this subject can be found in December 6, 1816; December 8, 1816, ABC 16.1.1, vol. 1. These discussions were similar in tone and emphasis to the missionary descriptions of sati described by Lata Mani.

17. BMJ, January 1816, ABC 16.1.1, vol. 1.

18. Bombay missionaries to Samuel Worcester, Bombay, July 20, 1820, ABC 16.1.1, vol. 1.

19. Newell, Bardwell, and Hall to SW, Bombay, Feb. 4, 1817; Bombay missionaries to SW, Bombay, April 18, 1817, ABC 16.1.1, vol. 1.

20. Hall, Newell, Bardwell, Nichols, and Graves to SW, Bombay, August 18, 1819.

21. BMJ, March 30, 1816, ABC 16.1.1, vol. 1.

22. Hall, Newell, Bardwell, Nichols, Graves to SW, Bombay, Aug. 18, 1819; Hall, Newell, Bardwell, Nichols, Graves to SW, Bombay, Jan. 1820, ABC 16.1.1, vol. 1.

23. Hall, Newell, Bardwell, Nichols, Graves to SW, Bombay, Jan. 1820, ABC 16.1.1, vol. 1.

24. Read, vol. 1, 14–15.

25. Graves, Garrett, Stone and Allen to Jeremiah Evarts, Bombay, July 1, 1829, ABC 16.1, vol. 4.

26. Bardwell, "Religious Intelligence," *The Panoplist and Missionary Herald* (October 1820), 457.

27. "Native Schools at Bombay," *The Panoplist and Missionary Herald* (December 1818), 558; ABCFM, *Annual Report* (Boston: Printed for the Board by Crocker and Brewster, 1825), 31–32. Two of these schools, the Andover School and the Salem School, were named for the New England towns from which individuals paid for their support.

28. "Native Schools at Bombay," *The Panoplist and Missionary Herald* (December 1818), 558.

29. Graves, Garrett, C. Stone, D.O. Allen to Jeremiah Evarts, Bombay, July 10, 1828, ABC 16.1, vol. 4.

30. Ibid.

31. S. Worcester to Rev. Messrs. Gordon Hall, S. Newell, H. Bardwell, J. Nichols and A. Graves, Salem, March 6, 1820, ABC 8.1, vol. 4.

32. Charlestown, Jan. 4, 1817, J. Evarts to Messrs. S. Newell and Gordon Hall, or either of them; Charlestown May 24, 1817, Jeremiah Evarts to Rev. Messrs. Hall and Newell; Jeremiah Evarts to Messrs. Gordon Hall, Samuel Newell, and Horatio Bardwell, Charlestown, Oct. 1, 1817; Jeremiah Evarts to Rev. Messrs. Hall, Nott and Bardwell, Boston Dec. 8, 1817, ABC 8.1, vol. 4.

33. By 1826, the ABCFM sent a new missionary to serve as superintendent of a boarding school there. Jeremiah Evarts to Rev. Gordon Hall, Boston, Aug. 28, 1826, ABC 8.1, vol. 4.

34. Hall, Graves, Frost, Garrett to Jeremiah Evarts, Bombay, July 19, 1825; Hall, Graves, Frost, Garrett to JE, Bombay, Aug. 27, 1825; Graves and Garrett to JE, Bombay, March 9, 1827, ABC 16.1, vol. 4.

35. Hall, Newell, Bardwell, Nichols, and Graves to Samuel Worcester, Bombay, Aug. 18, 1819, ABC 16.1.1, vol. 1.

36. See, for example, Read, vol. 1, 96.

37. Graves, Read, Allen, Stone to RA, Bombay, August 1832, ABC 16.1, vol. 5.

38. Read, vol. 2, 152–154.

39. Read, vol. 1, x, 40.

40. Ibid., 17–22.

41. Ibid., 20–21.

42. Ibid., 22–26.

43. Ibid., 22–26.

44. Ibid., 42–58.

45. Ibid., 30–37.

46. Ibid., 68–69.

47. Ibid., ch. 8.

48. Ibid., 71–75.

49. Ibid., ch. 8.

50. Emphasis in original. Ibid., 144.

51. Ibid., 23, 102.

52. Ibid., 32.

53. His biographer incorrectly notes the date of their marriage as December 1832. News of the marriage reached the United States in 1831, with the enclosure of an article from the *Oriental Christian Spectator* entitled "Marriage of a Converted Brahmun." Hollis Read, DO Allen, William Hervey, William Ramsey, and Cyrus Stone to Jeremiah Evarts, Bombay, July 20. 1831, ABC 16.1, vol. 5.

54. Graves, Read, Allen, Stone to RA, Bombay, August 1832, ABC 16.1, vol. 5.

55. Read, vol. 2, ch. 1.

56. Ramsey and Stone to RA, Bombay, Sept. 2, 1833, ABC 16.1, vol. 5.

57. Bombay Mission Journal, Dec. 14, 1816, ABC 16.1.1, vol. 1.

58. Read, vol. 1, 77–79.

59. Ibid., 92–94.

4. Missions as Settler Colonies

1. Peter Kanouse to Samuel Worcester, Rockaway, Feb. 18 1819; Barnabas King to Samuel Worcester, Rockaway, Feb. 7, 1819, ABC 6, vol. 1.

2. Alijah Conger to Samuel Worcester, Rockaway, May 12, 1819; Alijah Conger to Samuel Worcester, Rockaway, June 9, 1819; Alijah Conger to Samuel Worcester, Rockaway, June 27, 1819; Barnabas King to Samuel Worcester, Rockaway, June 28, 1819; Joseph Jackson to Samuel Worcester, Rockaway, June 30, 1819; Alijah Conger to Samuel Worcester, Rockaway, June 27, 1819, ABC 6, vol. 1.

3. Anderson, *Memorial of the First Fifty Years*, appendix V.

4. On settler colonialism, see Margaret D. Jacobs, *White Mother to a Dark Race: Settler Colonialism, Maternalism, and the Removal of Indigenous Children in the American West and Australia, 1880–1940* (Lincoln: University of Nebraska Press, 2009), 2–9.

5. "Mission and School among the Cherokees," *The Panoplist and Missionary Magazine* (August 1817), 384. On the dual policies of civilization and removal, see Francis Paul Prucha, *American Indian Policy in the Formative Years: The Indian Trade and Intercourse Acts, 1790–1834* (Cambridge: Harvard University Press, 1962), 213–227.

6. R. Pierce Beaver, *Church, State, and the American Indians: Two and a Half Centuries of Partnership in Missions between Protestant Churches and Government* (St. Louis, MO: Concordia, 1966), 63–69; Bernard W. Sheehan, *Seeds of Extinction: Jeffersonian Philanthropy and the American Indian* (Chapel Hill: University of North Carolina Press, 1973).

7. KC [Cyrus Kingsbury], "Sketch of a Plan for Instructing the Indians," *The Panoplist and Missionary Magazine* (April 1816), 150; Cyrus Kingsbury to Jeremiah Evarts, Washington DC, April 26, 1816; Cyrus Kingsbury to Mr. Eleazer Lord, Washington, DC, April 30, 1816, ABC 8.2.9.

8. ABCFM, *Annual Report* (1816), in *First Ten Annual Reports*, 136–138.

9. ABCFM, *First Ten Annual Reports*, 198.

10. ABCFM, *Annual Report* (1820), 320.

11. J. C. Calhoun, "Circular," September 3, 1819, in "Letter from the Secretary of War, Transmitting (Pursuant to a Resolution of the House of Representatives on the 6th January inst.) A Report of the Progress which has been Made in the Civilization of the Indian Tribes

and the sums which have been expended on that object" (January 17, 1820. Read, and ordered to lie upon the table) (Washington: Printed by Gales and Beaton, 1820), 102.

12. President James Monroe, "Message from the President of the United States, Transmitting a Report of the Secretary of War, of the Measures Hitherto Devised and Pursued For the Civilization of the several Indian Tribes, within the United States" (February 11, 1822 Read, and Referred to the Committee on Indian Affairs) (Washington: Printed by Gales and Beaton, 1822), 59.

13. William G. McLoughlin, *Cherokee Renascence in the New Republic* (Princeton: Princeton University Press, 1986); William G. McLoughlin, *Cherokees and Missionaries, 1789–1839* (New Haven: Yale University Press, 1984).

14. McLoughlin, *Cherokee Renascence*, ch. 16.

15. Ard Hoyt, Copy of Report to the Secretary of War, Brainerd, Cherokee Nation, Oct. 1, 1820; Copy of Report to J. C. Calhoun, Sec. of War, Brainerd, C.N., Oct. 1, 1821, ABC 18.3.1, vol. 2.

16. Ard Hoyt, Copy of Annual Report to Sec. of War, Brainerd, Oct. 23, 1823; Ard Hoyt to Hon. J.C. Calhoun, Brainerd, Cherokee Nation, Oct. 1, 1823, ABC 18.3.1, vol. 2.

17. Isaac Anderson, Matthew Donald, and David Campbell to the Prudential Committee of the ABCFM, Brainerd, Cherokee Nation, May 29, 1818, ABC 18.3.1, vol. 2.

18. J.C. Calhoun to "Sir," Dec. 12, 1821, ABC 18.3.1, vol. 2.

19. Gideon Blackburn, "Letter 1," *The Panoplist* (June 1807), 39; Return J. Meigs, "Circular, September 8, 1806," *The Panoplist and Missionary Magazine* (August 1808), 139; Blackburn, "Letter IV," *The Panoplist* (March 1808), 416, 475; Blackburn, "Letter II," *The Panoplist* (July 1807), 84; Blackburn, "Letter III," *The Panoplist* (Dec. 1807), 322; "Religious Intelligence," *The Panoplist and Missionary Magazine* (July 1808), 83; KC, "Sketch of a Plan for Instructing the Indians," 150.

20. Lorrin Andrews, "Essay on the Best practicable Method of conducting Native Schools at the Sandwich Islands," in ABCFM *Annual Report* (Printed for the Board by Crocker and Brewster, 1834), 162.

21. KC, "Sketch of a Plan for Instructing the Indians," 150.

22. ABCFM *Annual Report* (Boston: Crocker and Brewster, 1821), 49.

23. The Ceylon mission also adopted this practice in their extensive boarding schools. Charlestown, Jan. 4, 1817, J. Evarts to Messrs. S. Newell and Gordon Hall, or either of them; Charlestown May 24, 1817, Jeremiah Evarts to Rev. Messrs. Hall and Newell; Jeremiah Evarts to Messrs. Gordon Hall, Samuel Newell, and Horatio Bardwell, Charlestown, Oct. 1, 1817; Jeremiah Evarts to Rev. Messrs. Hall, Nott and Bardwell, Boston Dec. 8, 1817, ABC 8.1, vol. 4.

24. Cyrus Kingsbury to Samuel Worcester, Knoxville, TN, Nov. 28, 1816, ABC 8.2.9.

25. Ibid.

26. Samuel Worcester, "Report of the Prudential Committee," *The Panoplist and Missionary Magazine* (Oct. 1816), 446.

27. Samuel Worcester to Hon. John C. Calhoun, Secretary of War, Salem, Feb. 3, 1820, ABC 1.01, vol. 4.

28. ABCFM *Annual Report* (Printed for the Board by Crocker and Brewster, 1822), 35–36.

29. Ibid. (1822), 38.

30. ABCFM, *Annual Report* (1821), 50.

31. Leonard Worcester to Samuel Worcester, Peachian [?], August 16, 1820, ABC 6, vol. 1.

32. Ainsworth Emery Blunt letters, ABC 6, vol. 4.

33. Erastus Dean letters, ABC 6, vol. 4.

34. William Potter letters, ABC 6, vol. 1.

35. Thomson initially hoped to go to the Hawaiian mission, further indicating the connections between the setup at the two locations. John Thomson letters, ABC 6, vol. 6.

36. Hannah Kelly letters, ABC 6, vol. 5.

37. William Potter to Samuel Worcester, Lisbon, CT, Sept. 24, 1819, ABC 6, vol. 1.

38. Emphasis in original. Ann Paine to Samuel Worcester, Athens, PA, Dec. 21, 1819, ABC 6, vol. 1.

39. Samuel Worcester to Ann Paine, Salem, January 22, 1820, ABC 1.01, vol. 4; Hendrik Hartog, *Man and Wife in America: A History* (Cambridge: Harvard University Press, 2000), 76–86; Clement Paine and Ann Paine, Separation Agreement, ABC 6, vol. 1, Item 103; Ann Paine to Samuel Worcester, Athens, PA, Dec. 21, 1819; Ann Paine to Samuel Worcester, Athens, PA, Feb. 24, 1820, ABC 6, vol. 1.

40. Emphasis in original. Samuel Worcester to Ann Paine, Salem, January 22, 1820; Samuel Worcester to Ephraim Strong, Esq., Salem, April 20, 1820, ABC 1.01, vol. 4.

41. Ann Paine to Jeremiah Evarts, Athens, August 23, 1821, ABC 18.3.1, vol. 3.

42. Ann Paine to Jeremiah Evarts, Athens, November 8, 1821, ABC 18.3.1, vol. 3. LAP, "Religious Reading," *New York Evangelist*, April 19, 1860, 6.

43. Mr. William H. Mamaring letters, ABC 6, vol. 5.

44. ABCFM, *Annual Report* (1820), 305.

45. ABCFM, *Annual Report* (Boston: Printed for the Board by Crocker and Brewster, 1830), 65; ABCFM *Annual Report* (Boston: Printed for the Board by Crocker and Brewster, 1831).

46. Jennifer Thigpen, *Island Queens and Mission Wives: How Gender and Empire Remade Hawai'i's Pacific World* (Chapel Hill: The University of North Carolina Press, 2014).

47. Thomas H. Gallaudet, "An Address delivered at a Meeting for Prayers, with reference to the Sandwich Mission, in the Brick Church in Hartford, Oct. 11, 1819," in *Selected Writings of Hiram Bingham, 1814–1869, Missionary to the Hawaiian Islands: To Raise the Lord's Banner*, ed. Char Miller (Lewiston/Queenston, ME: Edwin Mellen Press, 1988), 112–114; 132–133; and "Instructions, From the Prudential Committee of the American Board of Commissioners for Foreign Missions to the Rev. Hiram Bingham and the Rev. Asa Thurston, Messrs. Daniel Chamberlain, Thomas Holman, Samuel Whitney, Samuel Ruggles and Elisha Loomis, John Honoore, Thomas Hopoo and William Tennooe, Members of the Mission to the Sandwich Islands," in Miller, *Selected Writings of Hiram Bingham*, 121–143.

48. "Instructions, From the Prudential Committee," in Miller, *Selected Writings of Hiram Bingham*, 134; Hiram Bingham to Rev. Samuel Worcester, Oahu, May 13, 1820 in Miller, *Selected Writings of Hiram Bingham*, 169–175.

49. Ralph S. Kuykendall, *The Hawaiian Kingdom*, vol. 1 (Honolulu: University of Hawaii Press, 1938), 61–70.

50. Hiram Bingham et al to Samuel Worcester, July 23, 1820, in Miller, *Selected Writings of Hiram Bingham*, 175–180.

51. Hiram Bingham to his parents, Honolulu, Jan. 12, 1823 in Miller, *Selected Writings of Hiram Bingham*, 212–213.

52. Hiram Bingham to Jeremiah Evarts, Oahu, Dec. 15, 1827 in Miller, *Selected Writings of Hiram Bingham*, 283–293.

53. Hiram Bingham to Lydia Bingham, Oahu, April 4, 1829 in Miller, *Selected Writings of Hiram Bingham*, 302–306.

54. ABCFM *Annual Report* (Boston: Printed for the Board by Crocker and Brewster, 1827), 72.

55. ABCFM, *Annual Report* (Boston: Printed for the Board by Crocker and Brewster, 1828), 60–62

56. Hiram Bingham to the Prudential Committee, Sandwich Islands, Oahu, Nov. 25, 1821 in Miller, *Selected Writings of Hiram Bingham*, 200–201; ABCFM *Annual Report* (1827), 75–85; ibid. (1828), 61; Bingham's statements of these events can be found in Miller, *Selected Writings of Hiram Bingham*, 307–331; Jennifer Fish Kashay, "Agents of Imperialism: Missionaries and Merchants in Early-Nineteenth-Century Hawaii," *New England Quarterly* 80, no. 2 (June 2007): 280–298.

57. Emphasis in original. ABCFM *Annual Report* (Boston: Printed for the Board by Crocker and Brewster, 1832).

58. Ibid., 83.

59. Lorrin Andrews, "Essay on the Best practicable Method," 156–168.

60. Joint Letter of the missionaries [1823], in Miller, *Selected Writings of Hiram Bingham*, 220–225; Hiram Bingham et al to Jeremiah Evarts, Honolulu, Jan. 11, 1823, in Miller, *Selected Writings of Hiram Bingham*, 207–208.

61. Hiram Bingham to Dwight Baldwin, Oahu, April 12, 1837 in Miller, *Selected Writings of Hiram Bingham*, 388.

62. Linda K. Menton, "A Christian and 'Civilized' Education: The Hawaiian Chiefs' Children's School, 1839–50," *History of Education Quarterly* 32, no. 2 (summer 1992): 213–242.

5. American Politics and the Cherokee Mission

1. ABCFM, *Annual Report* (Boston: Printed for the Board by Crocker and Brewster, 1826), 57.

2. Elias Cornelius, "Mission to the Cherokees," *The Panoplist and Missionary Magazine* (Dec. 1817), 563.

3. Elias Cornelius, "Wants of the Indians," *The Panoplist and Missionary Magazine* (Dec. 1817), 572.

4. Return J. Meigs, "Circular, September 8, 1806," *The Panoplist and Missionary Magazine* (August 1808), 139; President James Monroe, "Message from the President of the United States, Transmitting a Report of the Secretary of War, of the Measures Hitherto Devised and Pursued For the Civilization of the several Indian Tribes, within the United States," (February 11, 1822, Read and Referred to the Committee on Indian Affairs) (Washington: Printed by Gales and Beaton, 1822), 59.

5. Cyrus Kingsbury to Jeremiah Evarts, E. Tennessee, September 9, 1816, ABC 8.2.9.

6. ABCFM, *Annual Report* (Boston: Published by Samuel T. Armstrong, 1819), 39.

7. Ibid., 40.

8. McLoughlin, *Cherokee Renascence*, 258; 314–315.

9. Ronald N. Satz, *American Indian Policy in the Jacksonian Era*, rev. ed. (Norman: University of Oklahoma Press, 2002), ch. 1; Phillips, *Protestant America and the Pagan World*, 73; Prucha, *American Indian Policy*, 233–249.

10. Beaver, *Church, State, and the American Indians*, ch. 3; Jedidiah Morse, *A Report to the Secretary of War of the United States on Indian Affairs, Comprising a Narrative of a Tour* (1822; reprint New York: Augustus M. Kelley, 1970).

11. Margaret Bender, *Signs of Cherokee Culture: Sequoyah's Syllabary in Eastern Cherokee Life* (Chapel Hill: University of North Carolina Press, 2002); Sean P. Harvey, "'Must Not their Languages Be Savage and Barbarous Like Them?': Philology, Indian Removal, and Race Science," *Journal of the Early Republic* 30 (winter 2010): 505–532; McLoughlin, *Cherokee Renascence*, ch. 17; Willard Walker and James Sarbaugh, "The Early History of the Cherokee Syllabary," *Ethnohistory* 40, no. 1 (winter 1993): 70–94.

12. "Miscellanies: The Cherokee Constitution," *Missionary Herald*, June 1828, 193.

13. McLoughlin, *Cherokee Renascence*, ch. 13, 19, 20; Prucha, *American Indian Policy*, 227–233.

14. David Green to Isaac Procter, Boston, March 24, 1829, ABC 1.01, vol. 8.

15. Elizur Butler to D. Greene, March 28, 1830; Elizur Butler to Jeremiah Evarts, Haweis, Sept. 22, 1830; Elizur Butler to D. Greene, March 28, 1830, ABC 18.3.1, vol. 7.

16. Samuel A. Worcester to Jeremiah Evarts, New Echota Oct. 27, 1830, ABC 18.3.1, vol. 7.

17. Ibid., emphasis in the original; McLoughlin, *Cherokee Renascence*, ch. 21; Beaver, *Church, State, and the American Indians*, ch. 3.

18. Theodore Frelinghuysen to David Greene, Newark, August 25, 1831; "Prudential Committee Acts, Jan. 1831–Oct. 1831," ABC 18.3.1, vol. 7

19. Jeremiah Evarts to Samuel A. Worcester, Boston, Jan. 19, 1829, David Greene to Samuel A. Worcester, Boston, Feb. 9, 1829, ABC 1.01, vol. 8.

20. Jeremiah Evarts, *Cherokee Removal: The 'William Penn' Essays and Other Writings*, ed., with an Introduction by Francis Paul Prucha (Knoxville: University of Tennessee Press, 1981), essays 1, 22.

21. Jeremiah Evarts to Samuel A. Worcester, Boston, Sept. 26, 1829, ABC 1.01, vol. 8.

22. Jeremiah Evarts to Samuel A. Worcester, Boston, June 9, 1830; June 17, 1830; Nov. 6, 1830; Nov. 18, 1830, ABC 1.01, vol. 9.

23. Samuel A. Worcester to David Greene, New Echota, March 23, 1831, ABC 18.3.1, vol. 7; Elizur Butler to David Green, Haweis, June 20, 1831, ABC 18.3.1, vol. 7. McLoughlin, *Cherokee Renascence*, ch. 21.

24. Elizur Butler to Governor George Gilmer, June 7, 1831, ABC 18.3.1, vol. 7; "Prudential Committee Acts, Jan. 1831–Oct. 1831," ABC 18.3.1, vol. 7.

25. Samuel A. Worcester to David Greene, April 13, 1831; Samuel A. Worcester to David Greene, New Echota, May 25, 1831, ABC 18.3.1, vol. 7.

26. Samuel A. Worcester to Jeremiah Evarts, New Echota Jan. 28, 1831, ABC 18.3.1, vol. 7.

27. Samuel A. Worcester to George R. Gilmer, New Echota, June 10, 1831, ABC 18.3.1, vol. 7.

28. Jeremiah Evarts to Samuel A. Worcester, Boston, Sept. 26, 1826, ABC 1.01, vol. 8; Satz, *American Indian Policy in the Jacksonian Era*, 44–45.

29. William Wirt to Samuel A. Worcester, Baltimore, July 19, 1831, ABC 18.3.1, vol. 7.

30. William Wirt to John Williams, Baltimore, Sept. 21, 1831, ABC 18.3.1, vol. 7.

31. Samuel A. Worcester to David Greene, Brainerd, August 26 1831; Samuel A. Worcester to David Greene, New Echota, Sept. 8, 1831, ABC 18.3.1, vol. 7.

32. Samuel A. Worcester to David Greene, Lawrenceville, GA, Sept. 16, 1831; Samuel A. Worcester to David Greene, Penitentiary, Milledgeville, GA, Nov. 8, 1831; Samuel A. Worcester to David Greene, Penitentiary, Milledgeville, Nov. 14, 1831; Samuel A. Worcester to David Greene, Penitentiary, Nov. 27, 1831; Samuel A. Worcester to David Greene, Penitentiary, Jan. 28, 1832; Samuel A. Worcester to David Greene, Penitentiary Milledgeville, Feb. 28, 1832, ABC 18.3.1, vol. 7.

33. *Worcester v. Georgia*, 31 U.S. 515 (1832); Satz, *American Indian Policy in the Jacksonian Era*, 48–49.

34. McLoughlin, *Cherokee Renascence*, ch. 21; Samuel A. Worcester to David Greene, Penitentiary Milledgeville, April 4, 1832; Samuel A. Worcester and Butler to David Greene, Penitentiary Milledgeville, April 15, 1832; Samuel A. Worcester and Butler to David Greene, Penitentiary Milledgeville, April 28, 1832, ABC 18.3.1, vol. 7; Samuel A. Worcester and Butler to David Greene, Penitentiary Milledgeville, April 15, 1832, ABC 18.3.1, vol. 7.

35. W. Wirt to J. Sargent, Baltimore, Dec. 24, 1832; T. King to D. Greene, Milledgeville, GA, Dec. 18, 1832; Nott to Wisner, Dec. 1832; Nott to Wisner, Dec. 1832; C. McIntire to H. Hill, Charleston, Dec. 7, 1832; Van Rensselaer to Hubbard, Albany, Dec. 12, 1832; E. Porter to Wisner, Charleston, Dec. 11, 1832; Thomas Goulding to Wisner, Columbia Seminary, S.C., Dec. 25, 1832; S. Talmadge, etc. to Wisner, and Executive Committee of the American Board of Foreign Missions Dec. 28, 1832; J. Sergeant to Wisner, Philadelphia, Dec. 24, 1832, ABC 18.3.1, vol. 7. Italics in the original.

36. Samuel A. Worcester to David Greene, Penitentiary Milledgeville, May 7, 1832, ABC 18.3.1, vol. 7.

37. Samuel A. Worcester to David Greene, Penitentiary Milledgeville, Dec. 7, 1832; Samuel A. Worcester and Elizur Butler to David Greene, Milledgeville, Jan. 14, 1833; "Release of the Missionaries, Jan. 14, 1833," ABC 18.3.1, vol. 7.

38. "Reasons as to why the Cherokees should make a treaty, copied from Mr. Christies' Memoranda," May 1832, ABC 18.3.1, vol. 7.

39. The debates among the committee largely concerned what sort of pardon the missionaries ought to accept and how much blame they could accept from the Governor. "Prud. Comm. Opinions, Dec. 25, 1832," ABC 18.3.1, vol. 7.

40. Frelinghuysen was a former director of the ABCFM. T. Frelinghuysen to Dr. Wisner, Washington, Jan. 4, 1833; T. Frelinghuysen to Dr. Wisner, Washington, Jan. 11, 1833, ABC 18.3.1, vol. 7.

41. Butler to David Greene, March 18, 1833; Elizur Butler to David Greene, Haweis, July 9, 1833; Elizur Butler to David Greene, Brainerd, Feb. 18, 1834, ABC 18.3.1, vol. 7.

42. For the ABCFM's support of the treaty, see Phillips, *Protestant America and the Pagan World*, ch. 3.

43. Satz, *American Indian Policy in the Jacksonian Era*, 99–101.

44. "General Order Concerning Execution of Cherokee Treaty," Nov. 3, 1836, ABC 18.3.1, vol. 7.

45. ABC 18.3.1, vol. 4.

46. D. S. Butrick to Jeremiah Evarts, Hightower, March 26, 1829, ABC 18.3.1, vol. 4.

47. Wisner to Rev. D. S. Butrick, Mr. Isaac Proctor, Missionary Rooms, Boston, April 9, 1833; D. S. Butrick to Rev. B.B. Wisner (Boston, Candry's Creek, May 22, 1833, 18.3.3, vol. 2.

48. D. S. Butrick to Cor. Secretaries of the ABCFM, Candry's Creek, April 15, 1833, ABC 18.3.3, vol. 2.

49. [D. S. Butrick], "Papers relating to the Controversy with Georgia over the Indians, 1833–1840," ABC 18.3.3, vol. 2.

50. Ibid.

51. Elizur Butler to David Green, Haweis, May 9, 1831, ABC 18.3.1, vol. 7; Elizur Butler to Samuel Worcester, Sharon, June 1, 1819, ABC 6, vol. 1.

6. Missionaries and Colonies

1. On religious influences in colonization, see J. Kofi Agbeti, *West African Church History: Christian Missions and Church Foundations: 1482–1919* (Leiden: E.J. Brill, 1986), 113–114; Eric Burin, *Slavery and the Peculiar Solution: A History of the American Colonization Society* (Gainesville: University Press of Florida, 2005), intro. For other explanations, see Kazanjian, *The Colonizing Trick*, 94.

2. Burin, *Slavery and the Peculiar Solution*, 18–22; Douglas R. Egerton, "'Its Origin Is Not a Little Curious': A New Look at the American Colonization Society," *Journal of the Early Republic* 5, no. 4 (winter 1985): 463–480.

3. Burin, *Slavery and the Peculiar Solution*, ch. 7.

4. Ibid.; David Brion Davis, *Inhuman Bondage: The Rise and Fall of Slavery in the New World* (New York: Oxford University Press, 2006), 256–258.

5. Bruce Dorsey, *Reforming Men and Women: Gender in the Antebellum City* (Ithaca: Cornell University Press, 2002), ch. 4.

6. Kazanjian, *The Colonizing Trick*, 95; David Brion Davis, "Exodus, Black Colonization, and Promised Lands," Jefferson Memorial Lecture, University of California, Berkeley (2004), 33; John Saillant, "Missions in Liberia and Race Relations in the United States," in *The Foreign Missionary Enterprise at Home: Explorations in North American Cultural History*, ed. Daniel H. Bays and Grant Wacker (Tuscaloosa: University of Alabama Press, 2003), 13–28.

7. "American Colonization Society. Colony at Liberia," *Missionary Herald* (Sept. 1831), 290.

8. "Liberia," *Missionary Herald* (March 1830), 86.

9. "Sketch of the Life of the Rev. Lott Cary," in Ralph Randolph Gurley, *Life of Jehudi Ashmun, Late Colonial Agent in Liberia, with an Appendix* (Washington, DC: James C. Dunn, 1835), 148, 160; Alexander, *A History of Colonization*, chs. 16, 27, p. 393.

10. James Edon to John Leighton Wilson, Monrovia, Jan. 29, 1833; "Report of the State of the Colony of Liberia, March 24, 1834. Misters J. Leighton Wilson and Stephen R. Wynkoop to the Prud. Committee of the Am. Board of Com. Foreign Missions," ABC 15.1, vol. 1.

11. "Report of the State of the Colony of Liberia, March 24, 1834. Misters J. Leighton Wilson and Stephen R. Wynkoop to the Prud. Committee of the Am. Board of Com. Foreign Missions," ABC 15.1, vol. 1.

12. Rufus Anderson, "Instructions of the Prudential Committee to the Rev. John Leighton Wilson, missionary to West Africa; read at a public meeting, held at Philadelphia, Sept. 22, 1833," ABC 8.1, vol. 2.

13. Emphasis in the original. "Report of the State of the Colony of Liberia, March 24, 1834. Misters J. Leighton Wilson and Stephen R. Wynkoop to the Prud. Committee of the Am. Board of Com. Foreign Missions," ABC 15.1, vol. 1.

14. Penelope Campbell, *Maryland in Africa: The Maryland State Colonization Society, 1831–1857* (Urbana: University of Illinois Press, 1971). John Leighton Wilson, "Journal of J. Leighton Wilson on a Missionary Tour to Western Africa in the Year 1834," ABC 15.1, vol. 1, no. 3; J. Leighton Wilson and Stephen R. Wynkoop "To the Prudential Committee of the ABCFM . . . ," ABC 15.1, vol. 1.

15. Wilson Journal ABC 15.1, vol. 1; Wilson, "Missionary Tour to Western Africa"; J. Leighton Wilson and Stephen R. Wynkoop report "To the Prudential Committee of the ABCFM . . . ," ABC 15.1, vol. 1.

16. "Western Africa," *Missionary Herald* (November 1836), 409.

17. Journal, 14 ABC 15.1, vol. 1; John Leighton Wilson to John Latrobe, March 18, 1837, Maryland State Colonization Society Papers, Maryland Historical Society, Baltimore, MD (MSCS) Reel 3.

18. Rufus Anderson to John Leighton Wilson, Boston, July 2, 1836, ABC 2.1, vol. 1.

19. John Leighton Wilson to Rufus Anderson, Fair Hope, Cape Palmas, April 1, 1836, ABC 15.1, vol. 1. For a description of the schools, see Erskine Clarke, *By the Rivers of Water: A Nineteenth-Century Atlantic Odyssey* (New York: Basic Books, 2013), 162–168.

20. John Leighton Wilson to Rufus Anderson, Fair Hope, Cape Palmas, Jan. 7, 1835 ABC 15.1, vol. 1.

21. Clarke, *By the Rivers of Water*, 113, 123–124.

22. Emphasis in original. "Extracts from a Letter of Mr. Wilson," *Missionary Herald* (Feb. 1836), 64–65; Clarke, *By the Rivers of Water*, 111–112.

23. John Leighton Wilson to Rufus Anderson, Fair Hope, Cape Palmas, March 13, 1838 ABC 15.1, vol. 2.

24. Campbell, *Maryland in Africa*, 90–91.

25. Ibid., 124. For a modern biography of Russwurm that places him as a pan-African leader, see Winston James, *The Struggles of John Brown Russwurm: The Life and Writings of a Pan-Africanist Pioneer, 1799–1851* (New York: NYU Press, 2010).

26. N. J. Bayard to Rufus Anderson, Savannah, July 10, 1838, ABC 15.1, vol. 2.

27. Emphasis in the original. John Leighton Wilson to Rufus Anderson, Fair Hope, Cape Palmas, March 28, 1838, ABC 15.1, vol. 2.

28. John Leighton Wilson to John Latrobe, March 18, 1837. MSCS, Correspondence Received, Reel 3. Eugene S. Van Sickle, "A Transnational Vision: John H.B. Latrobe and Maryland's African Colonization Movement" (Ph.D. diss., West Virginia University, 2005), 123.

29. Maryland Colonization Society Board of Managers, quoted in Campbell, *Maryland in Africa*, 125.

30. Latrobe quoted in Van Sickle, "A Transnational Vision," 115–120.

31. Campbell, *Maryland in Africa*, 127–135.

32. John Leighton Wilson to Rufus Anderson, Fair Hope, Cape Palmas, March 28, 1838, ABC 15.1, vol. 2. Emphasis in original. D. Francis Bacon to Rufus Anderson, Sierra Leone, May 20, 1838 ABC 14, vol. 2.

33. John Leighton Wilson to Rufus Anderson, Fair Hope, Cape Palmas, March 28, 1838, ABC 15.1, vol. 2. Emphasis in original. D. Francis Bacon to Rufus Anderson, Sierra Leone, May 20, 1838 ABC 14, vol. 2.

34. Van Sickle, "A Transnational Vision," 126–140.

35. John Leighton Wilson to Rufus Anderson, Fair Hope, Cape Palmas, March 28, 1838, ABC 15.1, vol. 2.

36. Ibid., Sept. 25, 1838, ABC 15.1, vol. 2.

37. Rufus Anderson to John Leighton Wilson, Boston, July 16, 1838, ABC 2.1, vol. 2.

38. Ibid.

39. John Leighton Wilson to Rufus Anderson, Fair Hope, Cape Palmas, Sept. 25, 1838, ABC 15.1, vol. 2; for Anderson's response, see Rufus Anderson to John Leighton Wilson, Mission Rooms, Boston, Feb. 25, 1839, ABC 2.1, vol. 3.

40. John Leighton Wilson to Rufus Anderson, Fair Hope, Cape Palmas, Sept. 25, 1838, ABC 15.1, vol. 2.

41. John Leighton Wilson to Rufus Anderson, Colonization Letter no. 5 (n.d.), John Leighton Wilson to Rufus Anderson, Cape Palmas, Dec. 24, 1838, and John Leighton Wilson to Rufus Anderson, Fair Hope, Cape Palmas, Jan. 14, 1839, ABC 15.1, vol. 2.

42. Van Sickle, "A Transnational Vision," 130–131.

43. John Latrobe to John Russwurm, Baltimore, July 18, 1838; Latrobe Letter Book, MSCS.

44. John Leighton Wilson to Rufus Anderson, Colonization Letter no. 1, Fair Hope, Cape Palmas, March 13, 1838, ABC 15.1, vol. 2.

45. John Leighton Wilson to Rufus Anderson, letters on colonialism no. 2 (n.d.), ABC 15.1, vol. 2.

46. Rufus Anderson to John Leighton Wilson, Missionary Rooms, Boston, Feb. 25, 1839, ABC 2.1, vol. 3; John Leighton Wilson to Rufus Anderson, Colonization Letter no. 4 (n.d.), ABC 15.1, vol. 2. John Leighton Wilson to Rufus Anderson Fair Hope, Cape Palmas, March 7, 1836, ABC 15.1, vol. 1.; John Leighton Wilson to Rufus Anderson, Fair Hope, Cape Palmas, April 1, 1836 ABC 15.1, vol. 1.

47. John Latrobe to Rufus Anderson, Baltimore, Nov. 29, 1838, Latrobe Letter Book, MSCS.

48. John Latrobe to John Russwurm, July 18, 1838, Latrobe Letter Book, MSCS; John Latrobe to Rufus Anderson, Baltimore, Nov. 29, 1838, Latrobe Letter Book, MSCS; Latrobe quoted in Campbell, *Maryland in Africa*, 87; see also Tom W. Shick, "Rhetoric and Reality: Colonization and Afro-American Missionaries in Nineteenth-Century Liberia," in *Black Americans and the Missionary Movement in Africa*, ed. Sylvia M. Jacobs (Westport: Greenwood Press, 1982), 45–62.

49. John Leighton Wilson to Rufus Anderson, Fair Hope, Cape Palmas, April 25, 1839, ABC 15.1, vol. 2.

50. J.F.C. Finley to Rufus Anderson, Harper, Liberia, August 21, 1838 (copy), ABC 15.1, vol. 2.

51. John Leighton Wilson to Rufus Anderson, Colonization Letters, no. 4 (n.d.), ABC 15.1, vol. 2.; Van Sickle, "A Transnational Vision," 127–128.

52. Rufus Anderson to John Leighton Wilson, Boston, March 31, 1838, ABC 2.1, vol. 2.

53. Campbell, *Maryland in Africa*, 132–137.

54. Rufus Anderson to the Mission in West Africa, Boston, Dec. 3, 1841, ABC 2.1, vol. 4.

55. Ibid., Dec. 30, 1841, ABC 2.1, vol. 4.

56. "Very Late from Liberia," *African Repository and Colonial Journal* (June 1842), 185; "Extract from the Annual Report of the Maryland Colonization Society of 1843," *African Repository and Colonial Journal* (April 1843), 121.

57. Rufus Anderson to John Leighton Wilson, Missionary House, Boston, Jan. 23, 1841, Rufus Anderson to John Leighton Wilson, Boston, July 14, 1841, ABC 2.1, vol. 5; Genesis 13: 7–12.

58. John Leighton Wilson to Rufus Anderson Fair Hope, Cape Palmas, Sept. 25, 1838, ABC 15.1, vol. 2.

59. Rufus Anderson to John Leighton Wilson, Missionary House, Boston, Jan. 23, 1841, Rufus Anderson to John Leighton Wilson, Boston, July 14, 1841, ABC 2.1, vol. 5.

60. Rufus Anderson to John Leighton Wilson, Boston, July 16, 1838, ABC 2.1, vol. 2; Rufus Anderson to the Brethren of the West African Mission, Boston, March 31, 1838, ABC 2.1, vol. 3; Rufus Anderson to the Cape Palmas Mission, Missionary House, Boston, Jan. 23, 1841; Rufus Anderson to the Mission at Cape Palmas, Philadelphia, March 31, 1841; Rufus Anderson to the Mission of Cape Palmas, Boston, July 14, 1841, ABC 2.1, vol. 5; John Leighton Wilson to Rufus Anderson, Cape Palmas, April 13, 1839, John Leighton Wilson to Rufus Anderson, Fair Hope, Cape Palmas, Dec. 24, 1840, ABC 15.1, vol. 2; *Annual Report* (1838), 55–58.

61. John Leighton Wilson to Rufus Anderson, Gabon, June 25, 1842; John Leighton Wilson to Rufus Anderson, Gabon River, July 26, 1842; John Leighton Wilson to Rufus Anderson, Gabon River, Nov. 10, 1842, ABC 15.1, vol. 2; Wilson, "Missionary Tour to Western Africa," 291–298; Clarke, *By the Rivers of Water*, 221–227.

62. Hampden C. DuBose, *Memoirs of Rev. John Leighton Wilson, D.D., Missionary to Africa and Secretary of Foreign Missions* (Richmond, VA: Presbyterian Committee of Publication, 1895), 159–170; Clarke, *By the Rivers of Water*, 266–275.

63. John Leighton Wilson to Rufus Anderson, Fair Hope, Cape Palmas, March 28, 1838, ABC 15.1, vol. 2.

7. A "Christian Colony" in Singapore

1. Ira Tracy, Peter Parker, and Daniel Bradley to the Prudential Committee of the ABCFM, Singapore, July 1835, ABC 16.2.1, vol. 1.

2. Emphasis in the original. Rufus Anderson to American missionaries at Singapore, Boston, Feb. 18, 1836, ABC 2.1.1, vol. 1.

3. Rufus Anderson to American missionaries at Singapore, Boston, Feb. 18, 1836, ABC 2.1.1, vol. 1.

4. Samuel Newell and Gordon Hall to Samuel Worcester, Bombay, July 6, 1816 ABC 16.1.1, vol. 1.

5. ABCFM, *Annual Report* (1832), 55–60.

6. Ibid., 55.

7. "To the Rev. Ira Tracy, and Mr. Samuel Wells Williams, appointed to labor in connection with the China Mission," June 6, 1833, ABC 8.1, vol. 1.

8. Ibid.

9. Ibid.

10. L.A. Mills, "British Malaya, 1824–1867," *Journal of the Malayan Branch Royal Asiatic Society* 33, no. 191 (Nov. 1960): 60–85; C. M. Turnbull, *A History of Singapore, 1819–1988*, 2nd ed. (New York: Oxford University Press, 1989), ch. 1.

11. Sharom Ahmat, "American Trade with Singapore, 1819–65," *Journal of the Malaysian Branch of the Royal Asiatic Society* 38, no. 2 (December 1965): 241–257; Public Department Bengal, Feb. 2, 1835, IOR/E/4/746; Public Department, Feb. 2, 1836 IOR/E/4/947.

12. Sharom Ahmat, "Joseph B. Balestier: The First American Consul in Singapore, 1833–1852," *Journal of the Malaysian Branch of the Royal Asiatic Society* 39, no. 2 (December 1966): 108–122; India Political Department, Nov. 9, 1836, IOR/E/4/749.

13. ABCFM, *Annual Report* (Boston: Printed for the Board by Crocker and Brewster, 1835), 69.

14. Turnbull, *A History of Singapore*, ch. 2.

15. Emphasis in the original. Ira Tracy to Rufus Anderson, Canton, Dec. 14, 1833; Ira Tracy to Rufus Anderson, Canton, Dec. 21, 1833, ABC 16.2.1, vol. 1.

16. ABCFM, *Annual Report* (Boston: Printed for the Board by Crocker and Brewster, 1833), 68.

17. ABCFM *Annual Report* (Boston: Printed for the Board by Crocker and Brewster, 1834), 98–99; ABCFM *Annual Report* (1835), 68–70.

18. Dan. B. Bradley to R. Anderson, Moulmein, Burman Empire, Dec. 12, 1834, ABC 16.2.1, vol. 1.

19. Ira Tracy to Rufus Anderson, Singapore, August 5, 1834; Ira Tracy to Rufus Anderson, Singapore, Sept. 2, 1834; Ira Tracy to Rufus Anderson, Singapore, Sept. 4, 1834; Ira Tracy to Rufus Anderson, Sept. 8, 1834, ABC 16.2.1, vol. 1; R. L. O'Sullivan, "The Anglo-Chinese College and the Early 'Singapore Institution,'" *Journal of the Malaysian Branch of the Royal Asiatic Society* 61, no. 2 (1988): 45–62.

20. Ira Tracy, Peter Parker, and Daniel Bradley to the Prudential Committee of the ABCFM, Singapore, July 1835, ABC 16.2.1, vol. 1.

21. Daniel Bradley to Rufus Anderson, Singapore, April 25, 1835, ABC 16.2.1, vol. 1.

22. J. H. Moore, "Replies to Questions Relative to the Advantage of Establishing a Christian Colony of Americans on the Island of Singapore," ABC 16.2.1, vol. 1.

23. Ira Tracy, Peter Parker, and Daniel Bradley to the Prudential Committee of the ABCFM, Singapore, July 1835, ABC 16.2.1, vol. 1.

24. Daniel Bradley to Rufus Anderson, Bangkok, Feb. 9, 1836, ABC 16.2.1, vol. 1.

25. Ira Tracy, Peter Parker, and Daniel Bradley to the Prudential Committee of the ABCFM, Singapore, July 1835, ABC 16.2.1, vol. 1.

26. Ibid.

27. J. H. Moore, "Replies to Questions Relative to the advantage of establishing a Christian Colony of Americans on the Island of Singapore," ABC 16.2.1, vol. 1.

28. Ira Tracy, Peter Parker, and Daniel Bradley to the Prudential Committee of the ABCFM, Singapore, July 1835, ABC 16.2.1, vol. 1.

29. Rufus Anderson to the American Missionaries at Singapore, Boston, Feb. 18, 1836, ABC 2.1.1, v. 01; Alfred North, quoted in Rufus Anderson To Mr. Alfred North, Boston, May 20, 1837, ABC 2.1.1, v. 01; Rufus Anderson to William Ellis, Boston, Dec. 26, 1835, LMS 8, Folder 4, Jacket A.

30. Parker, Tracy, Bradley to the Hon. C. Murchison Esq., Governor of Prince of Wales Island, Malacca, and Singapore, Singapore, June 20, 1835, ABC 16.2.1, vol. 1.

31. J. H. Moore, "Replies to Questions Relative to the advantage of establishing a Christian Colony of Americans on the Island of Singapore," ABC 16.2.1, vol. 1.

32. Emphasis in original. Rufus Anderson to the Brethren at Singapore, Boston, June 29, 1836, ABC 2.1.1, vol. 01.

33. Rufus Anderson to William Ellis, Boston, Dec. 26, 1835, LMS 8, Box 1, Folder 4, Jacket A.

34. Ira Tracy to Rufus Anderson, Singapore, August 5, 1834; Ira Tracy to Rufus Anderson, Singapore, Sept. 2, 1834; Ira Tracy to Rufus Anderson, Singapore, Sept. 15, 1834; Ira Tracy Journal, entries dated Sept. 22, 1834, Sept. 24, 1834, ABC 16.2.1, vol. 1.

35. Bradley to Rufus Anderson, Singapore, Jan. 13, 1835, J. Balestier to D. Bradley, Singapore, June 16, 1835, ABC 16.2.1, vol. 1.

36. Rufus Anderson to Missionaries at Singapore, Boston, February 18, 1836; Rufus Anderson to Missionaries at Canton, Boston, March 8, 1836, ABC 2.1, vol. 1.

37. "Extracts from Instructions to Rev. Matthew B. Hope and Rev. Joseph Travelli," ABC 16.2.6, vol. 2.

38. *Singapore Mission Journal* (SMJ) May 3, 1836; May 17, 1836 ABC 16.2.6, vol. 1.

39. On the boarders, see SMJ Aug. 2 and 19, Sept. 20, 1836, ABC 16.2.6, vol. 1.

40. Emphasis in original. Charles Robinson to Rufus Anderson, Singapore, Jan. 14, 1834, ABC 16.2.1, v. 1; ABCFM, *Annual Report* (Boston: Printed for the Board by Crocker and Brewster, 1837), 89; Stephen Johnson to Rufus Anderson, Singapore, Feb. 15, 1834, ABC 16.2.1, vol. 1.

41. Stephen Johnson and Charles Robinson to the Secretaries of the ABCFM, Singapore, May 18, 1834, ABC 16.2.1, vol. 1.

42. Alfred North to Rufus Anderson, October 13, 1836, ABC 16.2.1, vol. 1.

43. Emphasis in the original. Alfred North to Rufus Anderson, Singapore, Dec. 24, 1836.

44. ABCFM, *Annual Report* (1837), 151–155; ABCFM, *Annual Report* (Boston: Printed for the Board by Crocker and Brewster, 1839), 122–124.

45. "Principles on Which Missionary Seminaries are to be Reared," ABCFM *Annual Report* (1837), 151–155.

46. John Demos, *The Heathen School: A Story of Hope and Betrayal in the Age of the Early Republic* (New York: Knopf, 2014); Hutchison, *Errand to the World*, 67.

47. ABCFM, *Annual Report* (Boston: Printed for the Board by Crocker and Brewster, 1838), 88–93; ABCFM, *Annual Report* (1839), 122–123.

48. O'Sullivan; Peter Wicks, "Education, British Colonialism, and a Plural Society in West Malaysia: The Development of Education in the British Settlements along the Straits of Malacca, 1786–1874," *History of Education Quarterly* 20, no. 2 (summer 1980): 163–187.

49. Samuel Worcester to the Rev. Messrs. Adoniram Judson, Samuel Nott, Samuel Newell, Gordon Hall, and Luther Rice, Salem, Feb. 11, 1812, ABC 8.1, vol. 4.

50. Charles Robinson to Rufus Anderson, Singapore, April 21, 1834, ABC 16.2.1, vol. 1.

51. Rufus Anderson to William Ellis, Boston, June 9, 1838 and Oct. 5, 1838, LMS 8, Box 1, Folder 4, Jacket C; November 12, 1838; June 24, 1839. LMS Home. Board Minutes, 1839–1847.

Conclusion

1. ABCFM, Annual Report (Boston: Printed for the Board by Crocker and Brewster, 1846), 221.

2. Ibid.

3. Hutchison, *Errand to the World*, 82; Anderson, *Memorial of the First Fifty Years*, 250.

4. Hall and Newell, *Conversion of the World*, 58.

5. John R. Mott, *The Evangelization of the World in This Generation* (New York: Student Volunteer Movement for Foreign Missions, 1900), 7.

Index